STAR WARS®

EPISODE II

ATTACK OF THE CLONES™

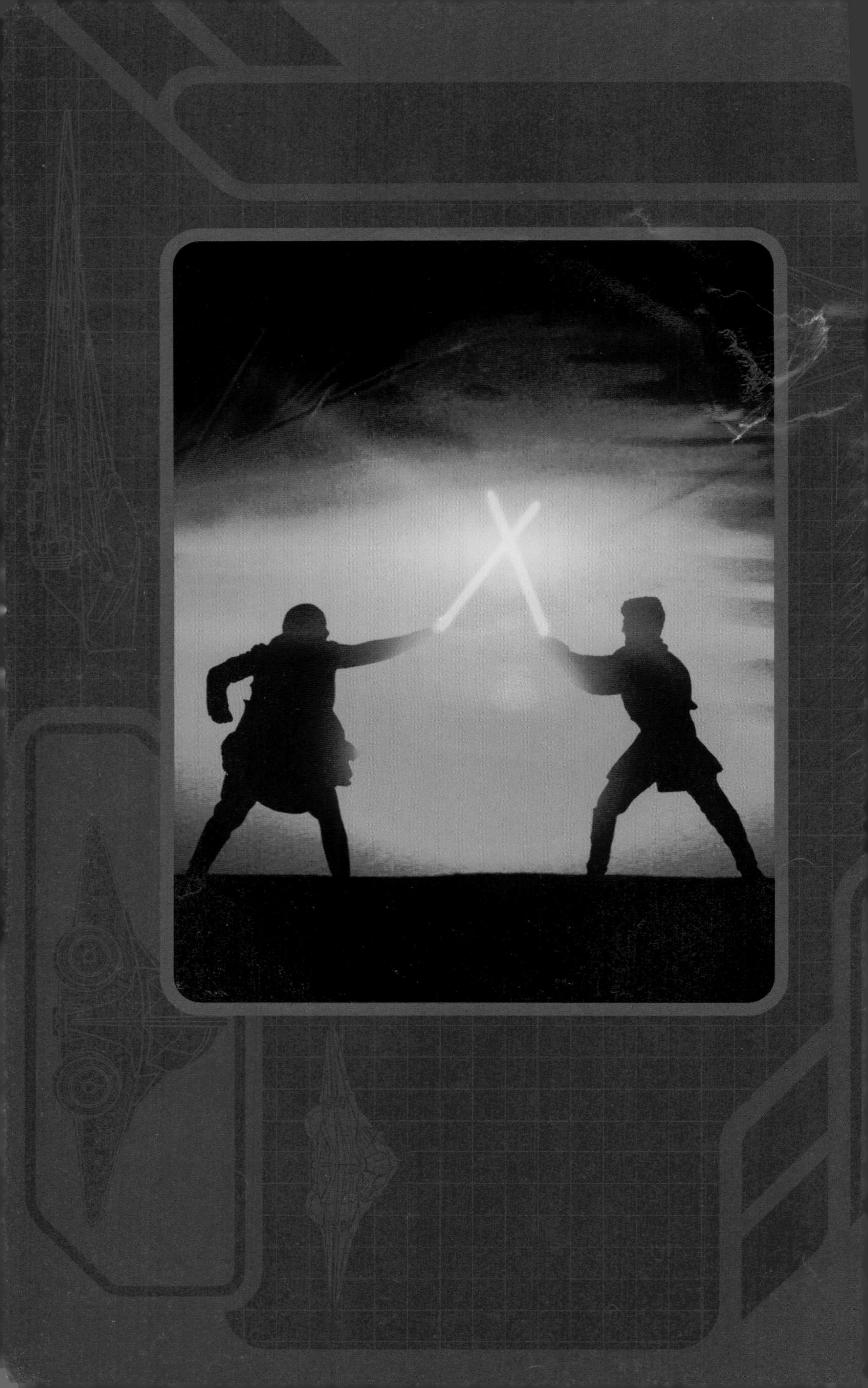

STAR WARS®

EPISODE II

ATTACK OF THE CLONES™

BASED ON THE STORY BY
GEORGE LUCAS
AND SCREENPLAY BY
GEORGE LUCAS AND
JONATHAN HALES

SCRIPT
HENRY GILROY

PENCILS
JAN DUURSEMA

INKS
RAY KRYSSING

COLORS
**CHRIS HORN, JASON HVAM, DAN JACKSON,
DAVE MCCAIG, DAVID NESTELLE,
AND DIGITAL CHAMELEON**

LETTERS
STEVE DUTRO

COVER ART
DREW STRUZAN

DARK HORSE COMICS®

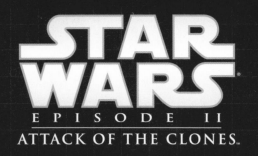

STAR WARS®
EPISODE II
ATTACK OF THE CLONES™

Publisher
MIKE RICHARDSON

Editor
DAVE LAND

Assistant Editor
PHILIP SIMON

Collection Designer
DAVID NESTELLE

Art Director
MARK COX

Special thanks to **CHRIS CERASI** and
LUCY AUTREY WILSON at Lucas Licensing

STAR WARS: EPISODE II — ATTACK OF THE CLONES

This book collects issues 1 through 4 of the Dark Horse comic book series
STAR WARS: EPISODE II — ATTACK OF THE CLONES.

DARK HORSE COMICS, INC.
10956 SE MAIN STREET
MILWAUKIE, OR 97222

WWW.DARKHORSE.COM

COMIC SHOP LOCATOR SERVICE: (888) 266-4226

FIRST EDITION: APRIL 2002
ISBN: 1-56971-609-9

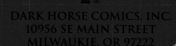

2 4 6 8 10 9 7 5 3 1

PRINTED IN CANADA

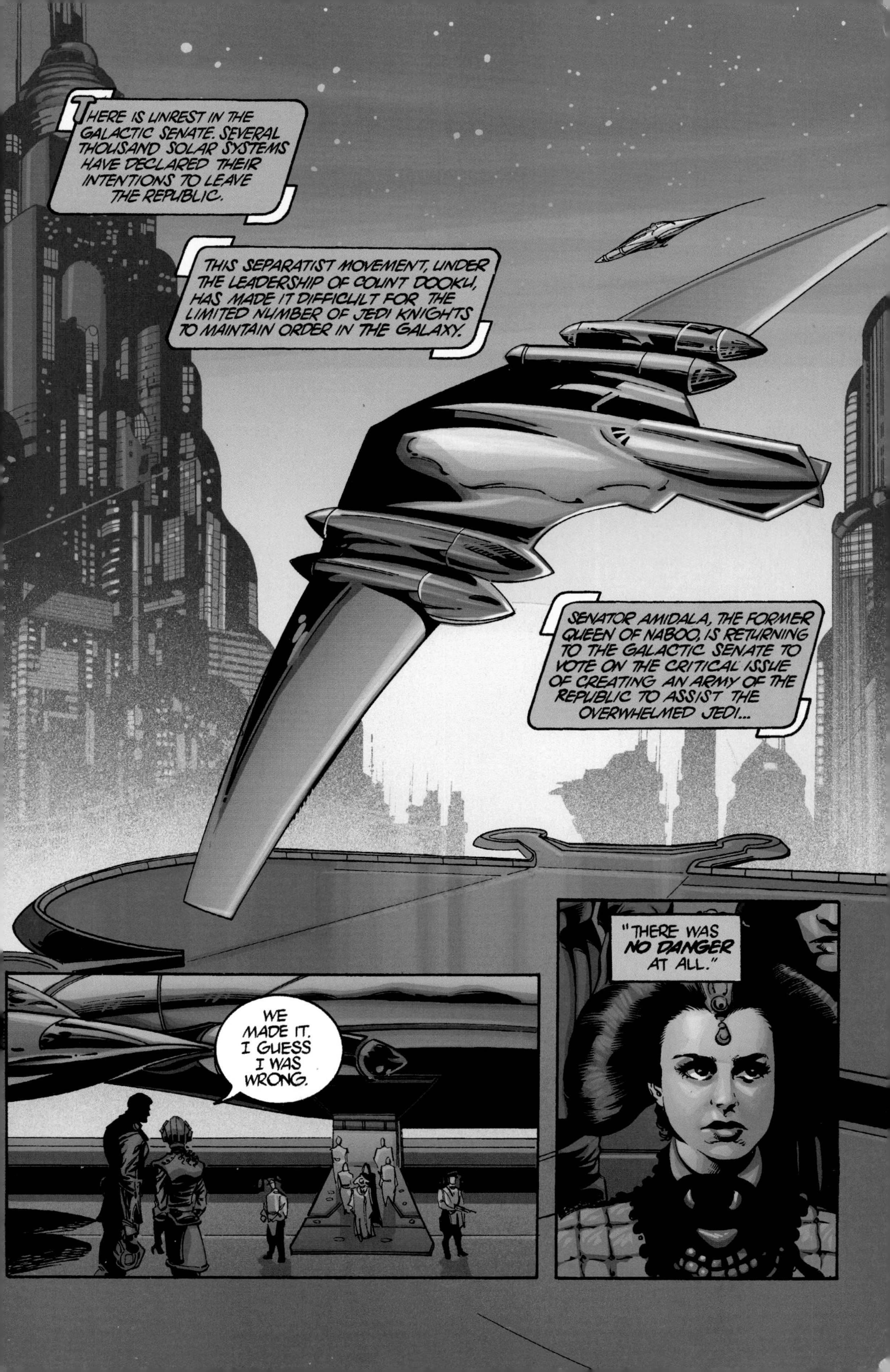
THERE IS UNREST IN THE GALACTIC SENATE. SEVERAL THOUSAND SOLAR SYSTEMS HAVE DECLARED THEIR INTENTIONS TO LEAVE THE REPUBLIC.
THIS SEPARATIST MOVEMENT, UNDER THE LEADERSHIP OF COUNT DOOKU, HAS MADE IT DIFFICULT FOR THE LIMITED NUMBER OF JEDI KNIGHTS TO MAINTAIN ORDER IN THE GALAXY.
SENATOR AMIDALA, THE FORMER QUEEN OF NABOO, IS RETURNING TO THE GALACTIC SENATE TO VOTE ON THE CRITICAL ISSUE OF CREATING AN ARMY OF THE REPUBLIC TO ASSIST THE OVERWHELMED JEDI...
WE MADE IT. I GUESS I WAS WRONG.
"THERE WAS NO DANGER AT ALL."

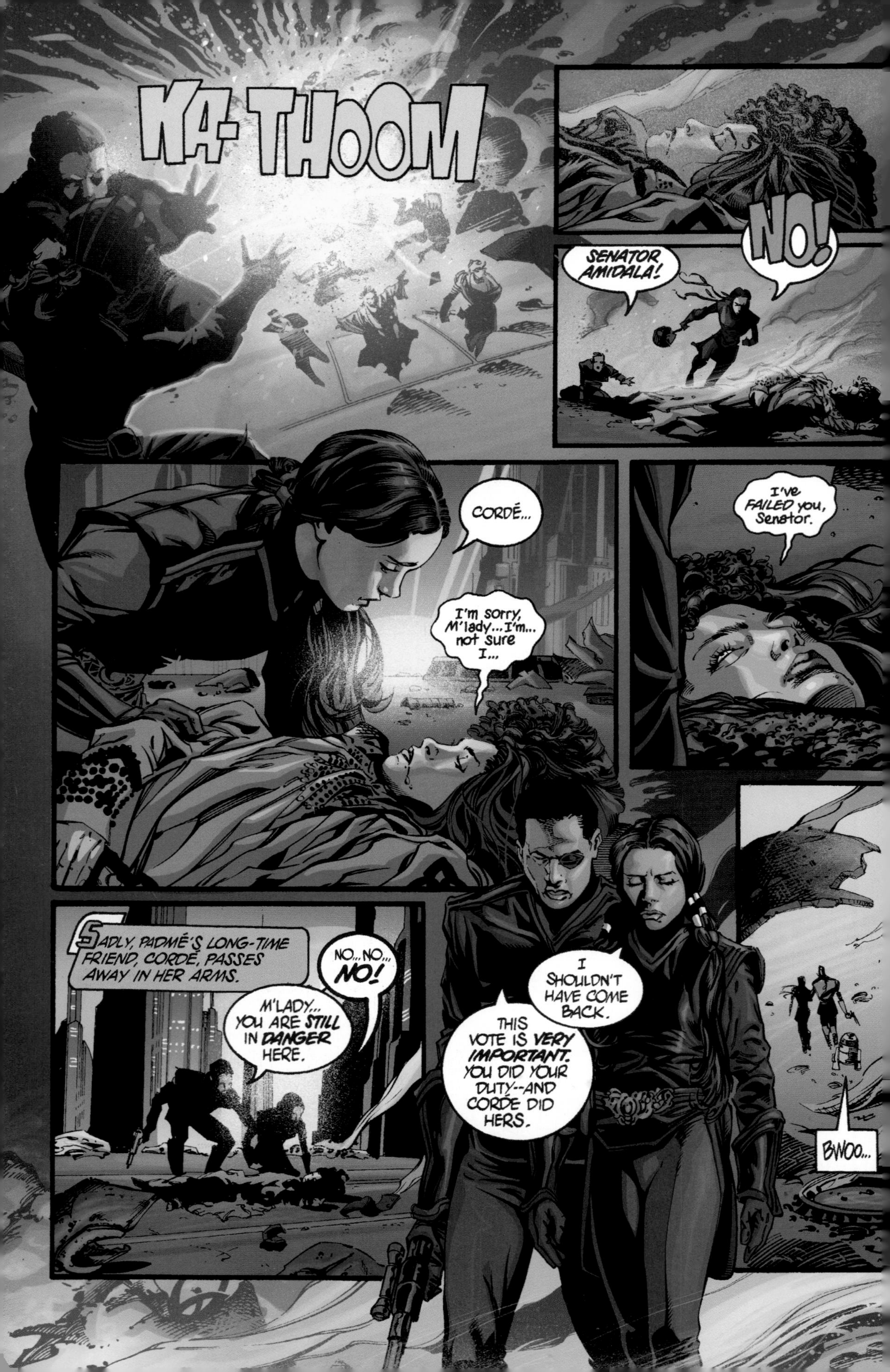
KA-THOOM
NO!
SENATOR AMIDALA!
CORDÉ...
I'm sorry, M'lady...I'm... not sure I...
I've FAILED you, Senator.
SADLY, PADMÉ'S LONG-TIME FRIEND, CORDÉ, PASSES AWAY IN HER ARMS.
NO... NO... NO!
M'LADY... YOU ARE STILL IN DANGER HERE.
I SHOULDN'T HAVE COME BACK.
THIS VOTE IS VERY IMPORTANT. YOU DID YOUR DUTY--AND CORDÉ DID HERS.
BWOO...

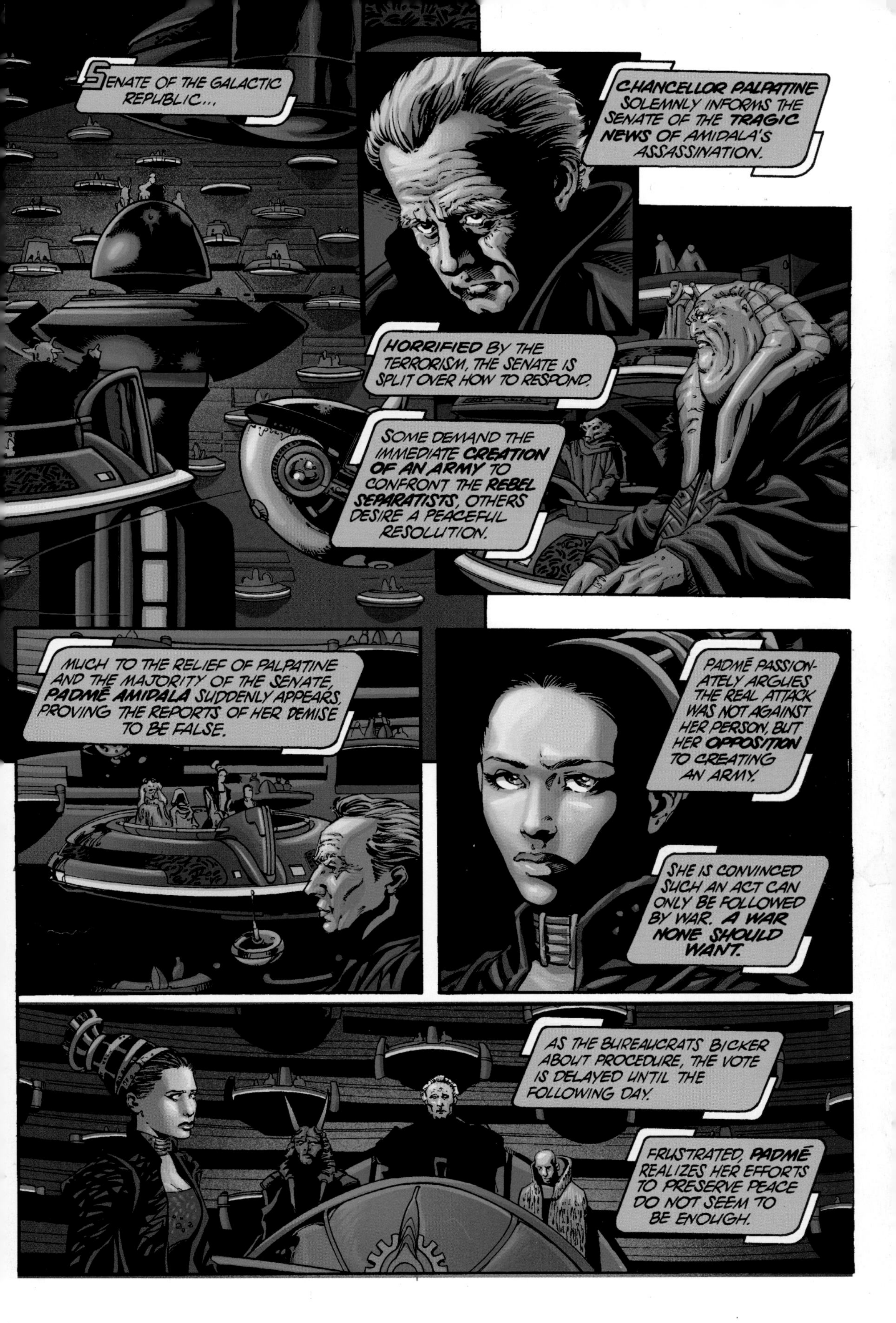
SENATE OF THE GALACTIC REPUBLIC...
CHANCELLOR PALPATINE SOLEMNLY INFORMS THE SENATE OF THE TRAGIC NEWS OF AMIDALA'S ASSASSINATION.
HORRIFIED BY THE TERRORISM, THE SENATE IS SPLIT OVER HOW TO RESPOND.
SOME DEMAND THE IMMEDIATE CREATION OF AN ARMY TO CONFRONT THE REBEL SEPARATISTS, OTHERS DESIRE A PEACEFUL RESOLUTION.
MUCH TO THE RELIEF OF PALPATINE AND THE MAJORITY OF THE SENATE, PADMÉ AMIDALA SUDDENLY APPEARS, PROVING THE REPORTS OF HER DEMISE TO BE FALSE.
PADMÉ PASSION-ATELY ARGUES THE REAL ATTACK WAS NOT AGAINST HER PERSON, BUT HER OPPOSITION TO CREATING AN ARMY.
SHE IS CONVINCED SUCH AN ACT CAN ONLY BE FOLLOWED BY WAR. A WAR NONE SHOULD WANT.
AS THE BUREAUCRATS BICKER ABOUT PROCEDURE, THE VOTE IS DELAYED UNTIL THE FOLLOWING DAY.
FRUSTRATED, PADMÉ REALIZES HER EFFORTS TO PRESERVE PEACE DO NOT SEEM TO BE ENOUGH.

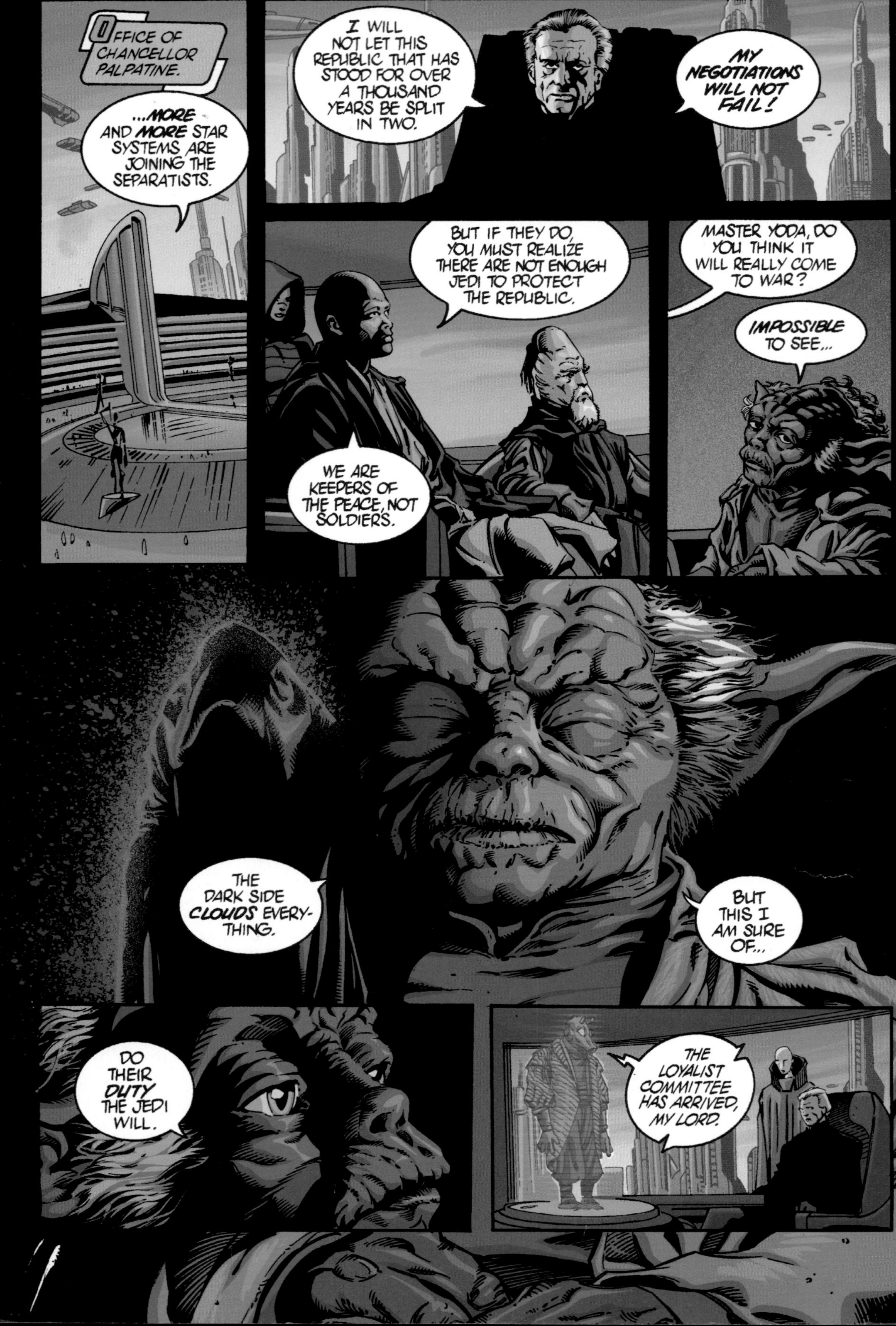
OFFICE OF CHANCELLOR PALPATINE.
...MORE AND MORE STAR SYSTEMS ARE JOINING THE SEPARATISTS.
I WILL NOT LET THIS REPUBLIC THAT HAS STOOD FOR OVER A THOUSAND YEARS BE SPLIT IN TWO.
MY NEGOTIATIONS WILL NOT FAIL!
BUT IF THEY DO, YOU MUST REALIZE THERE ARE NOT ENOUGH JEDI TO PROTECT THE REPUBLIC.
WE ARE KEEPERS OF THE PEACE, NOT SOLDIERS.
MASTER YODA, DO YOU THINK IT WILL REALLY COME TO WAR?
IMPOSSIBLE TO SEE...
THE DARK SIDE CLOUDS EVERY-THING.
BUT THIS I AM SURE OF...
DO THEIR DUTY THE JEDI WILL.
THE LOYALIST COMMITTEE HAS ARRIVED, MY LORD.

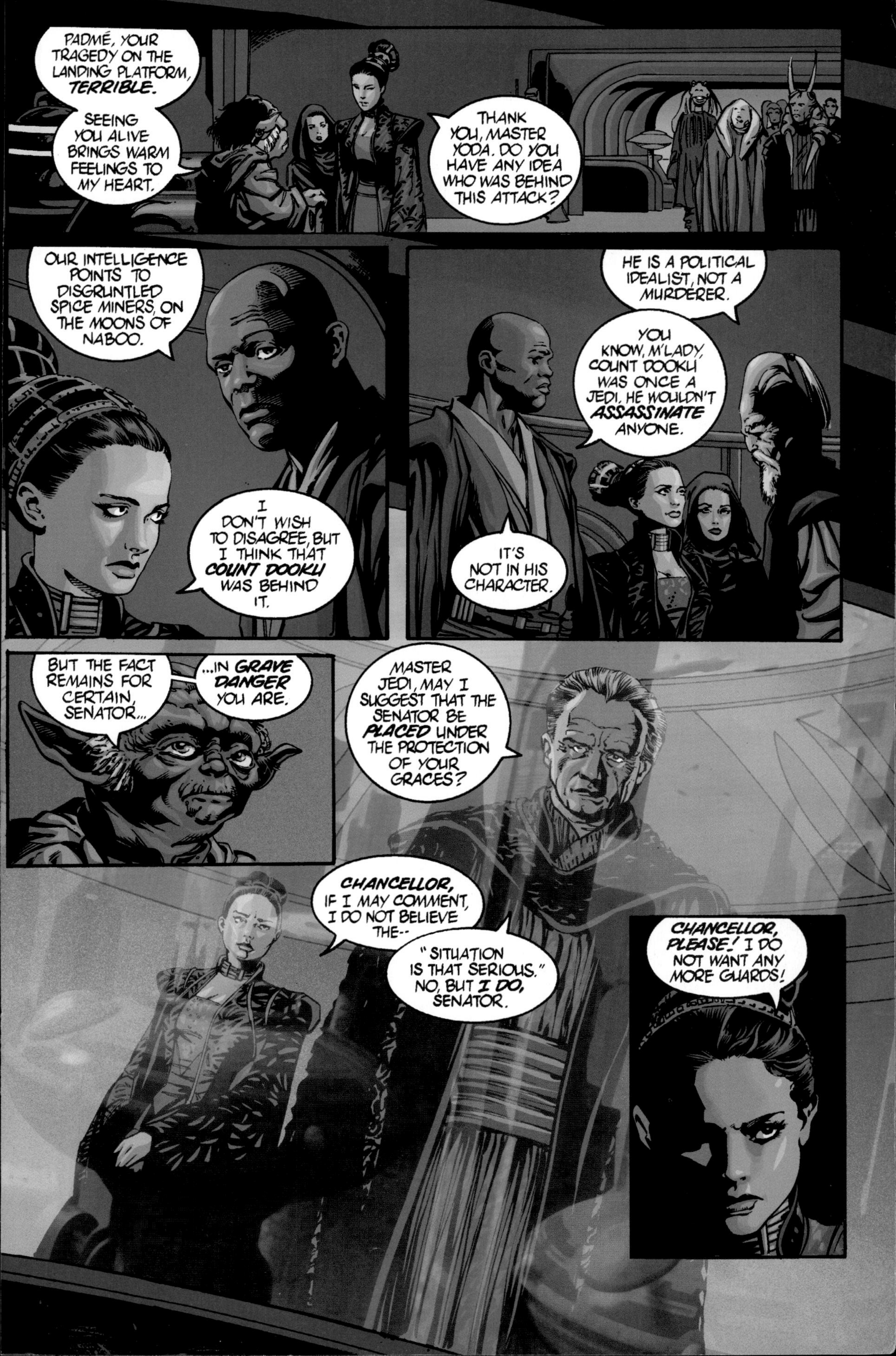
PADMÉ, YOUR TRAGEDY ON THE LANDING PLATFORM, TERRIBLE.
SEEING YOU ALIVE BRINGS WARM FEELINGS TO MY HEART.
THANK YOU, MASTER YODA. DO YOU HAVE ANY IDEA WHO WAS BEHIND THIS ATTACK?
OUR INTELLIGENCE POINTS TO DISGRUNTLED SPICE MINERS, ON THE MOONS OF NABOO.
I DON'T WISH TO DISAGREE, BUT I THINK THAT COUNT DOOKU WAS BEHIND IT.
HE IS A POLITICAL IDEALIST, NOT A MURDERER.
YOU KNOW, M'LADY, COUNT DOOKU WAS ONCE A JEDI. HE WOULDN'T ASSASSINATE ANYONE.
IT'S NOT IN HIS CHARACTER.
BUT THE FACT REMAINS FOR CERTAIN, SENATOR...
...IN GRAVE DANGER YOU ARE.
MASTER JEDI, MAY I SUGGEST THAT THE SENATOR BE PLACED UNDER THE PROTECTION OF YOUR GRACES?
CHANCELLOR, IF I MAY COMMENT, I DO NOT BELIEVE THE--
"SITUATION IS THAT SERIOUS." NO, BUT I DO, SENATOR.
CHANCELLOR, PLEASE! I DO NOT WANT ANY MORE GUARDS!

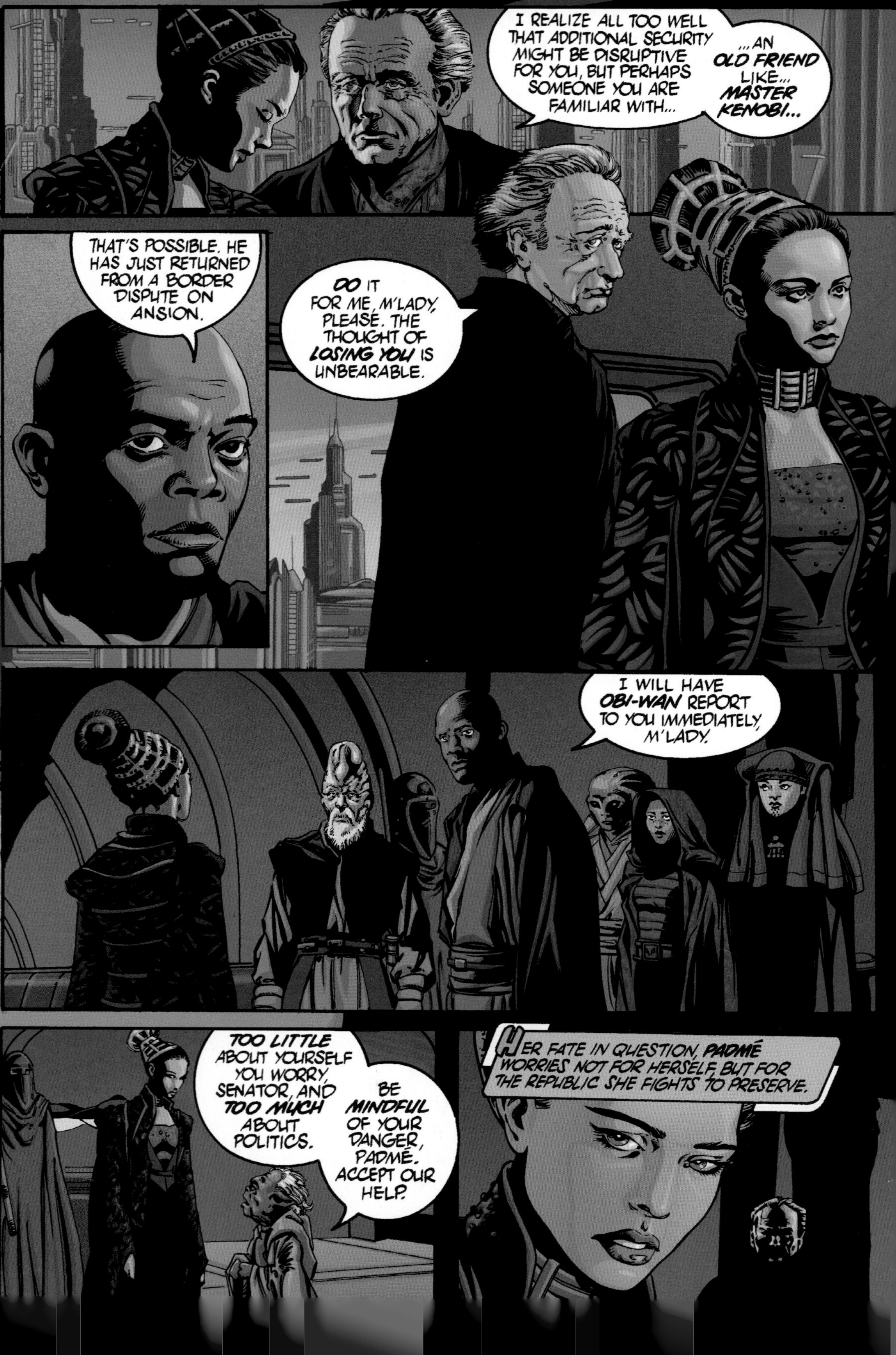

I REALIZE ALL TOO WELL THAT ADDITIONAL SECURITY MIGHT BE DISRUPTIVE FOR YOU, BUT PERHAPS SOMEONE YOU ARE FAMILIAR WITH...
...AN OLD FRIEND LIKE... MASTER KENOBI...
THAT'S POSSIBLE. HE HAS JUST RETURNED FROM A BORDER DISPUTE ON ANSION.
DO IT FOR ME, M'LADY, PLEASE. THE THOUGHT OF LOSING YOU IS UNBEARABLE.
I WILL HAVE OBI-WAN REPORT TO YOU IMMEDIATELY, M'LADY.
TOO LITTLE ABOUT YOURSELF YOU WORRY, SENATOR, AND TOO MUCH ABOUT POLITICS.
BE MINDFUL OF YOUR DANGER, PADMÉ. ACCEPT OUR HELP.
HER FATE IN QUESTION, PADMÉ WORRIES NOT FOR HERSELF, BUT FOR THE REPUBLIC SHE FIGHTS TO PRESERVE.

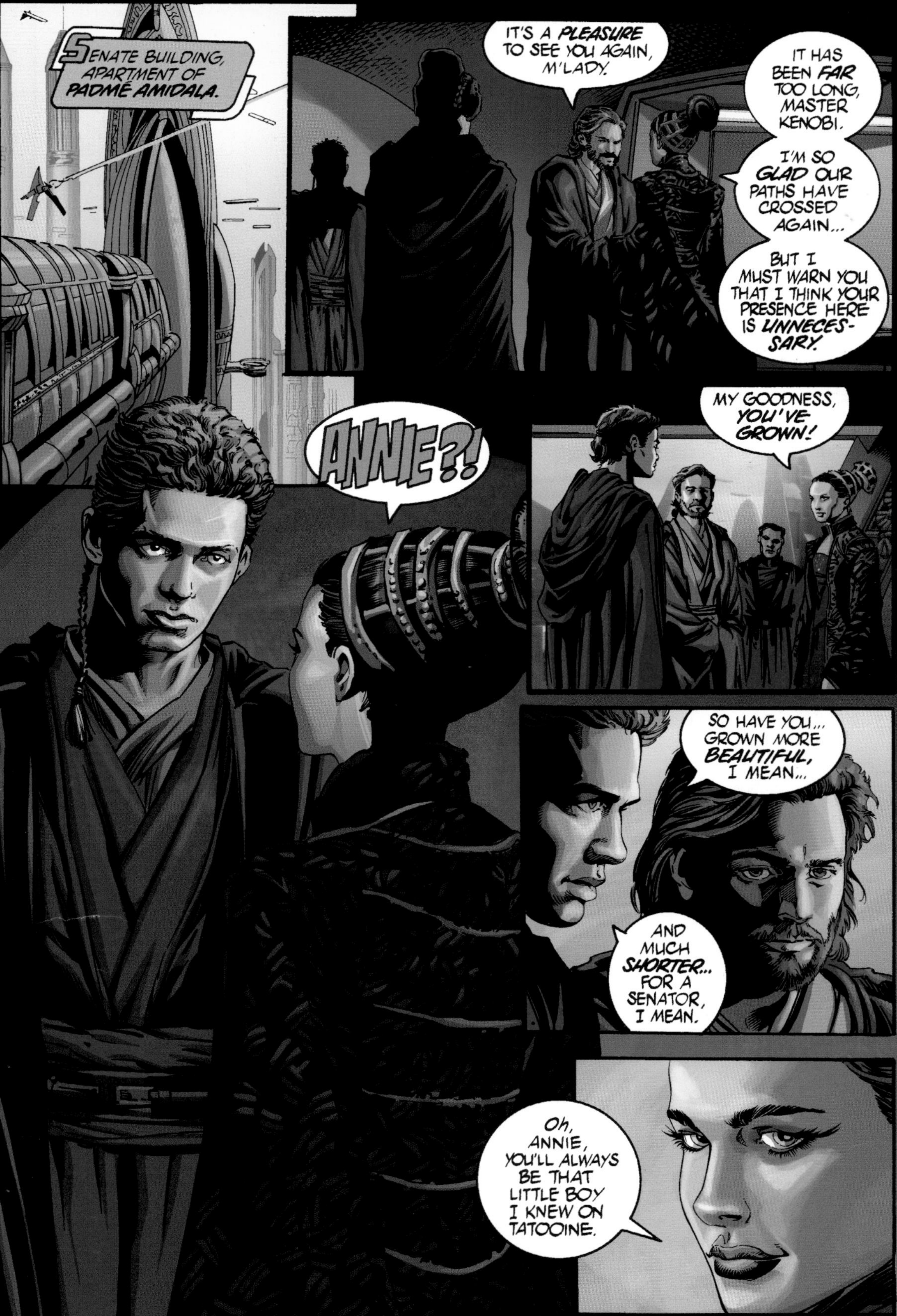
SENATE BUILDING, APARTMENT OF PADMÉ AMIDALA.
IT'S A PLEASURE TO SEE YOU AGAIN, M'LADY.
IT HAS BEEN FAR TOO LONG, MASTER KENOBI.
I'M SO GLAD OUR PATHS HAVE CROSSED AGAIN...
BUT I MUST WARN YOU THAT I THINK YOUR PRESENCE HERE IS UNNECES-SARY.
ANNIE?!
MY GOODNESS, YOU'VE GROWN!
SO HAVE YOU... GROWN MORE BEAUTIFUL, I MEAN...
AND MUCH SHORTER... FOR A SENATOR, I MEAN.
Oh, ANNIE, YOU'LL ALWAYS BE THAT LITTLE BOY I KNEW ON TATOOINE.

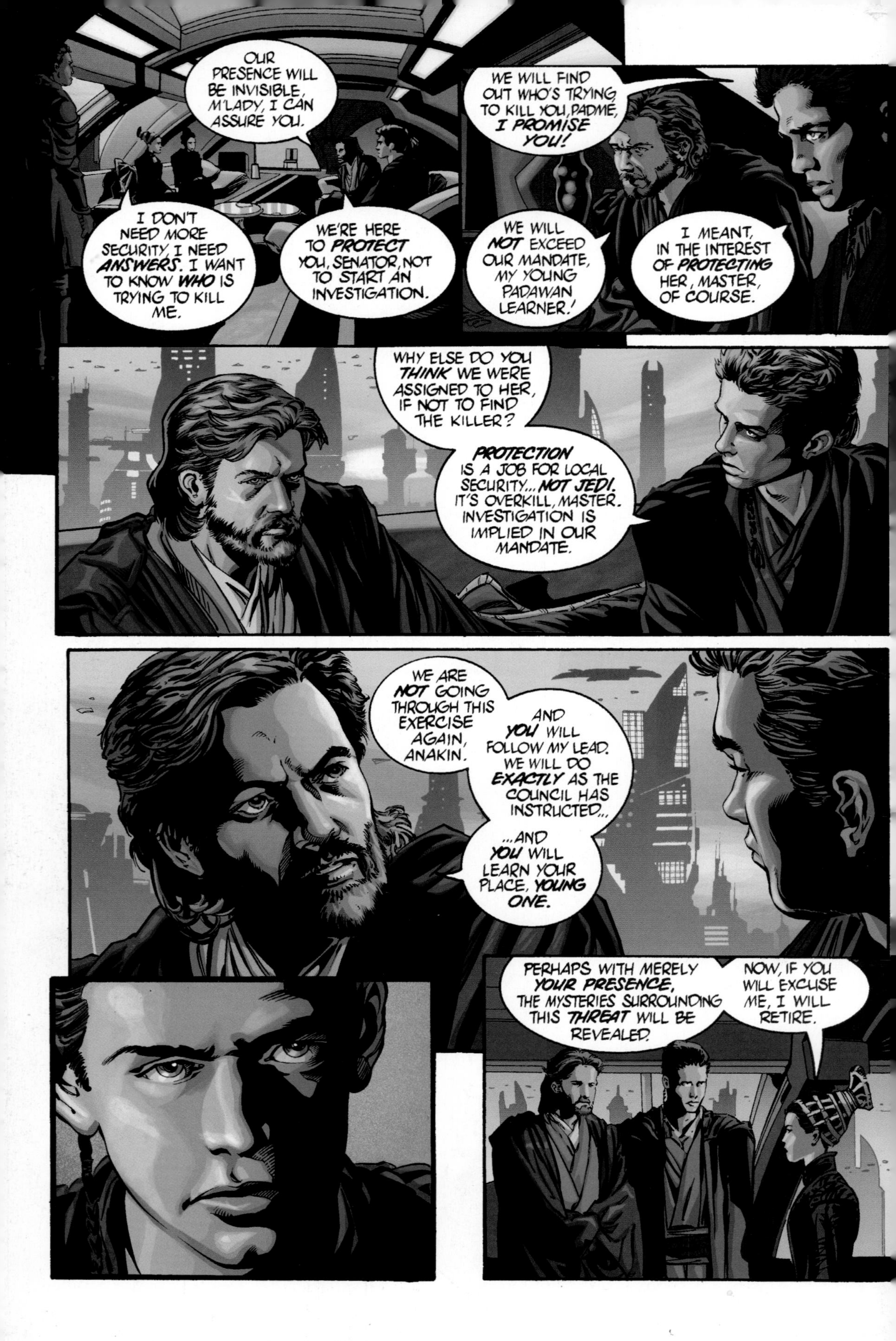
OUR PRESENCE WILL BE INVISIBLE, M'LADY, I CAN ASSURE YOU.
I DON'T NEED MORE SECURITY, I NEED ANSWERS. I WANT TO KNOW WHO IS TRYING TO KILL ME.
WE'RE HERE TO PROTECT YOU, SENATOR, NOT TO START AN INVESTIGATION.
WE WILL FIND OUT WHO'S TRYING TO KILL YOU, PADME, I PROMISE YOU!
WE WILL NOT EXCEED OUR MANDATE, MY YOUNG PADAWAN LEARNER!
I MEANT, IN THE INTEREST OF PROTECTING HER, MASTER, OF COURSE.
WHY ELSE DO YOU THINK WE WERE ASSIGNED TO HER, IF NOT TO FIND THE KILLER?
PROTECTION IS A JOB FOR LOCAL SECURITY... NOT JEDI. IT'S OVERKILL, MASTER. INVESTIGATION IS IMPLIED IN OUR MANDATE.
WE ARE NOT GOING THROUGH THIS EXERCISE AGAIN, ANAKIN.
AND YOU WILL FOLLOW MY LEAD. WE WILL DO EXACTLY AS THE COUNCIL HAS INSTRUCTED...
...AND YOU WILL LEARN YOUR PLACE, YOUNG ONE.
PERHAPS WITH MERELY YOUR PRESENCE, THE MYSTERIES SURROUNDING THIS THREAT WILL BE REVEALED.
NOW, IF YOU WILL EXCUSE ME, I WILL RETIRE.

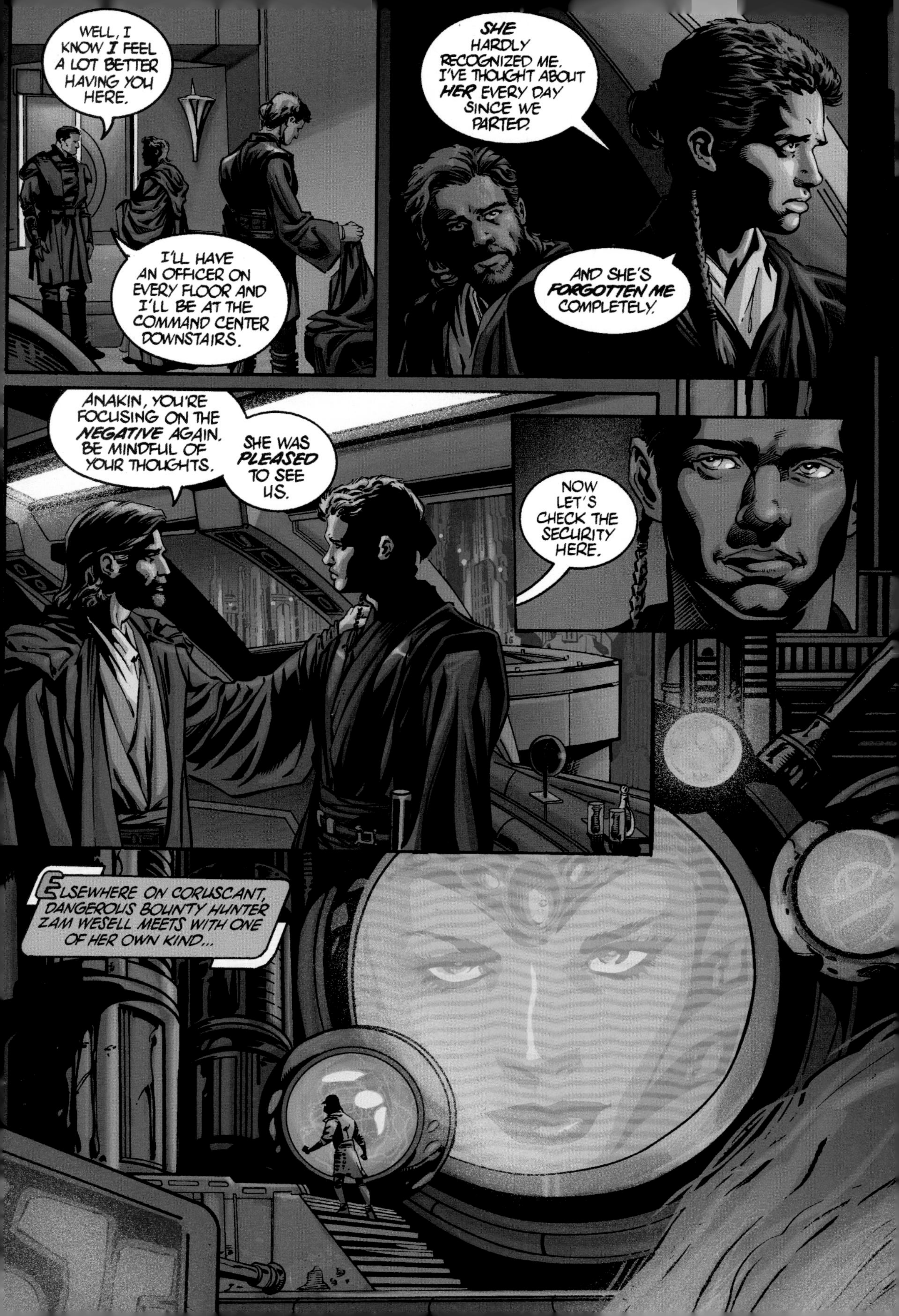

WELL, I KNOW I FEEL A LOT BETTER HAVING YOU HERE.
I'LL HAVE AN OFFICER ON EVERY FLOOR AND I'LL BE AT THE COMMAND CENTER DOWNSTAIRS.
SHE HARDLY RECOGNIZED ME. I'VE THOUGHT ABOUT HER EVERY DAY SINCE WE PARTED.
AND SHE'S FORGOTTEN ME COMPLETELY.
ANAKIN, YOU'RE FOCUSING ON THE NEGATIVE AGAIN. BE MINDFUL OF YOUR THOUGHTS.
SHE WAS PLEASED TO SEE US.
NOW LET'S CHECK THE SECURITY HERE.
ELSEWHERE ON CORUSCANT, DANGEROUS BOUNTY HUNTER ZAM WESELL MEETS WITH ONE OF HER OWN KIND...

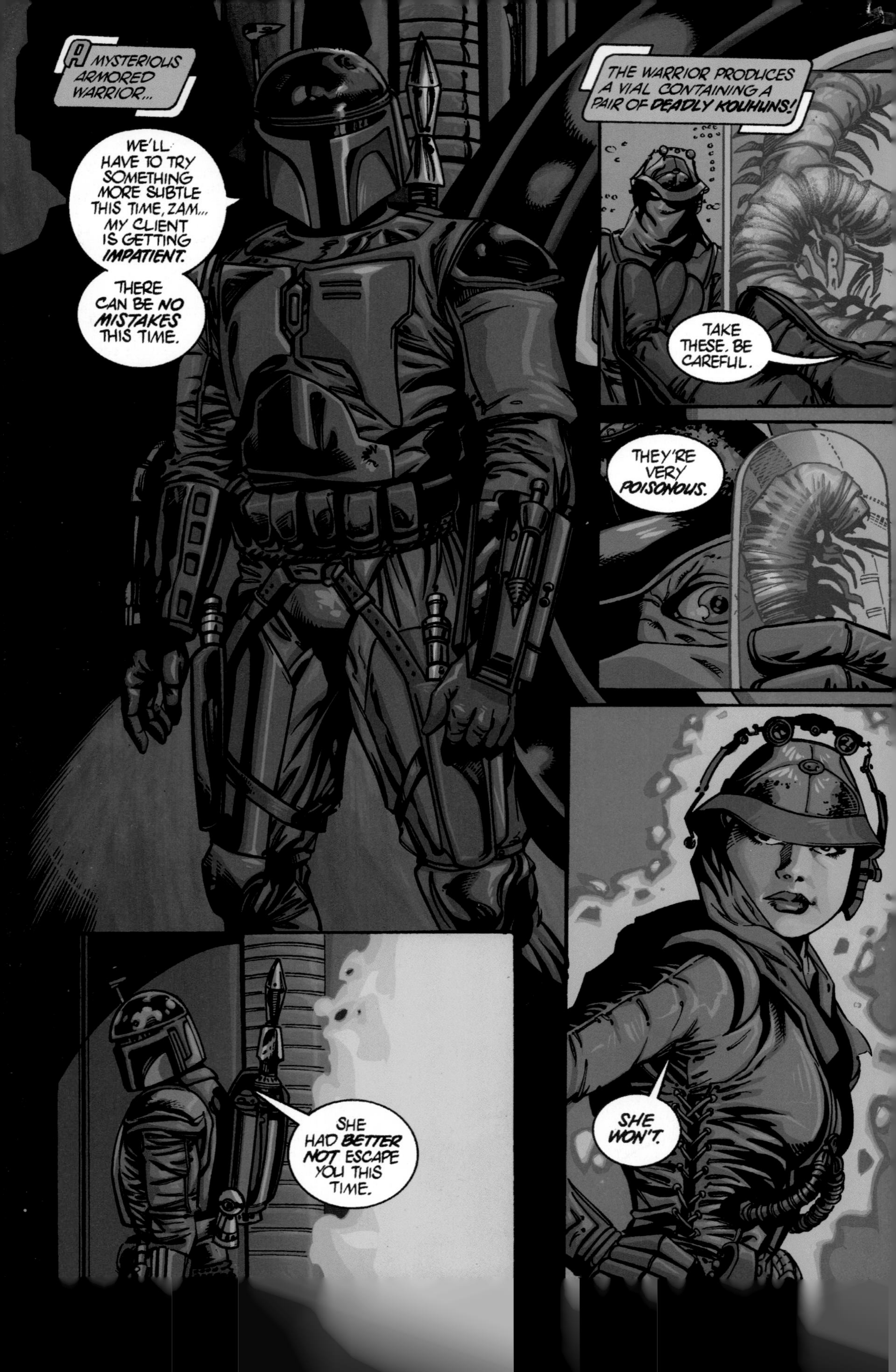
A MYSTERIOUS ARMORED WARRIOR...
WE'LL HAVE TO TRY SOMETHING MORE SUBTLE THIS TIME, ZAM... MY CLIENT IS GETTING IMPATIENT.
THERE CAN BE NO MISTAKES THIS TIME.
THE WARRIOR PRODUCES A VIAL CONTAINING A PAIR OF DEADLY KOUHUNS!
TAKE THESE. BE CAREFUL.
THEY'RE VERY POISONOUS.
SHE HAD BETTER NOT ESCAPE YOU THIS TIME.
SHE WON'T.

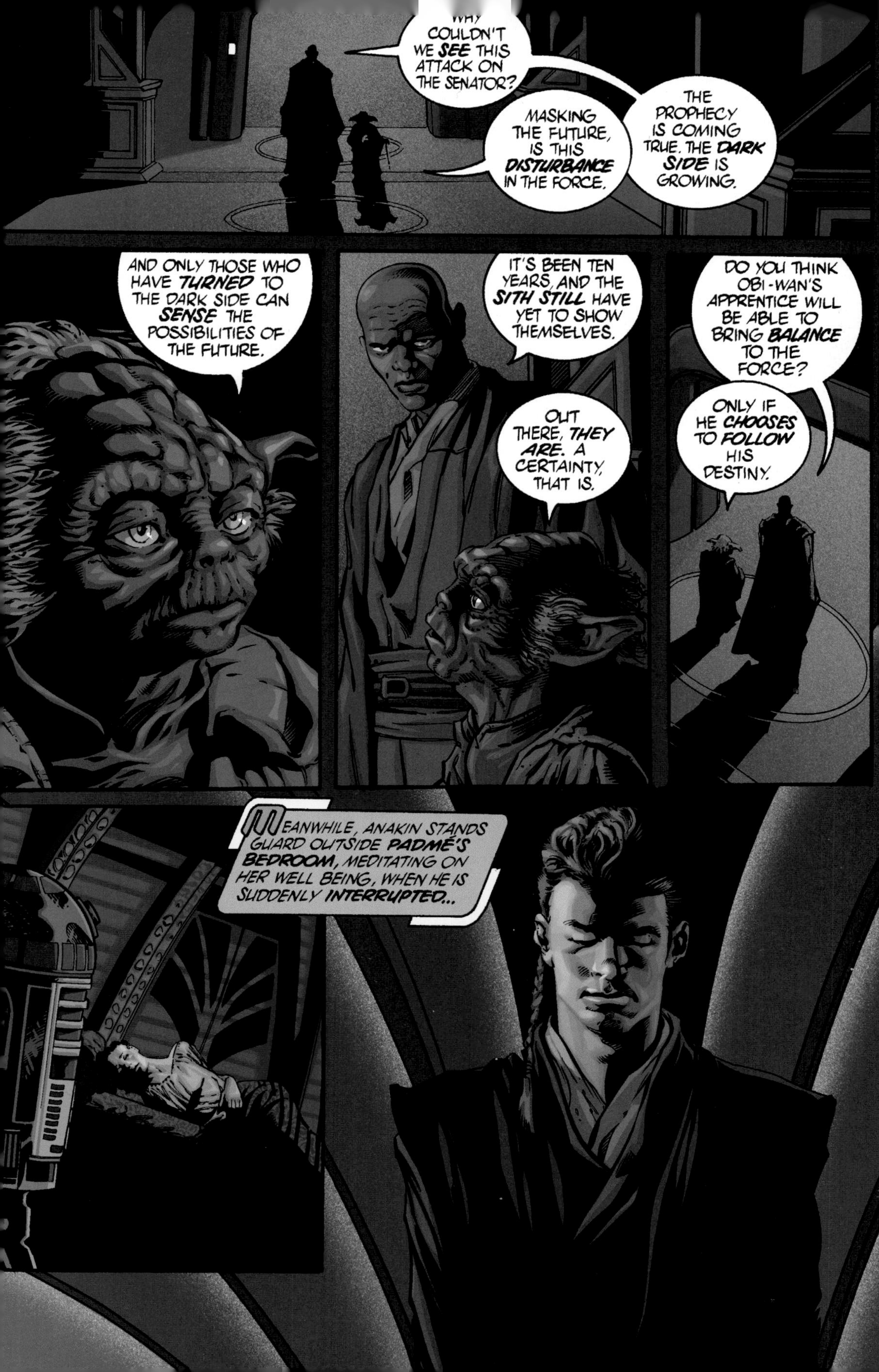
WHY COULDN'T WE SEE THIS ATTACK ON THE SENATOR?
MASKING THE FUTURE, IS THIS DISTURBANCE IN THE FORCE.
THE PROPHECY IS COMING TRUE. THE DARK SIDE IS GROWING.
AND ONLY THOSE WHO HAVE TURNED TO THE DARK SIDE CAN SENSE THE POSSIBILITIES OF THE FUTURE.
IT'S BEEN TEN YEARS, AND THE SITH STILL HAVE YET TO SHOW THEMSELVES.
OUT THERE, THEY ARE. A CERTAINTY, THAT IS.
DO YOU THINK OBI-WAN'S APPRENTICE WILL BE ABLE TO BRING BALANCE TO THE FORCE?
ONLY IF HE CHOOSES TO FOLLOW HIS DESTINY.
MEANWHILE, ANAKIN STANDS GUARD OUTSIDE PADMÉ'S BEDROOM, MEDITATING ON HER WELL BEING, WHEN HE IS SUDDENLY INTERRUPTED...

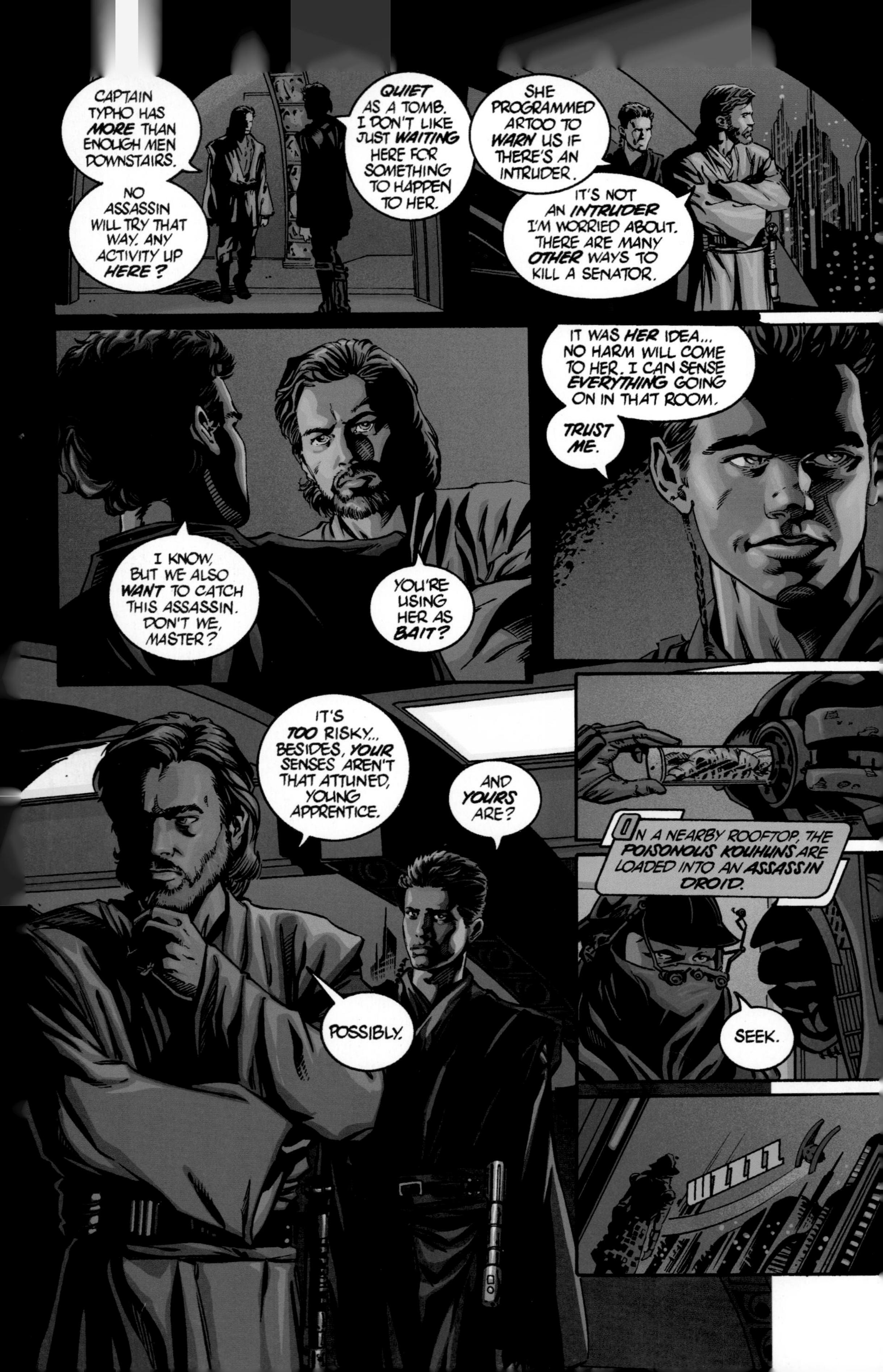
CAPTAIN TYPHO HAS MORE THAN ENOUGH MEN DOWNSTAIRS.
NO ASSASSIN WILL TRY THAT WAY. ANY ACTIVITY UP HERE?
QUIET AS A TOMB. I DON'T LIKE JUST WAITING HERE FOR SOMETHING TO HAPPEN TO HER.
SHE PROGRAMMED ARTOO TO WARN US IF THERE'S AN INTRUDER.
IT'S NOT AN INTRUDER I'M WORRIED ABOUT. THERE ARE MANY OTHER WAYS TO KILL A SENATOR.
I KNOW, BUT WE ALSO WANT TO CATCH THIS ASSASSIN. DON'T WE, MASTER?
YOU'RE USING HER AS BAIT?
IT WAS HER IDEA... NO HARM WILL COME TO HER. I CAN SENSE EVERYTHING GOING ON IN THAT ROOM.
TRUST ME.
IT'S TOO RISKY... BESIDES, YOUR SENSES AREN'T THAT ATTUNED, YOUNG APPRENTICE.
AND YOURS ARE?
POSSIBLY.
ON A NEARBY ROOFTOP, THE POISONOUS KOUHUNS ARE LOADED INTO AN ASSASSIN DROID.
SEEK.
WZZZZ

UNAWARE OF THE APPROACHING DANGER, *ANAKIN* AND *OBI-WAN* CONVERSE...

I DON'T SLEEP WELL ANYMORE.

BECAUSE OF YOUR *MOTHER?*

I DON'T KNOW WHY I KEEP *DREAMING* ABOUT HER NOW. I HAVEN'T SEEN *HER* SINCE I WAS LITTLE.

DREAMS PASS IN TIME.

I'D RATHER DREAM OF *PADMÉ.* JUST BEING AROUND HER AGAIN IS...

INTOXI- CATING.

MIND YOUR THOUGHTS, ANAKIN, THEY *BETRAY* YOU.

YOU'VE MADE A COMMITMENT TO THE JEDI ORDER... A *COMMITMENT* NOT EASILY BROKEN.

AND THEY *FORGET THE NICETIES* OF DEMOCRACY TO GET THOSE FUNDS.

AND DON'T FORGET SHE'S A POLITICIAN. THEY'RE *NOT* TO BE TRUSTED.

IT'S BEEN MY EXPERIENCE THAT SENATORS ARE ONLY FOCUSED ON *PLEASING THOSE* WHO FUND THEIR CAMPAIGNS.

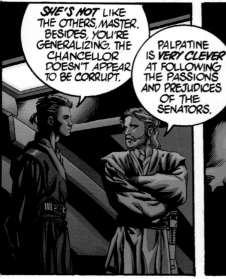

SHE'S NOT LIKE THE OTHERS, MASTER. BESIDES, YOU'RE GENERALIZING. THE CHANCELLOR DOESN'T APPEAR TO BE CORRUPT.

PALPATINE IS *VERY CLEVER* AT FOLLOWING THE PASSIONS AND PREJUDICES OF THE SENATORS.

I *THINK* HE IS A GOOD MAN. MY INSTINCTS ARE VERY *POSITIVE* ABOUT HIM.

MASTER...

I SENSE IT, TOO!

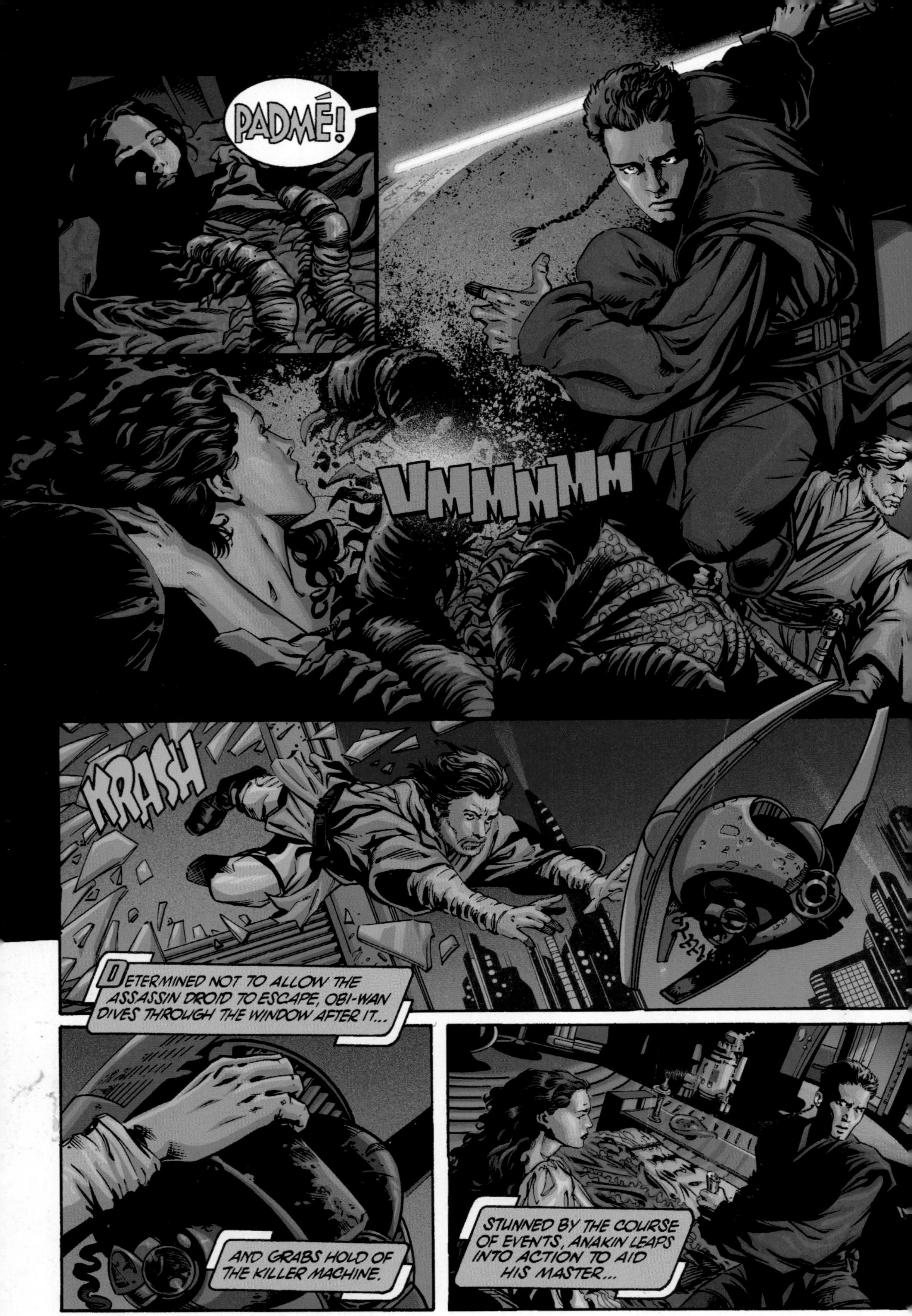
PADMÉ!
VMMMMMM
KRASH
DETERMINED NOT TO ALLOW THE ASSASSIN DROID TO ESCAPE, OBI-WAN DIVES THROUGH THE WINDOW AFTER IT...
AND GRABS HOLD OF THE KILLER MACHINE.
STUNNED BY THE COURSE OF EVENTS, ANAKIN LEAPS INTO ACTION TO AID HIS MASTER...

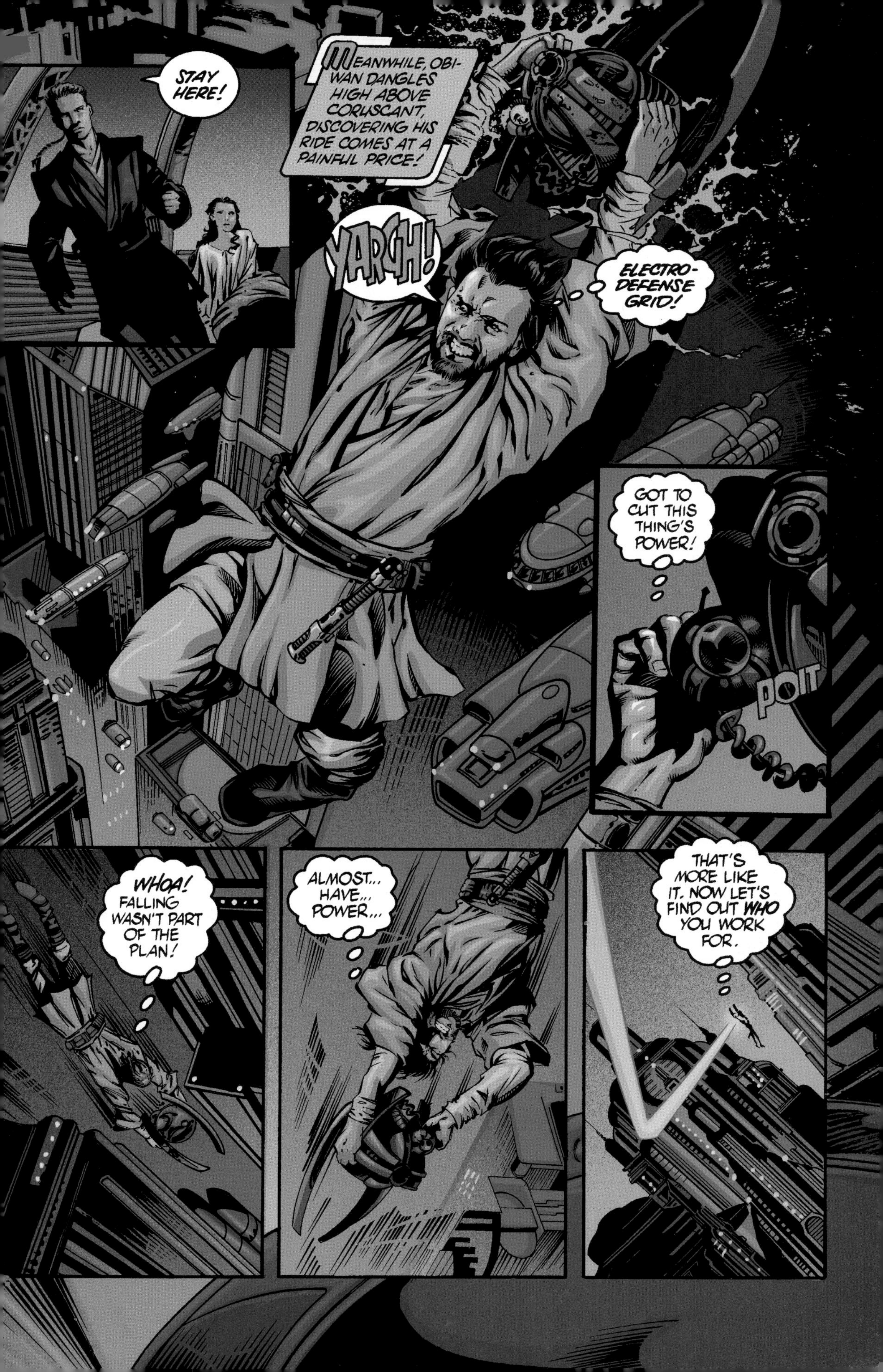
STAY HERE!
MEANWHILE, OBI-WAN DANGLES HIGH ABOVE CORUSCANT, DISCOVERING HIS RIDE COMES AT A PAINFUL PRICE!
YARGH!
ELECTRO-DEFENSE GRID!
GOT TO CUT THIS THING'S POWER!
POIT
WHOA! FALLING WASN'T PART OF THE PLAN!
ALMOST... HAVE... POWER...
THAT'S MORE LIKE IT. NOW LET'S FIND OUT WHO YOU WORK FOR.

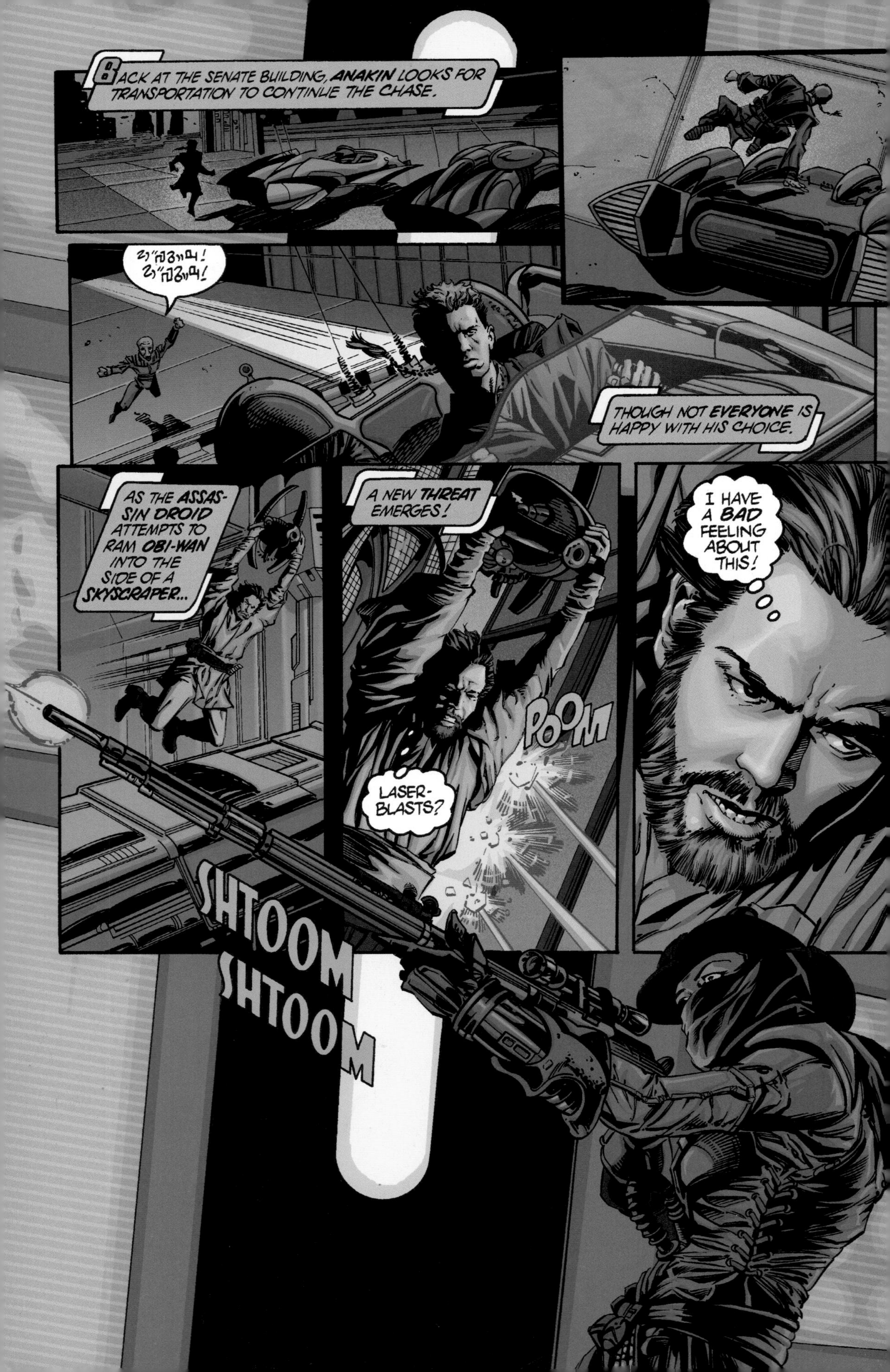
BACK AT THE SENATE BUILDING, ANAKIN LOOKS FOR TRANSPORTATION TO CONTINUE THE CHASE.
THOUGH NOT EVERYONE IS HAPPY WITH HIS CHOICE.
AS THE ASSASSIN DROID ATTEMPTS TO RAM OBI-WAN INTO THE SIDE OF A SKYSCRAPER...
A NEW THREAT EMERGES!
POOM
LASER-BLASTS?
I HAVE A BAD FEELING ABOUT THIS!
SHTOOM
SHTOOM

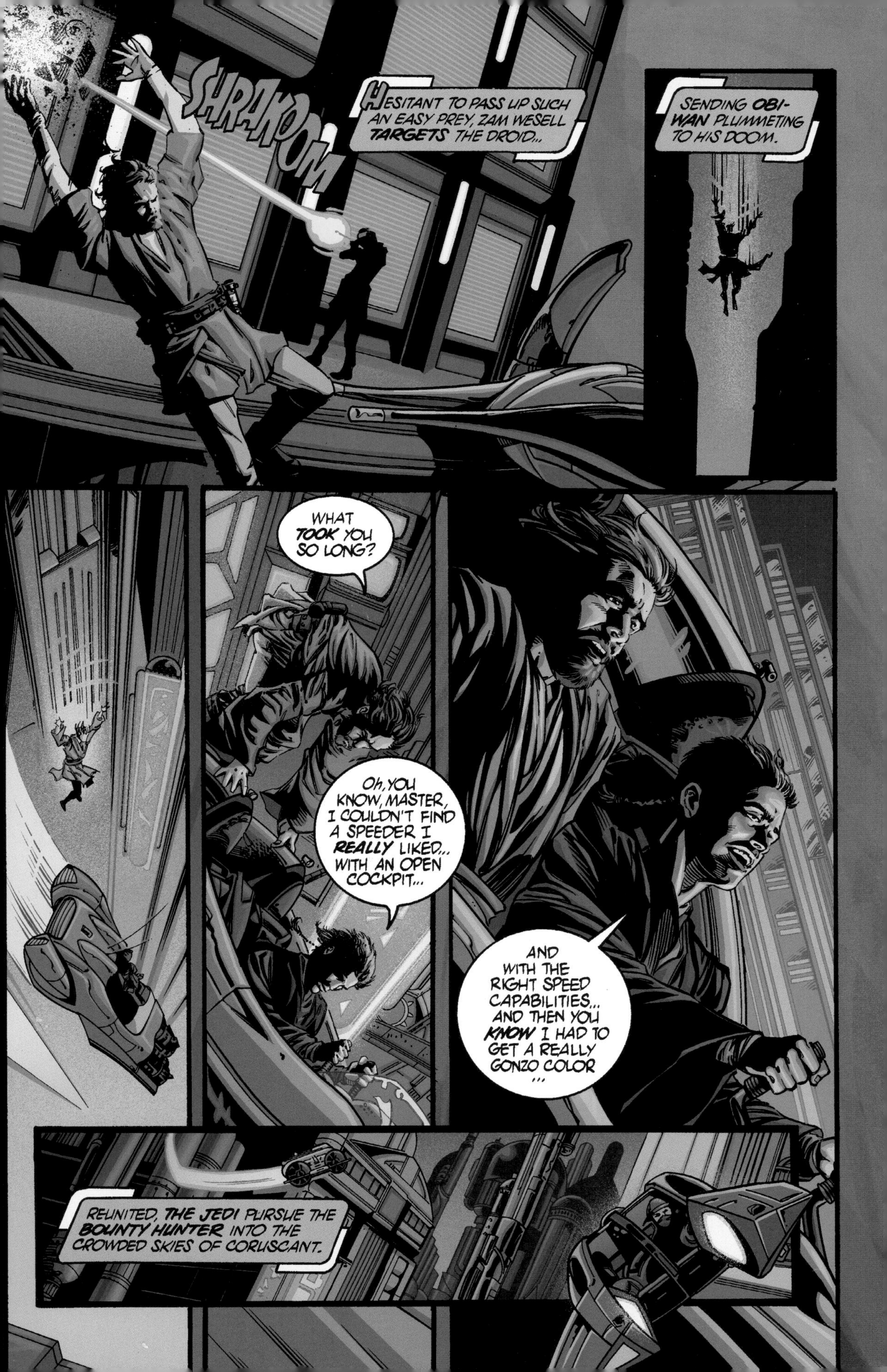
SHRAKOOM
HESITANT TO PASS UP SUCH AN EASY PREY, ZAM WESELL TARGETS THE DROID...
SENDING OBI-WAN PLUMMETING TO HIS DOOM.
WHAT TOOK YOU SO LONG?
OH, YOU KNOW, MASTER, I COULDN'T FIND A SPEEDER I REALLY LIKED... WITH AN OPEN COCKPIT...
AND WITH THE RIGHT SPEED CAPABILITIES... AND THEN YOU KNOW I HAD TO GET A REALLY GONZO COLOR ...
REUNITED, THE JEDI PURSUE THE BOUNTY HUNTER INTO THE CROWDED SKIES OF CORUSCANT.

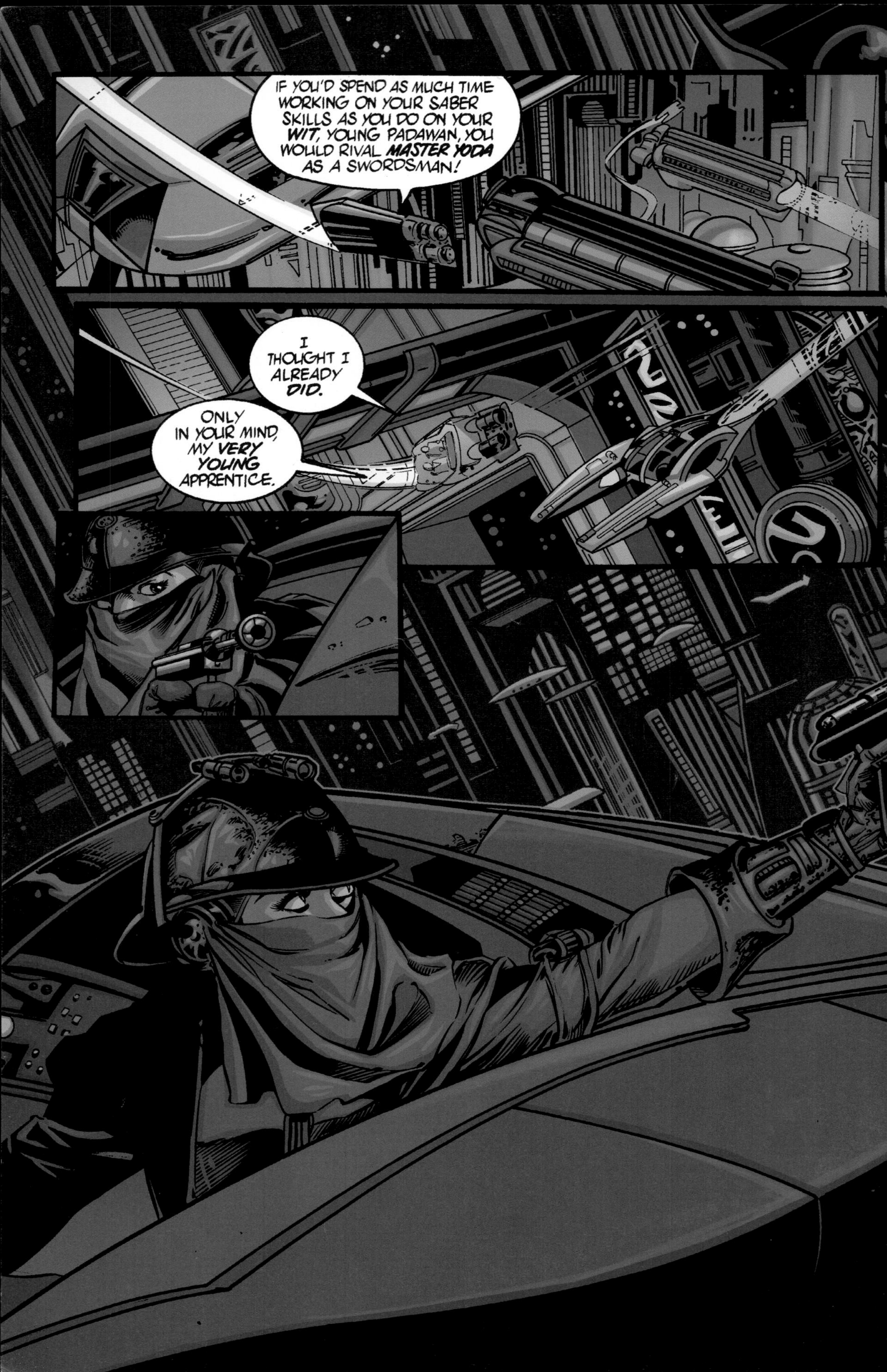
IF YOU'D SPEND AS MUCH TIME WORKING ON YOUR SABER SKILLS AS YOU DO ON YOUR WIT, YOUNG PADAWAN, YOU WOULD RIVAL MASTER YODA AS A SWORDSMAN!
I THOUGHT I ALREADY DID.
ONLY IN YOUR MIND, MY VERY YOUNG APPRENTICE.

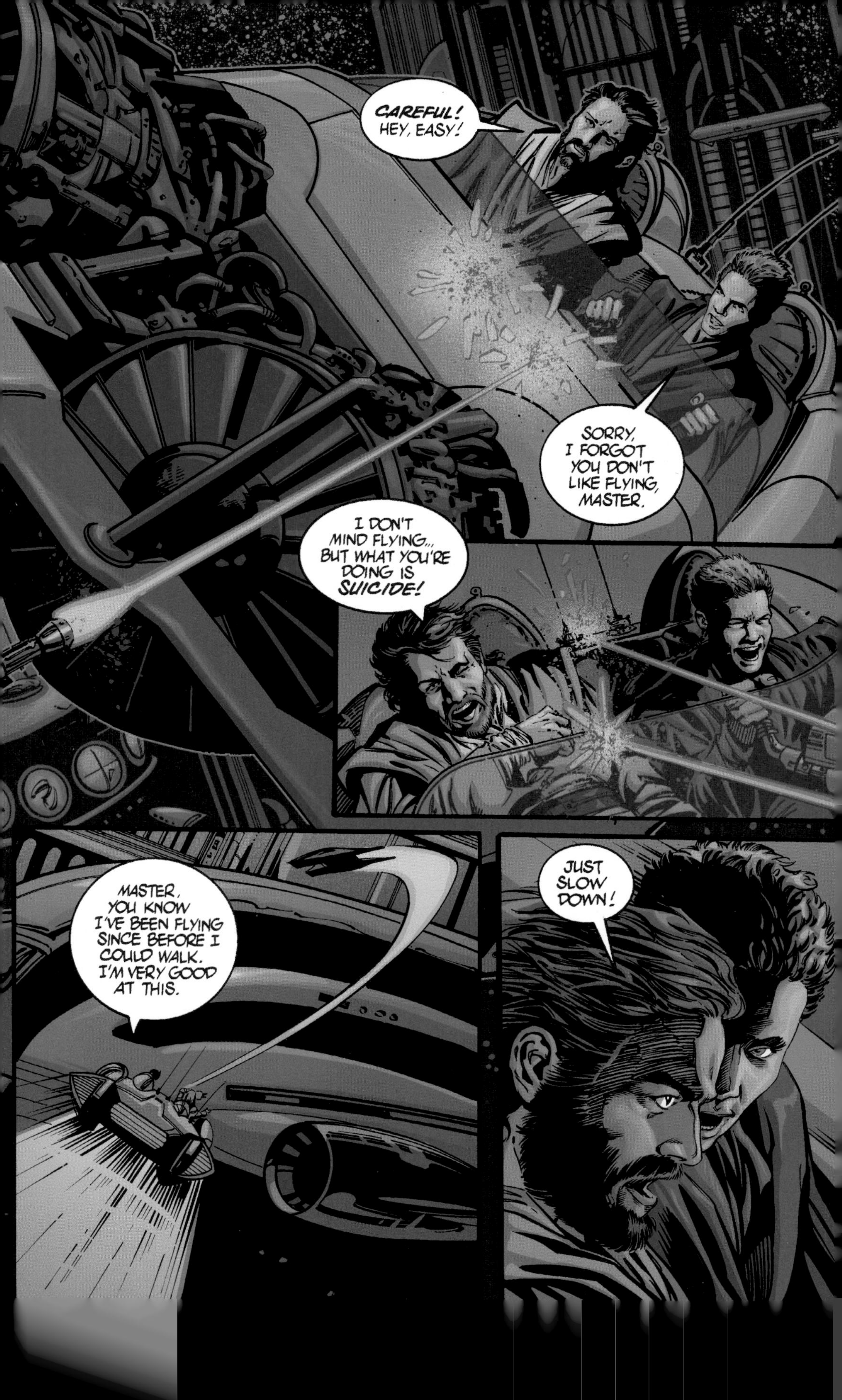
CAREFUL! HEY, EASY!
SORRY, I FORGOT YOU DON'T LIKE FLYING, MASTER.
I DON'T MIND FLYING... BUT WHAT YOU'RE DOING IS SUICIDE!
MASTER, YOU KNOW I'VE BEEN FLYING SINCE BEFORE I COULD WALK. I'M VERY GOOD AT THIS.
JUST SLOW DOWN!

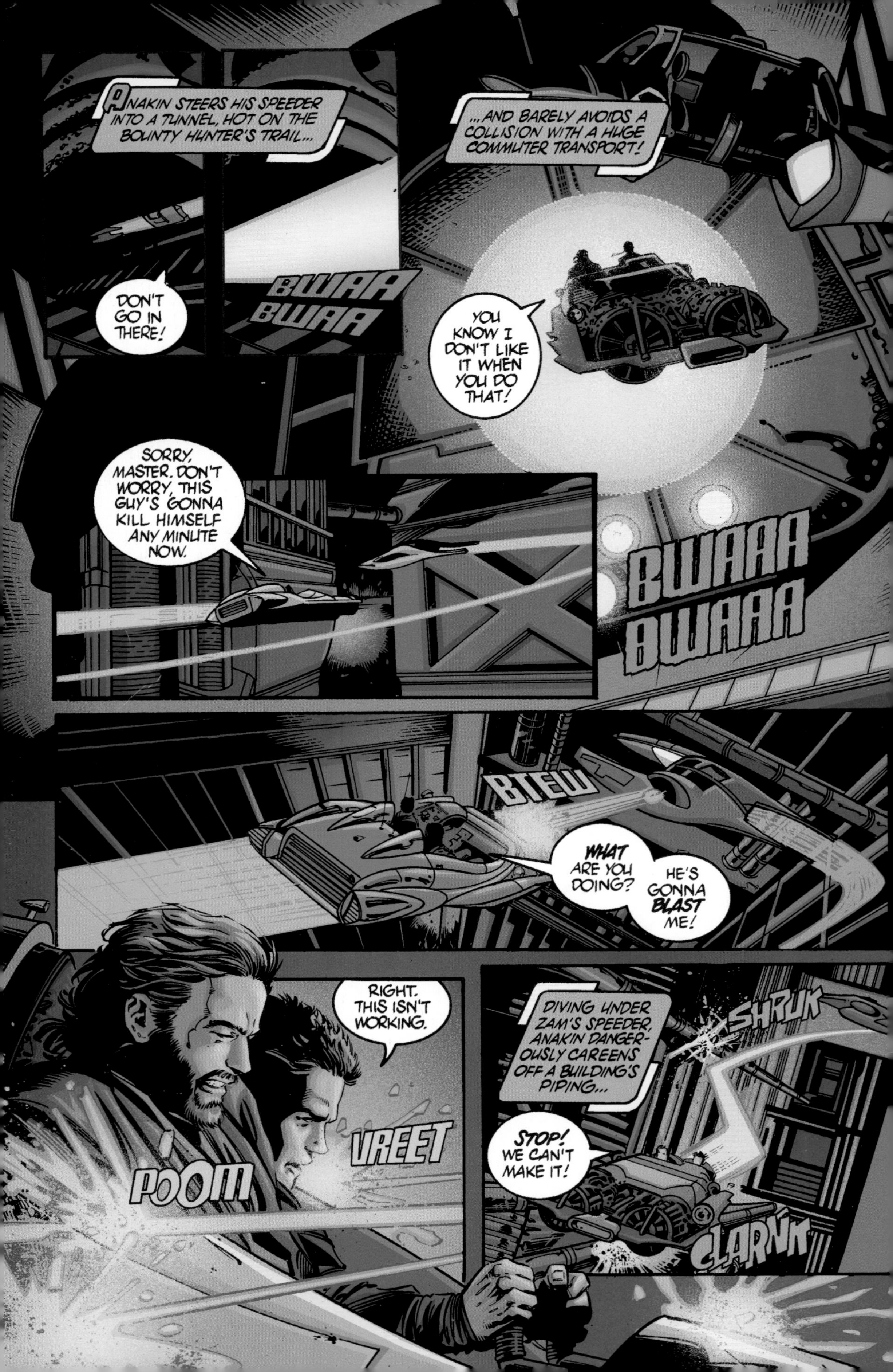

ANAKIN STEERS HIS SPEEDER INTO A TUNNEL, HOT ON THE BOUNTY HUNTER'S TRAIL...
DON'T GO IN THERE!
BWAA BWAA
...AND BARELY AVOIDS A COLLISION WITH A HUGE COMMUTER TRANSPORT!
YOU KNOW I DON'T LIKE IT WHEN YOU DO THAT!
SORRY, MASTER. DON'T WORRY, THIS GUY'S GONNA KILL HIMSELF ANY MINUTE NOW.
BWAAA BWAAA
BTEW
WHAT ARE YOU DOING?
HE'S GONNA BLAST ME!
RIGHT. THIS ISN'T WORKING.
VREET
POOM
DIVING UNDER ZAM'S SPEEDER, ANAKIN DANGEROUSLY CAREENS OFF A BUILDING'S PIPING...
SHRUK
STOP! WE CAN'T MAKE IT!
CLARNK

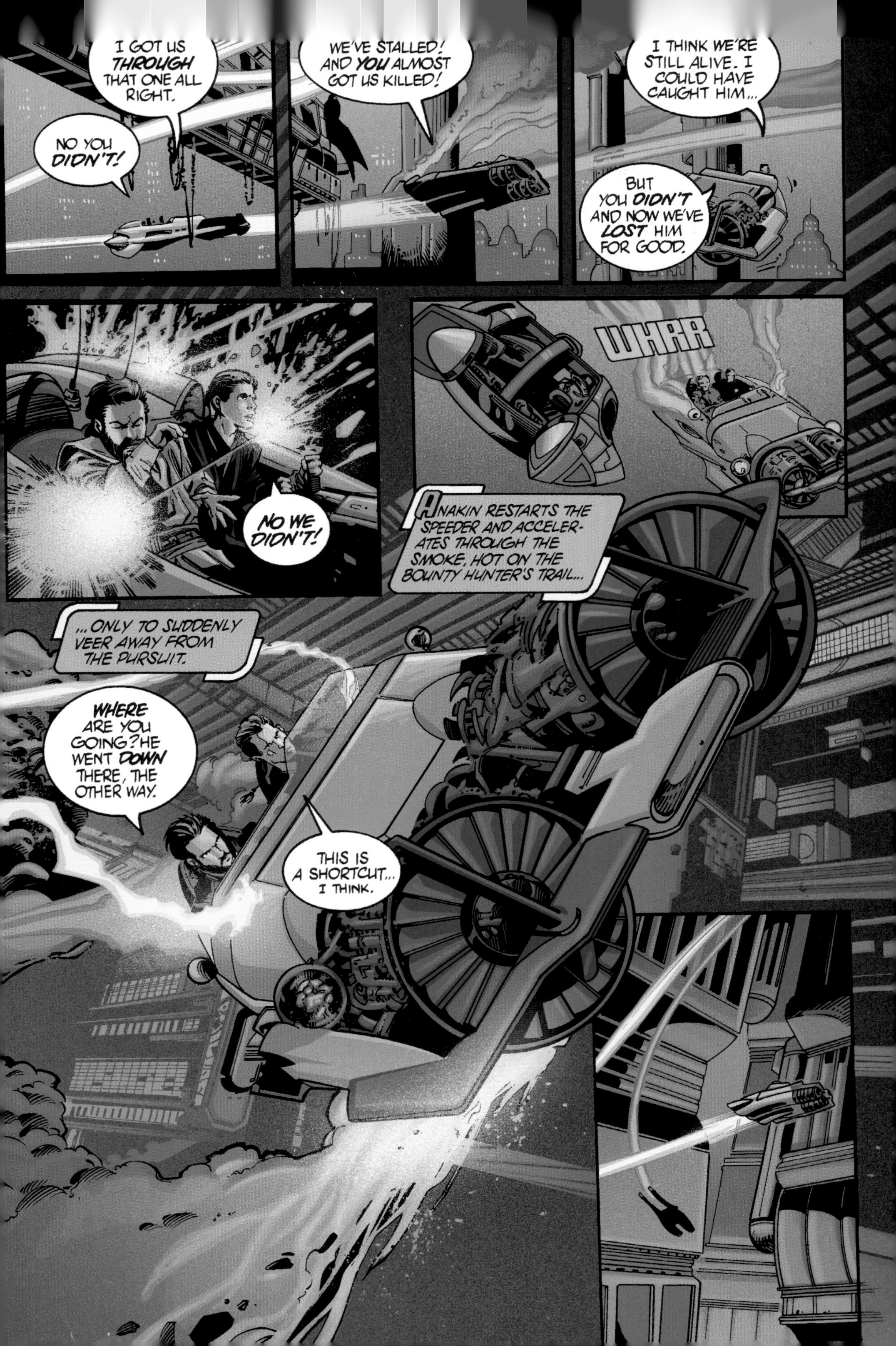
I GOT US THROUGH THAT ONE ALL RIGHT.
NO YOU DIDN'T!
WE'VE STALLED! AND YOU ALMOST GOT US KILLED!
I THINK WE'RE STILL ALIVE. I COULD HAVE CAUGHT HIM...
BUT YOU DIDN'T AND NOW WE'VE LOST HIM FOR GOOD.
NO WE DIDN'T!
WHRR
ANAKIN RESTARTS THE SPEEDER AND ACCELERATES THROUGH THE SMOKE, HOT ON THE BOUNTY HUNTER'S TRAIL...
...ONLY TO SUDDENLY VEER AWAY FROM THE PURSUIT.
WHERE ARE YOU GOING? HE WENT DOWN THERE, THE OTHER WAY.
THIS IS A SHORTCUT... I THINK.

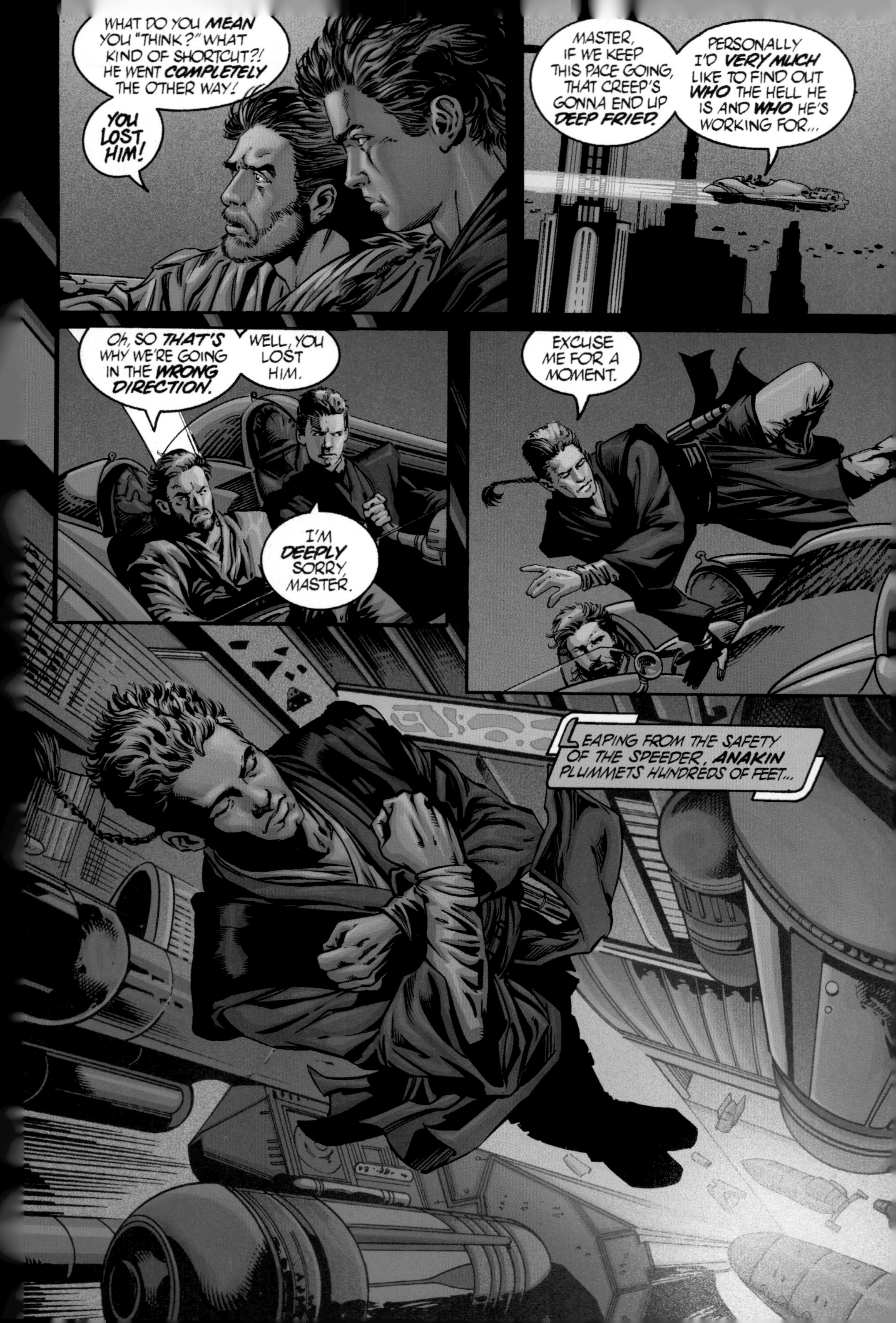

WHAT DO YOU MEAN YOU "THINK?" WHAT KIND OF SHORTCUT?! HE WENT COMPLETELY THE OTHER WAY!
YOU LOST HIM!
MASTER, IF WE KEEP THIS PACE GOING, THAT CREEP'S GONNA END UP DEEP FRIED.
PERSONALLY I'D VERY MUCH LIKE TO FIND OUT WHO THE HELL HE IS AND WHO HE'S WORKING FOR...
Oh, SO THAT'S WHY WE'RE GOING IN THE WRONG DIRECTION.
WELL, YOU LOST HIM.
I'M DEEPLY SORRY, MASTER.
EXCUSE ME FOR A MOMENT.
LEAPING FROM THE SAFETY OF THE SPEEDER, ANAKIN PLUMMETS HUNDREDS OF FEET...

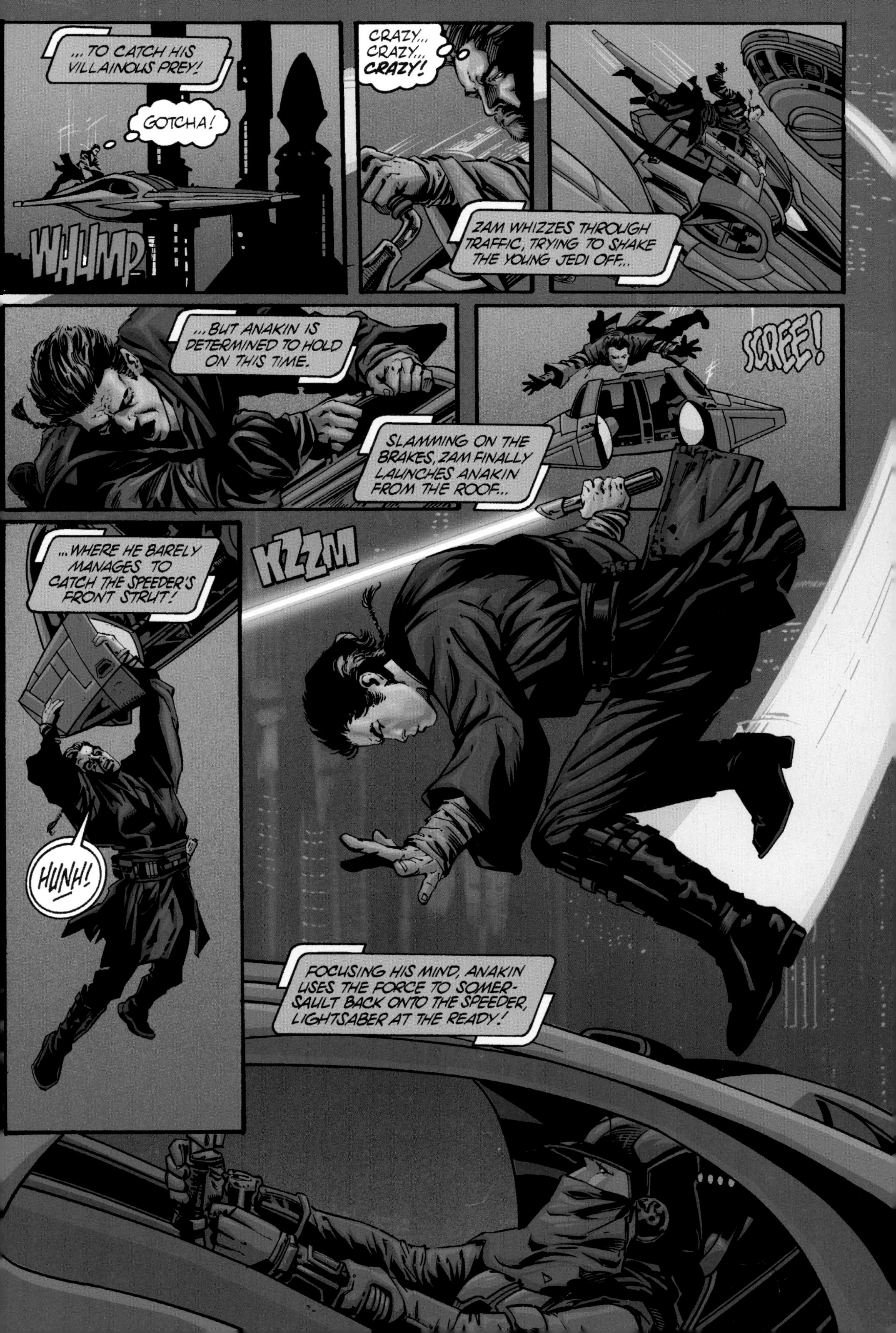

...TO CATCH HIS VILLAINOUS PREY!
GOTCHA!
WHUMP
CRAZY... CRAZY... CRAZY!
ZAM WHIZZES THROUGH TRAFFIC, TRYING TO SHAKE THE YOUNG JEDI OFF...
...BUT ANAKIN IS DETERMINED TO HOLD ON THIS TIME.
SCREE!
SLAMMING ON THE BRAKES, ZAM FINALLY LAUNCHES ANAKIN FROM THE ROOF...
...WHERE HE BARELY MANAGES TO CATCH THE SPEEDER'S FRONT STRUT!
KZZM
HUNH!
FOCUSING HIS MIND, ANAKIN USES THE FORCE TO SOMER-SAULT BACK ONTO THE SPEEDER, LIGHTSABER AT THE READY!

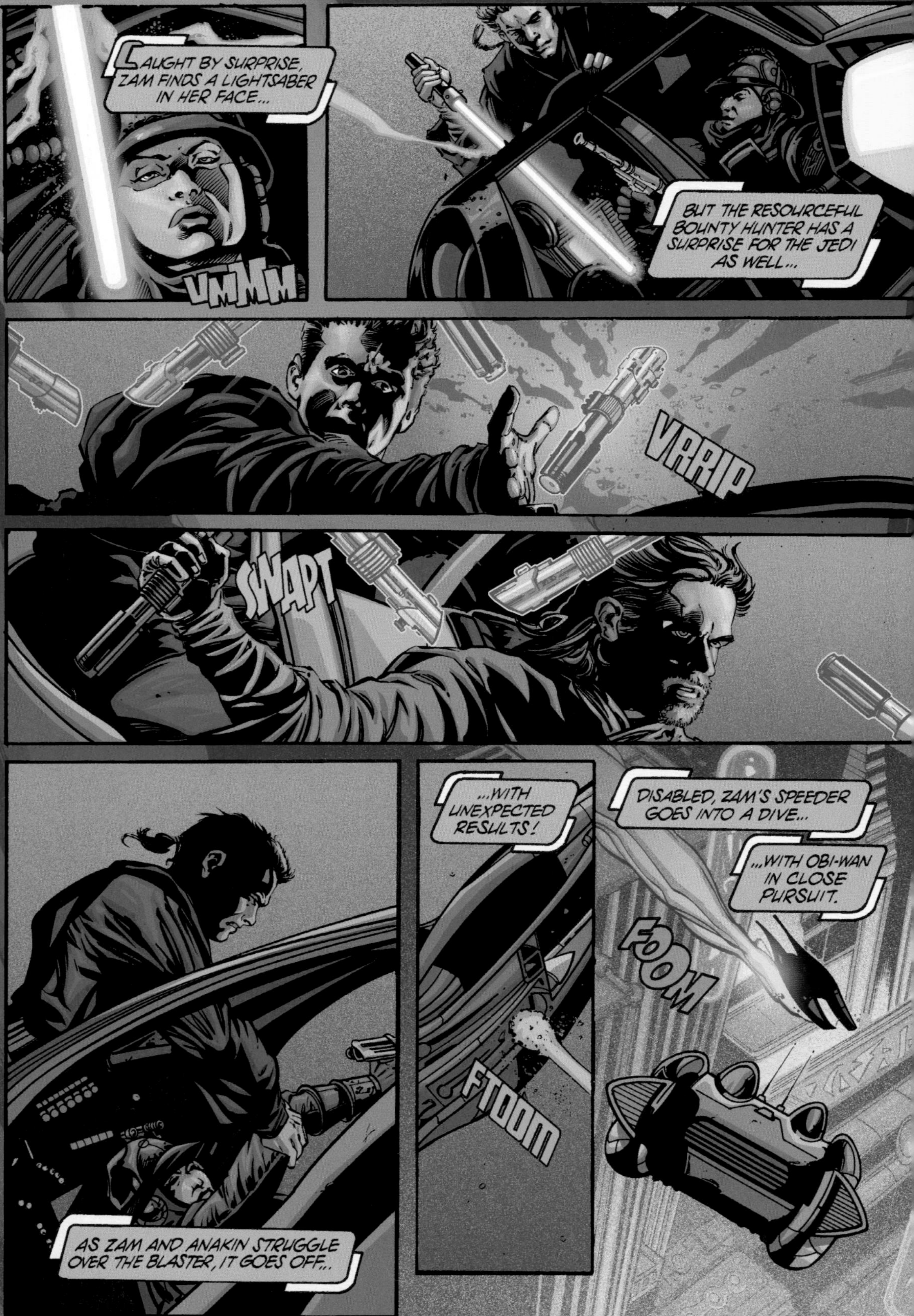
CAUGHT BY SURPRISE, ZAM FINDS A LIGHTSABER IN HER FACE...
UMMM
BUT THE RESOURCEFUL BOUNTY HUNTER HAS A SURPRISE FOR THE JEDI AS WELL...
VRRIP
SWAPT
AS ZAM AND ANAKIN STRUGGLE OVER THE BLASTER, IT GOES OFF...
...WITH UNEXPECTED RESULTS!
FTOOM
DISABLED, ZAM'S SPEEDER GOES INTO A DIVE...
...WITH OBI-WAN IN CLOSE PURSUIT.
FOOM

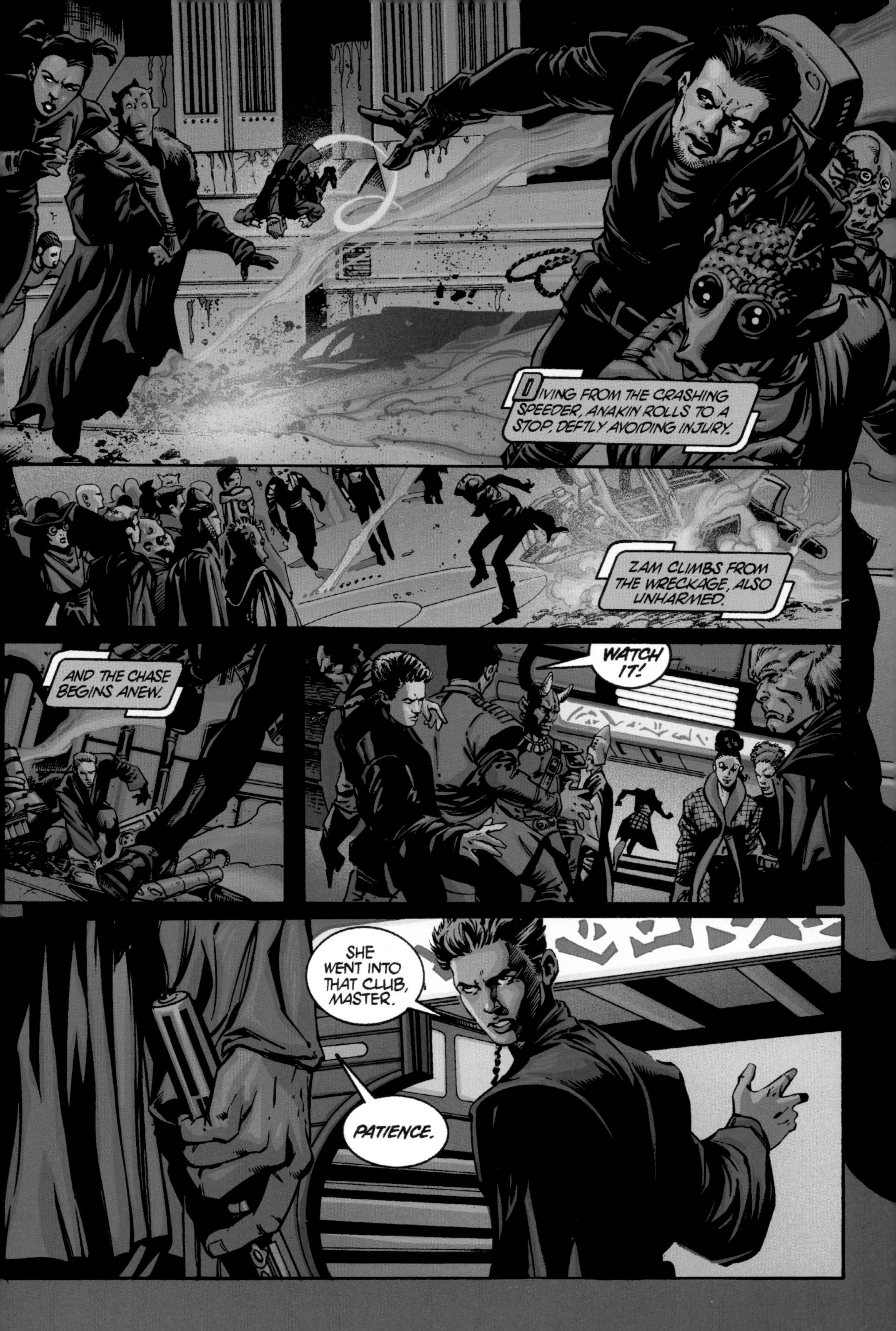
DIVING FROM THE CRASHING SPEEDER, ANAKIN ROLLS TO A STOP, DEFTLY AVOIDING INJURY.
ZAM CLIMBS FROM THE WRECKAGE, ALSO UNHARMED.
AND THE CHASE BEGINS ANEW.
WATCH IT!
SHE WENT INTO THAT CLUB, MASTER.
PATIENCE.

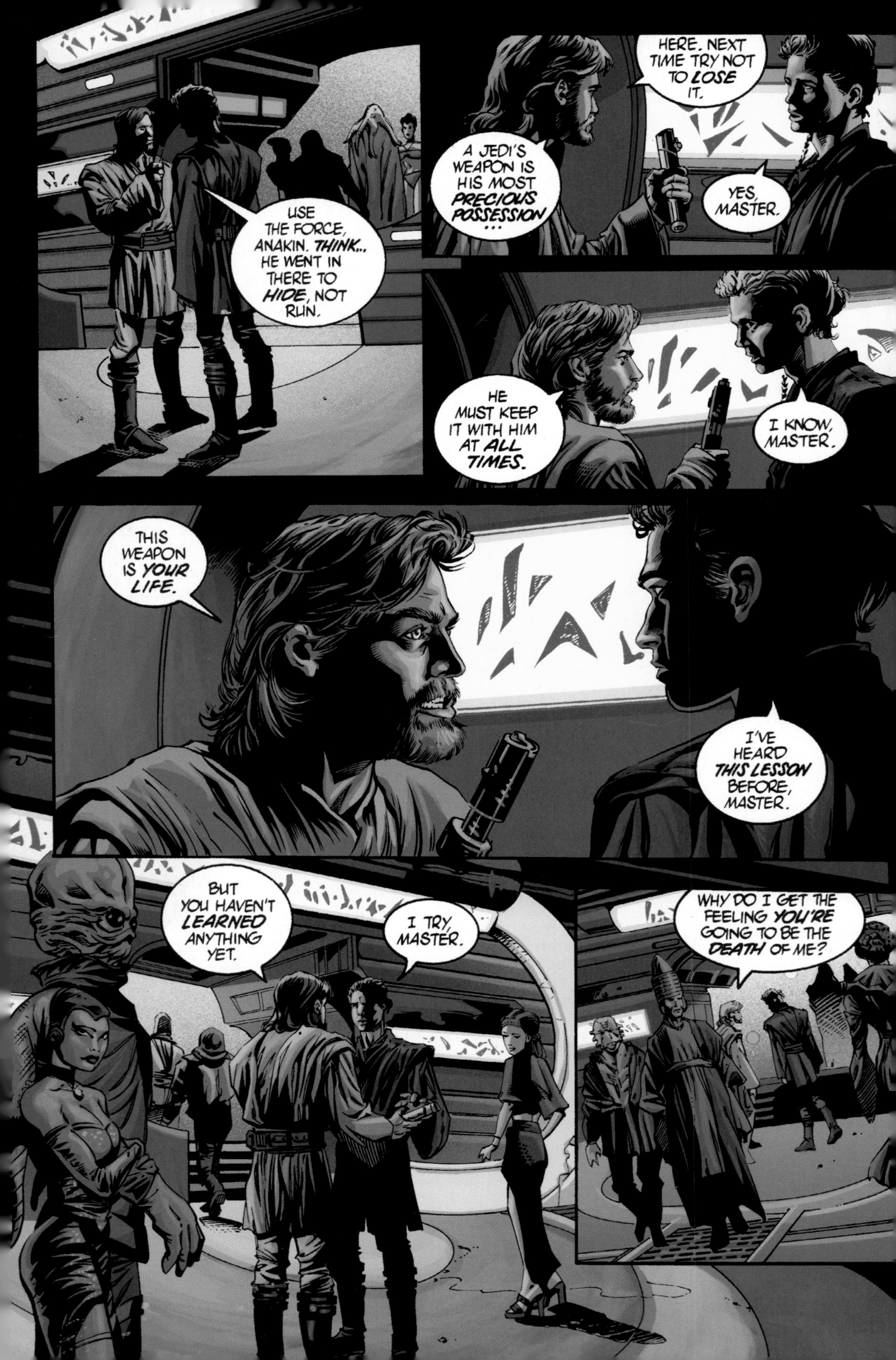

USE THE FORCE, ANAKIN. THINK... HE WENT IN THERE TO HIDE, NOT RUN.
HERE. NEXT TIME TRY NOT TO LOSE IT.
A JEDI'S WEAPON IS HIS MOST PRECIOUS POSSESSION...
YES, MASTER.
HE MUST KEEP IT WITH HIM AT ALL TIMES.
I KNOW, MASTER.
THIS WEAPON IS YOUR LIFE.
I'VE HEARD THIS LESSON BEFORE, MASTER.
BUT YOU HAVEN'T LEARNED ANYTHING YET.
I TRY, MASTER.
WHY DO I GET THE FEELING YOU'RE GOING TO BE THE DEATH OF ME?

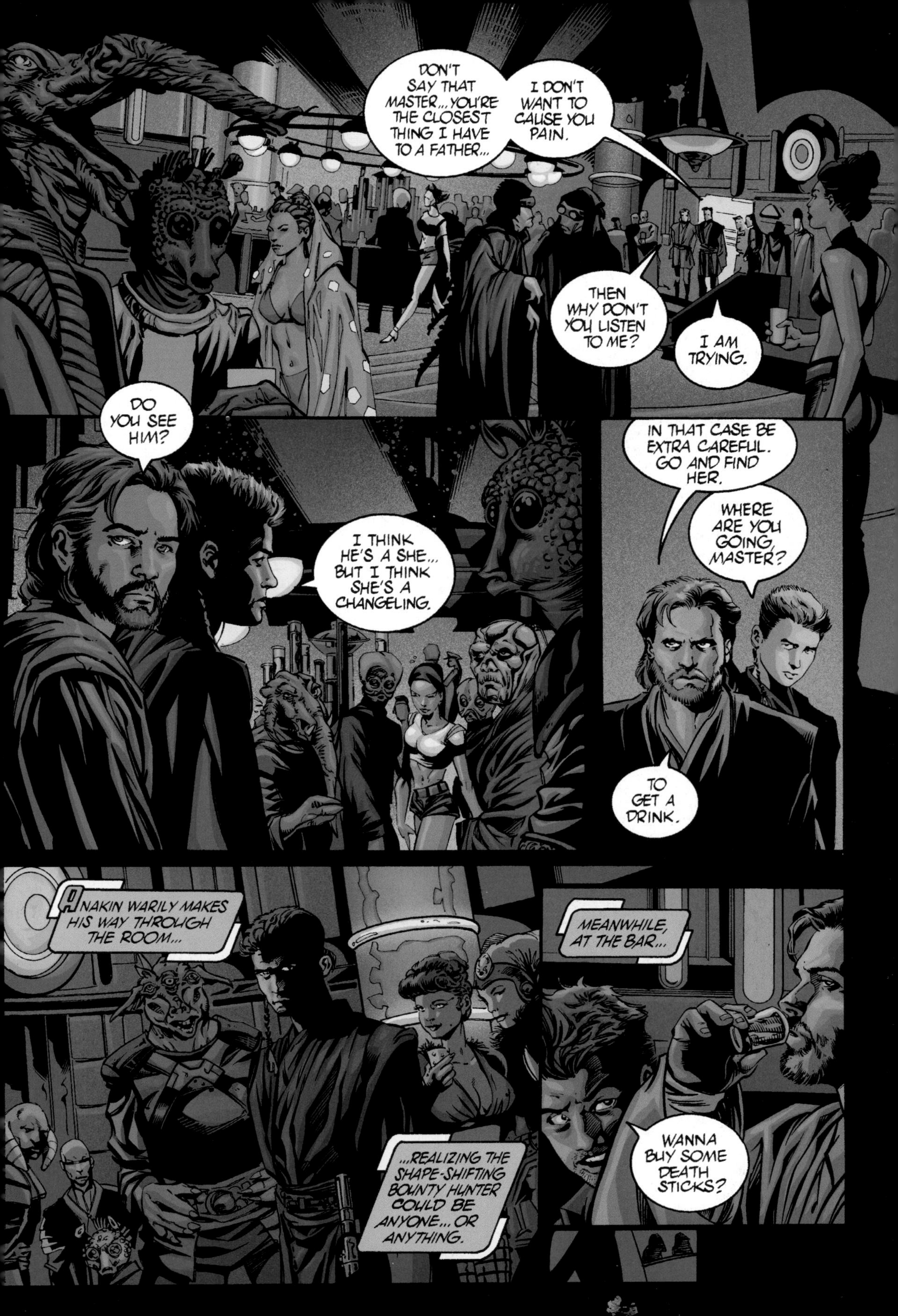
DON'T SAY THAT MASTER... YOU'RE THE CLOSEST THING I HAVE TO A FATHER...
I DON'T WANT TO CAUSE YOU PAIN.
THEN WHY DON'T YOU LISTEN TO ME?
I AM TRYING.
DO YOU SEE HIM?
I THINK HE'S A SHE... BUT I THINK SHE'S A CHANGELING.
IN THAT CASE BE EXTRA CAREFUL. GO AND FIND HER.
WHERE ARE YOU GOING, MASTER?
TO GET A DRINK.
ANAKIN WARILY MAKES HIS WAY THROUGH THE ROOM...
...REALIZING THE SHAPE-SHIFTING BOUNTY HUNTER COULD BE ANYONE... OR ANYTHING.
MEANWHILE, AT THE BAR...
WANNA BUY SOME DEATH STICKS?

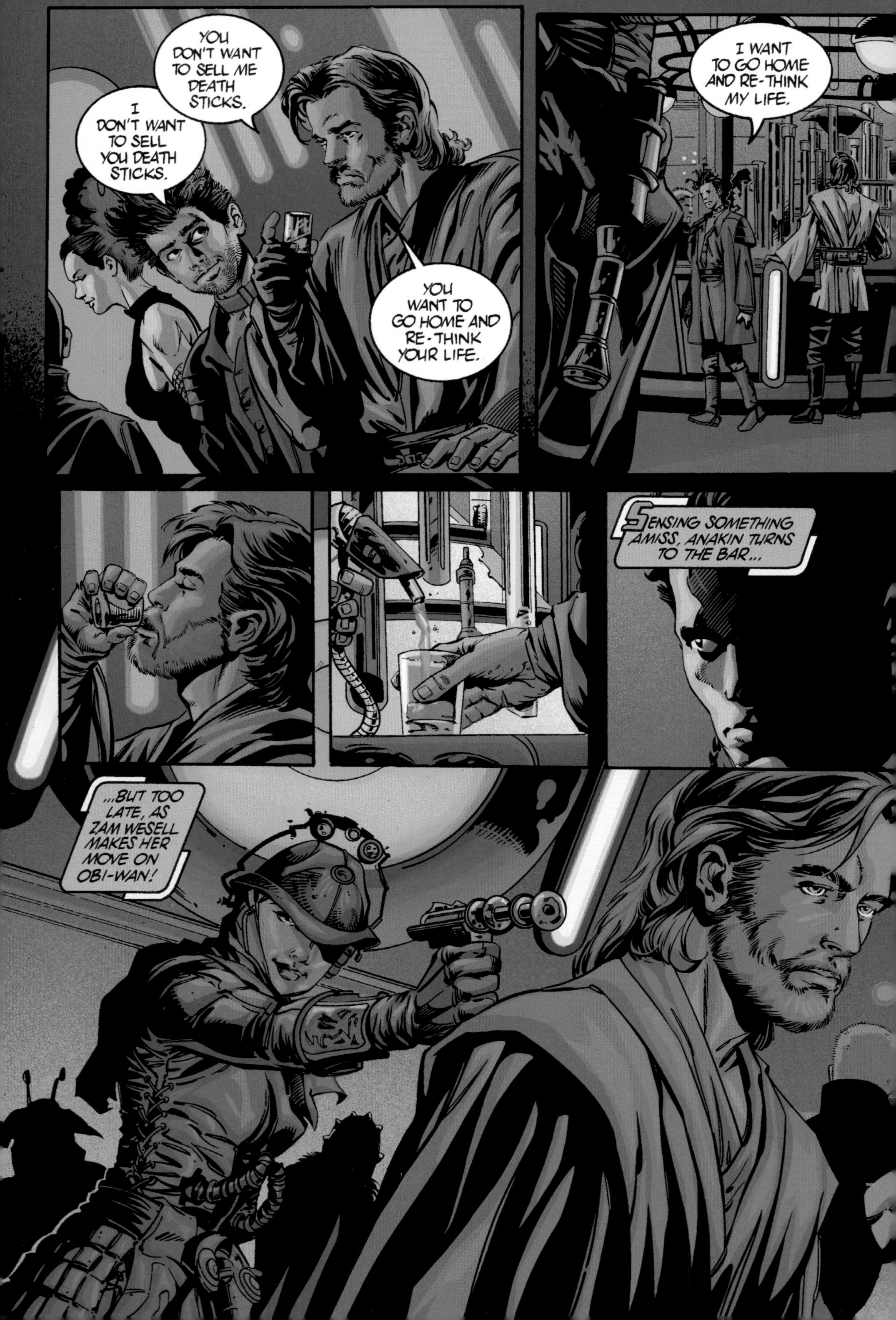
YOU DON'T WANT TO SELL ME DEATH STICKS.
I DON'T WANT TO SELL YOU DEATH STICKS.
YOU WANT TO GO HOME AND RE-THINK YOUR LIFE.
I WANT TO GO HOME AND RE-THINK MY LIFE.
SENSING SOMETHING AMISS, ANAKIN TURNS TO THE BAR...
...BUT TOO LATE, AS ZAM WESELL MAKES HER MOVE ON OBI-WAN!

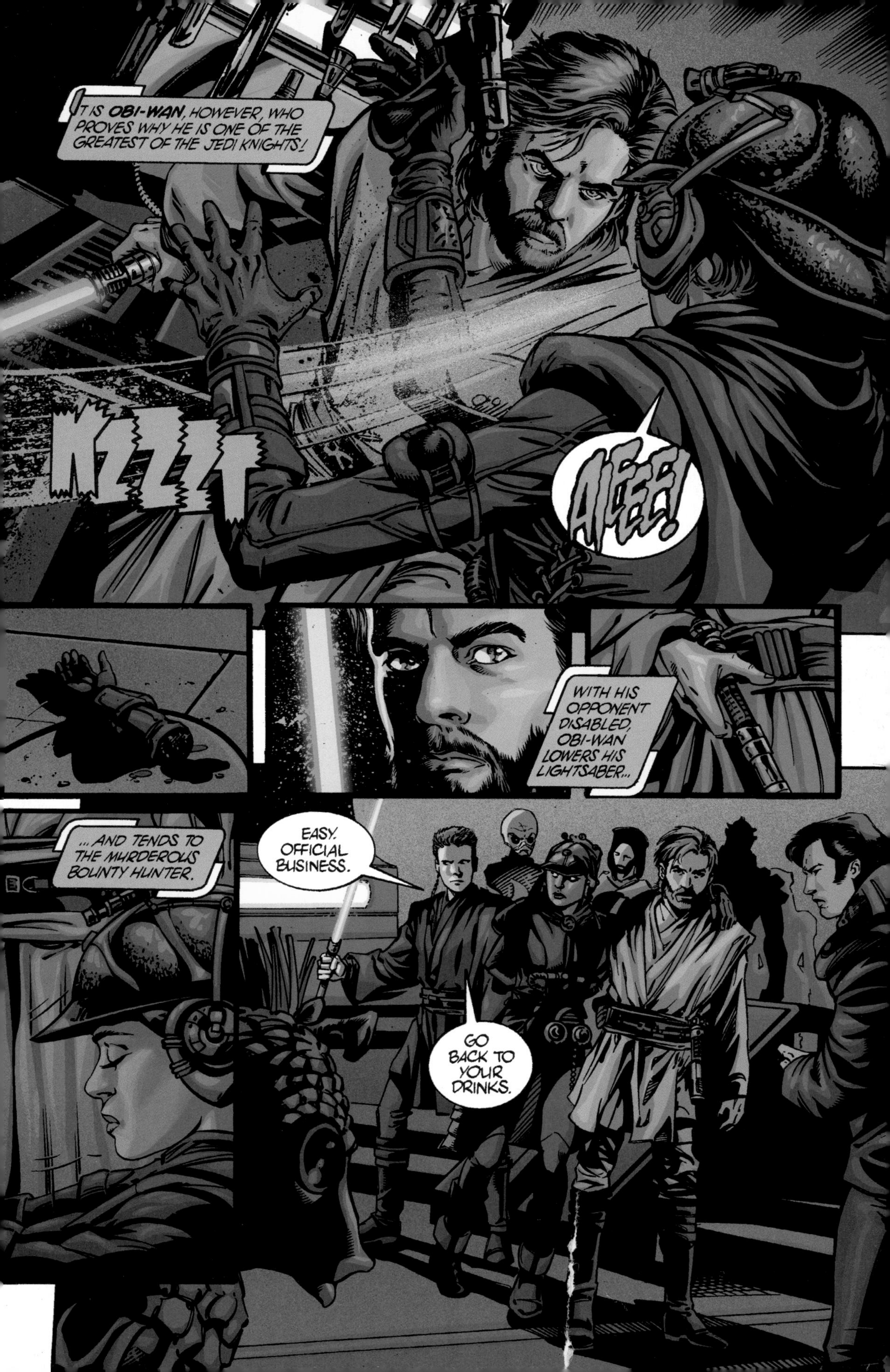
IT IS OBI-WAN, HOWEVER, WHO PROVES WHY HE IS ONE OF THE GREATEST OF THE JEDI KNIGHTS!
KZZZT
AIEEE!
WITH HIS OPPONENT DISABLED, OBI-WAN LOWERS HIS LIGHTSABER...
...AND TENDS TO THE MURDEROUS BOUNTY HUNTER.
EASY. OFFICIAL BUSINESS.
GO BACK TO YOUR DRINKS.

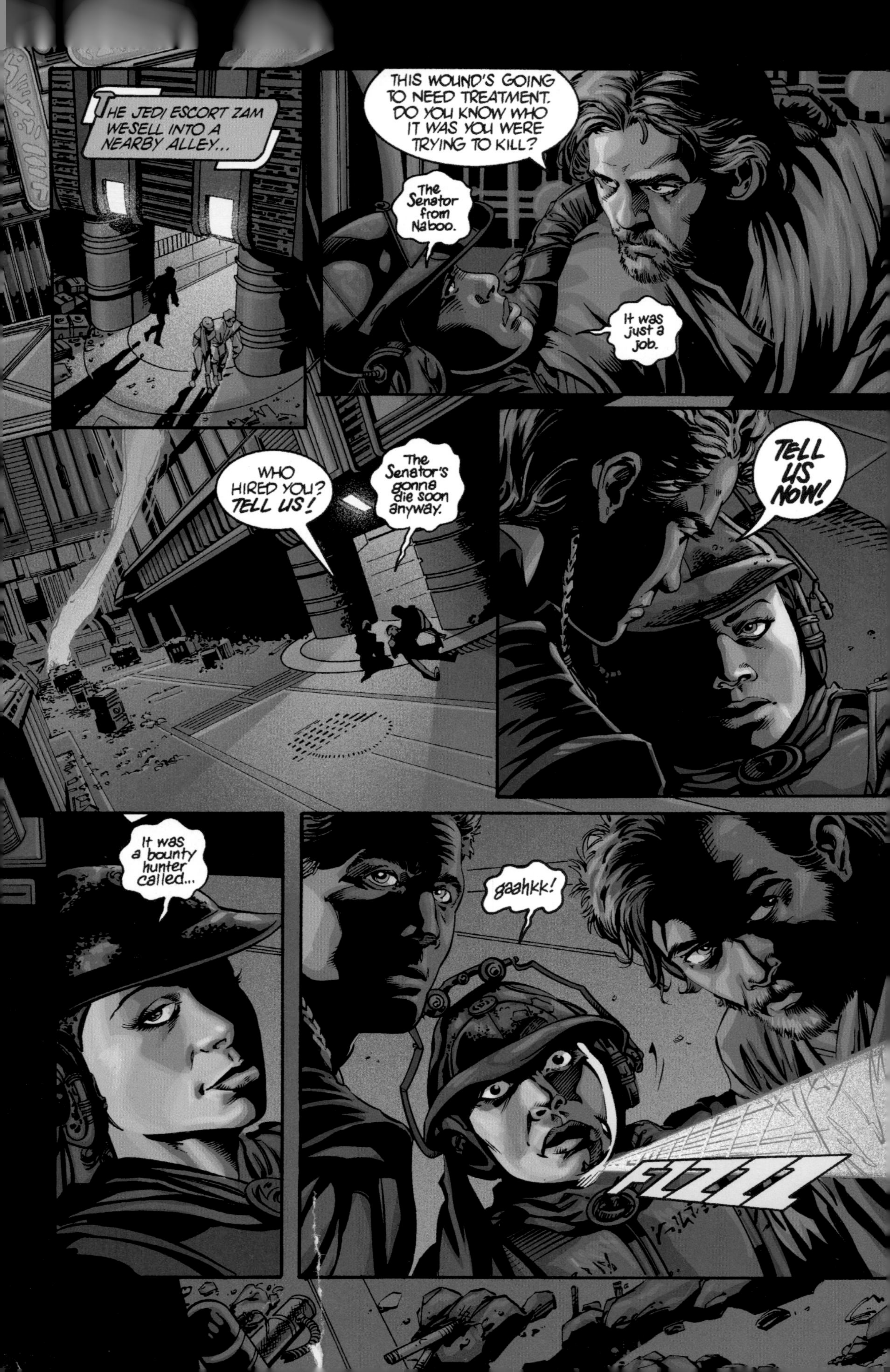

THE JEDI ESCORT ZAM WESELL INTO A NEARBY ALLEY...
THIS WOUND'S GOING TO NEED TREATMENT. DO YOU KNOW WHO IT WAS YOU WERE TRYING TO KILL?
The Senator from Naboo.
It was just a job.
WHO HIRED YOU? TELL US!
The Senator's gonna die soon anyway.
TELL US NOW!
It was a bounty hunter called...
gaahkk!
FZZZT

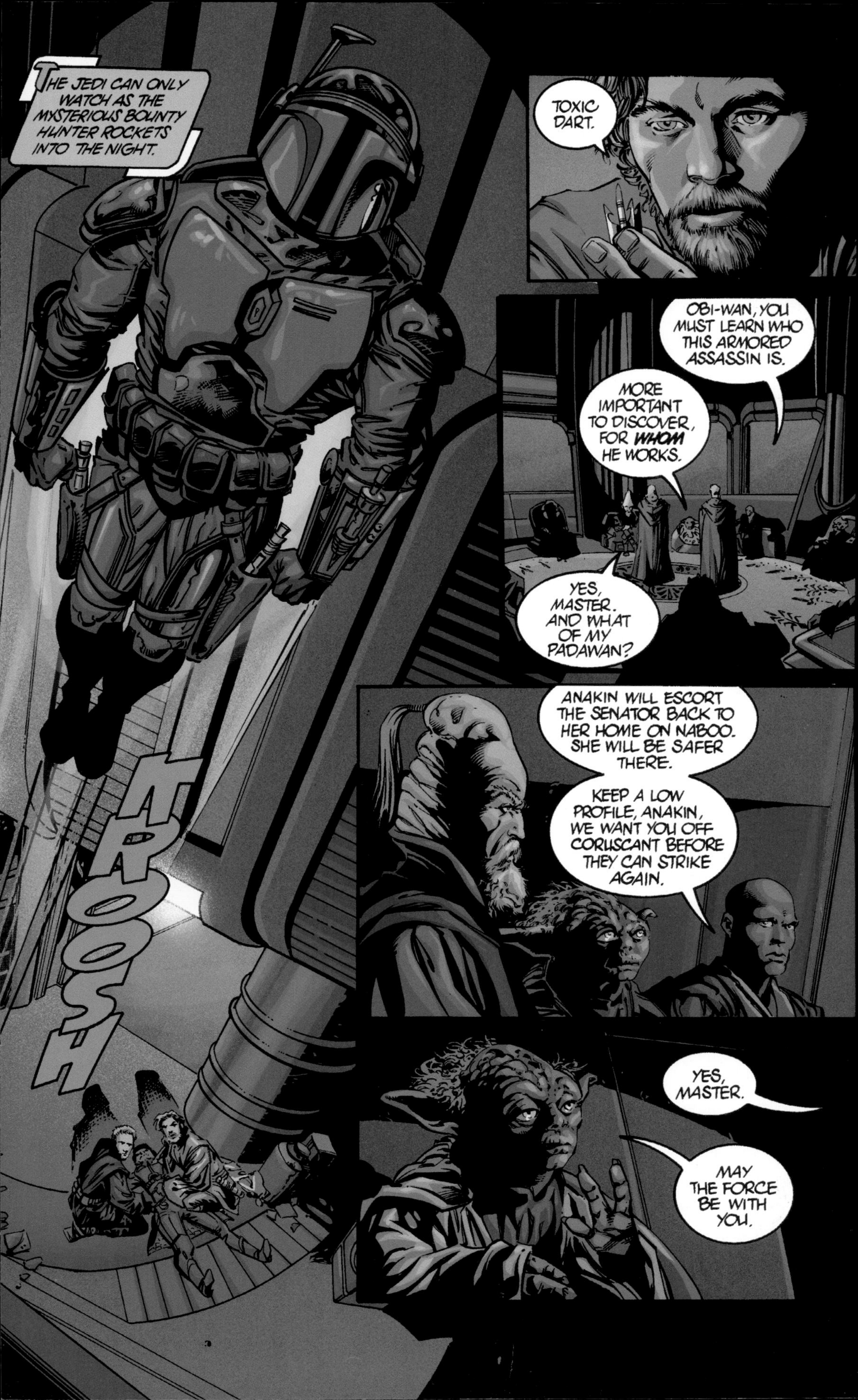
THE JEDI CAN ONLY WATCH AS THE MYSTERIOUS BOUNTY HUNTER ROCKETS INTO THE NIGHT.
KRROOOSH
TOXIC DART.
OBI-WAN, YOU MUST LEARN WHO THIS ARMORED ASSASSIN IS.
MORE IMPORTANT TO DISCOVER, FOR WHOM HE WORKS.
YES, MASTER. AND WHAT OF MY PADAWAN?
ANAKIN WILL ESCORT THE SENATOR BACK TO HER HOME ON NABOO. SHE WILL BE SAFER THERE.
KEEP A LOW PROFILE, ANAKIN, WE WANT YOU OFF CORUSCANT BEFORE THEY CAN STRIKE AGAIN.
YES, MASTER.
MAY THE FORCE BE WITH YOU.

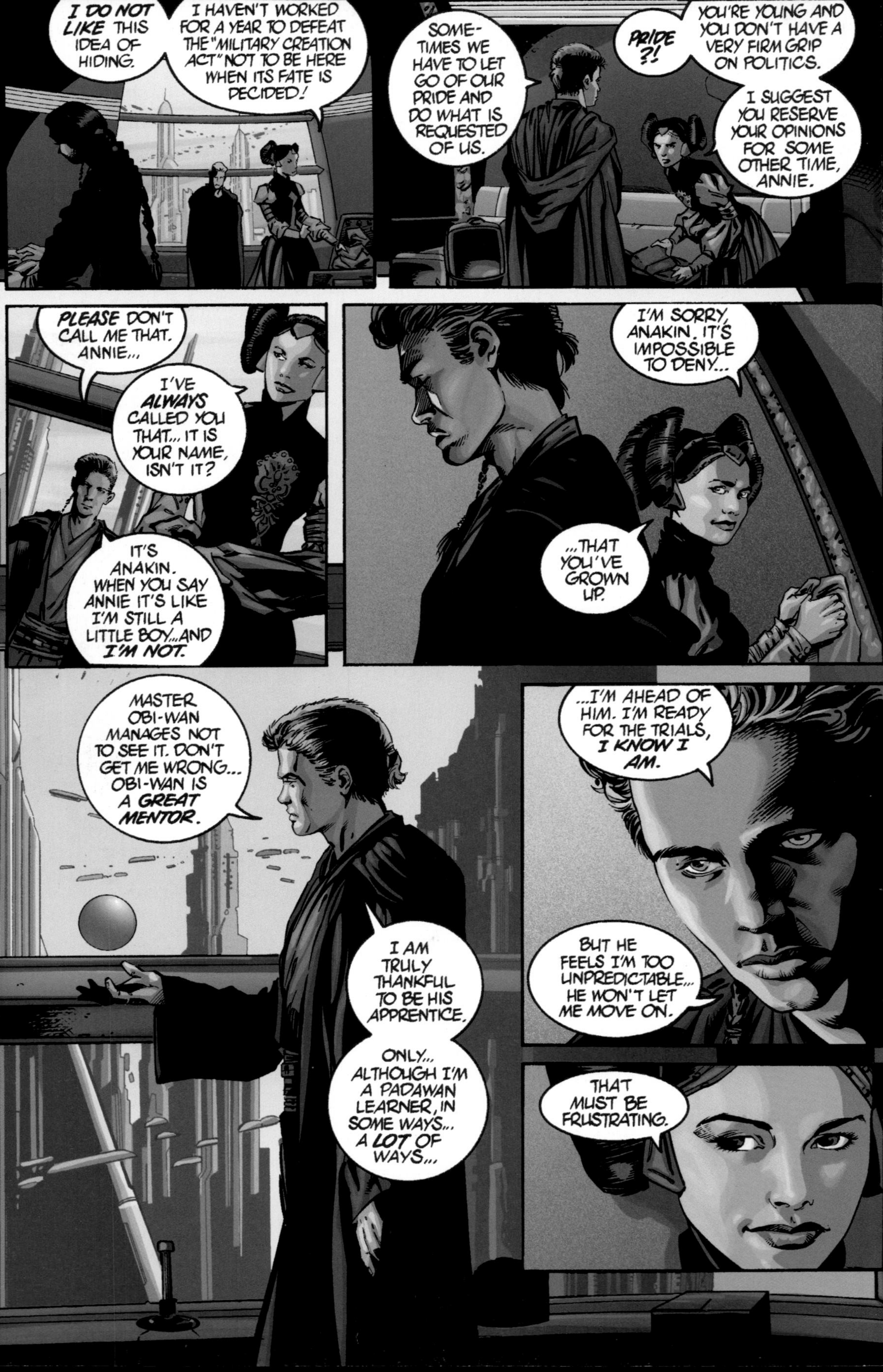
I DO NOT LIKE THIS IDEA OF HIDING.
I HAVEN'T WORKED FOR A YEAR TO DEFEAT THE "MILITARY CREATION ACT" NOT TO BE HERE WHEN ITS FATE IS DECIDED!
SOMETIMES WE HAVE TO LET GO OF OUR PRIDE AND DO WHAT IS REQUESTED OF US.
PRIDE ?!
YOU'RE YOUNG AND YOU DON'T HAVE A VERY FIRM GRIP ON POLITICS.
I SUGGEST YOU RESERVE YOUR OPINIONS FOR SOME OTHER TIME, ANNIE.
PLEASE DON'T CALL ME THAT. ANNIE...
I'VE ALWAYS CALLED YOU THAT... IT IS YOUR NAME, ISN'T IT?
IT'S ANAKIN. WHEN YOU SAY ANNIE IT'S LIKE I'M STILL A LITTLE BOY...AND I'M NOT.
I'M SORRY, ANAKIN. IT'S IMPOSSIBLE TO DENY...
...THAT YOU'VE GROWN UP.
MASTER OBI-WAN MANAGES NOT TO SEE IT. DON'T GET ME WRONG... OBI-WAN IS A GREAT MENTOR.
I AM TRULY THANKFUL TO BE HIS APPRENTICE.
ONLY... ALTHOUGH I'M A PADAWAN LEARNER, IN SOME WAYS... A LOT OF WAYS...
...I'M AHEAD OF HIM. I'M READY FOR THE TRIALS, I KNOW I AM.
BUT HE FEELS I'M TOO UNPREDICTABLE... HE WON'T LET ME MOVE ON.
THAT MUST BE FRUSTRATING.

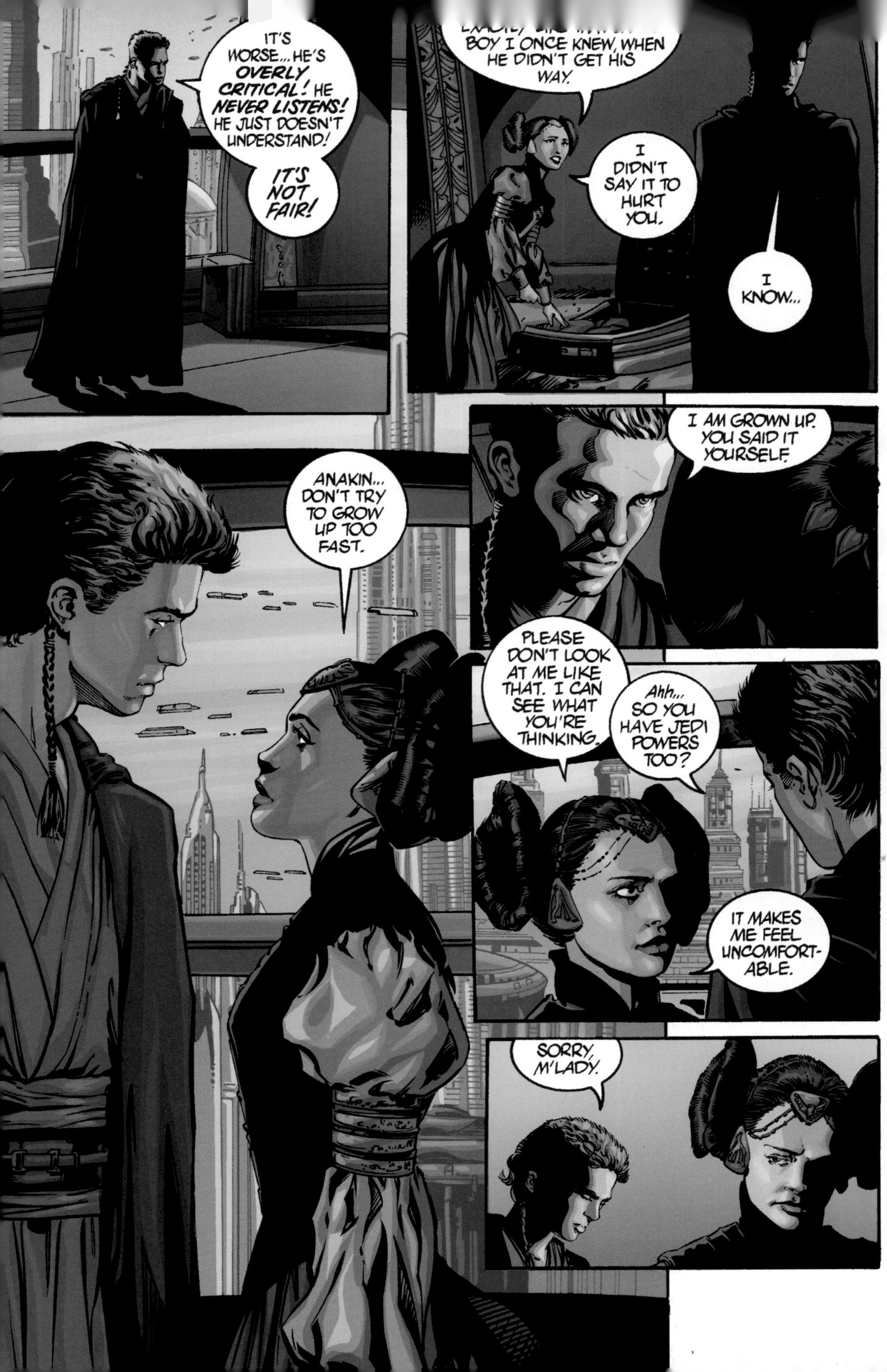
IT'S WORSE... HE'S OVERLY CRITICAL! HE NEVER LISTENS! HE JUST DOESN'T UNDERSTAND!
IT'S NOT FAIR!
BOY I ONCE KNEW, WHEN HE DIDN'T GET HIS WAY.
I DIDN'T SAY IT TO HURT YOU.
I KNOW...
ANAKIN... DON'T TRY TO GROW UP TOO FAST.
I AM GROWN UP. YOU SAID IT YOURSELF.
PLEASE DON'T LOOK AT ME LIKE THAT. I CAN SEE WHAT YOU'RE THINKING.
Ahh... SO YOU HAVE JEDI POWERS TOO?
IT MAKES ME FEEL UNCOMFORT-ABLE.
SORRY, M'LADY.

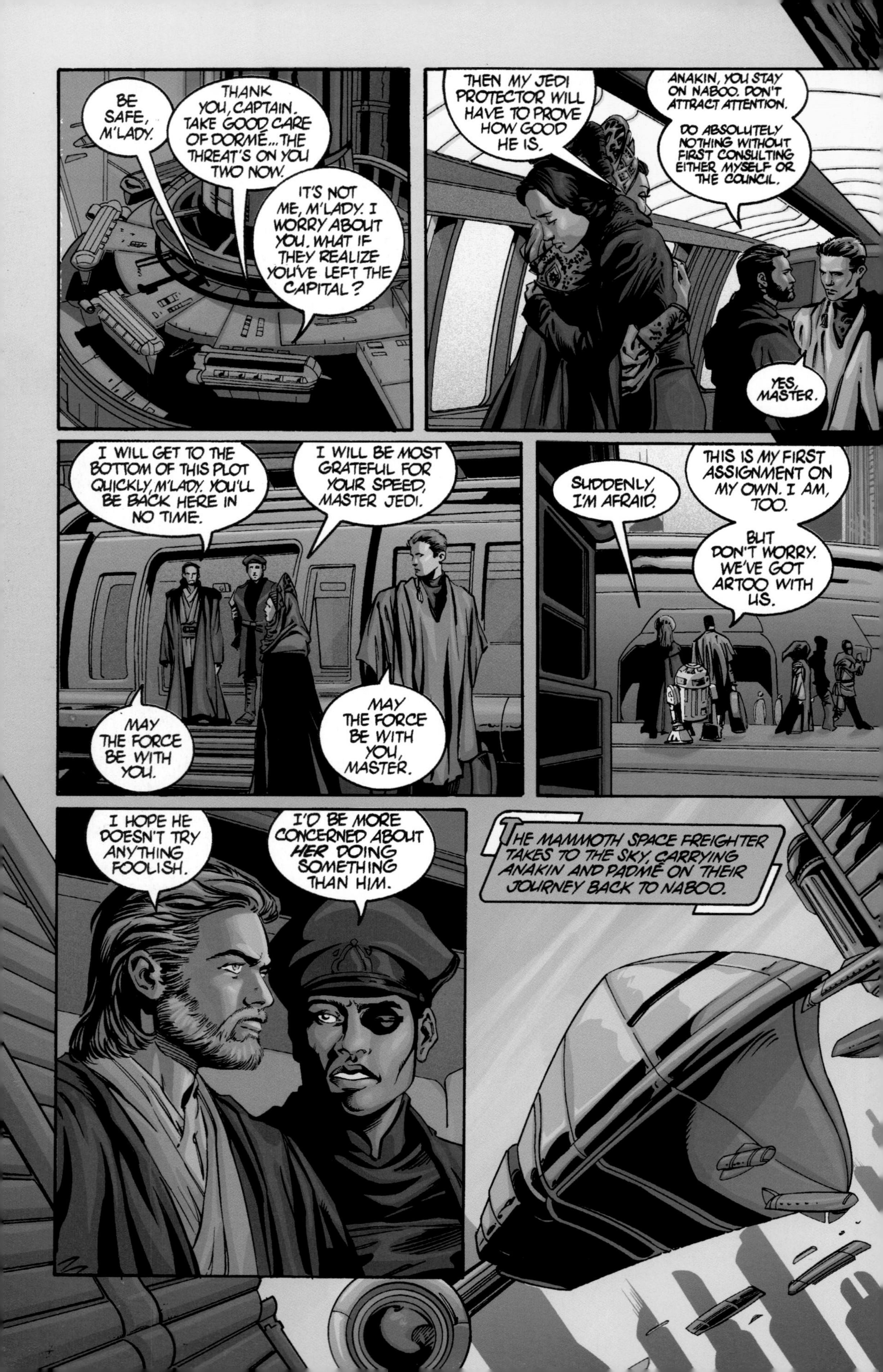
BE SAFE, M'LADY.
THANK YOU, CAPTAIN. TAKE GOOD CARE OF DORMÉ... THE THREAT'S ON YOU TWO NOW.
IT'S NOT ME, M'LADY. I WORRY ABOUT YOU. WHAT IF THEY REALIZE YOU'VE LEFT THE CAPITAL?
THEN MY JEDI PROTECTOR WILL HAVE TO PROVE HOW GOOD HE IS.
ANAKIN, YOU STAY ON NABOO. DON'T ATTRACT ATTENTION.
DO ABSOLUTELY NOTHING WITHOUT FIRST CONSULTING EITHER MYSELF OR THE COUNCIL.
YES, MASTER.
I WILL GET TO THE BOTTOM OF THIS PLOT QUICKLY, M'LADY. YOU'LL BE BACK HERE IN NO TIME.
I WILL BE MOST GRATEFUL FOR YOUR SPEED, MASTER JEDI.
MAY THE FORCE BE WITH YOU.
MAY THE FORCE BE WITH YOU, MASTER.
SUDDENLY, I'M AFRAID.
THIS IS MY FIRST ASSIGNMENT ON MY OWN. I AM, TOO.
BUT DON'T WORRY. WE'VE GOT ARTOO WITH US.
I HOPE HE DOESN'T TRY ANYTHING FOOLISH.
I'D BE MORE CONCERNED ABOUT HER DOING SOMETHING THAN HIM.
THE MAMMOTH SPACE FREIGHTER TAKES TO THE SKY, CARRYING ANAKIN AND PADMÉ ON THEIR JOURNEY BACK TO NABOO.

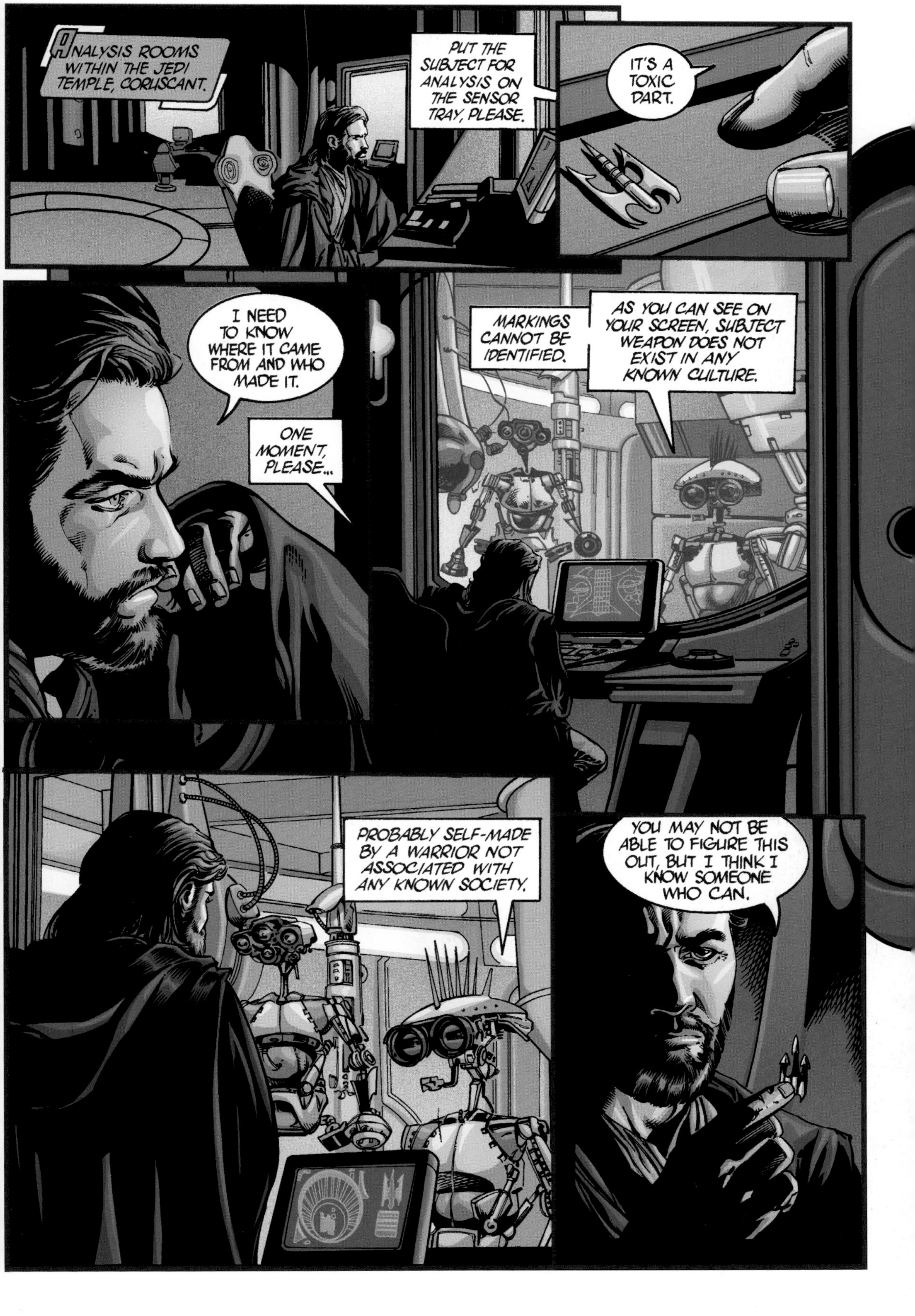
ANALYSIS ROOMS WITHIN THE JEDI TEMPLE, CORUSCANT.
PUT THE SUBJECT FOR ANALYSIS ON THE SENSOR TRAY, PLEASE.
IT'S A TOXIC DART.
I NEED TO KNOW WHERE IT CAME FROM AND WHO MADE IT.
ONE MOMENT, PLEASE...
MARKINGS CANNOT BE IDENTIFIED.
AS YOU CAN SEE ON YOUR SCREEN, SUBJECT WEAPON DOES NOT EXIST IN ANY KNOWN CULTURE.
PROBABLY SELF-MADE BY A WARRIOR NOT ASSOCIATED WITH ANY KNOWN SOCIETY.
YOU MAY NOT BE ABLE TO FIGURE THIS OUT, BUT I THINK I KNOW SOMEONE WHO CAN.

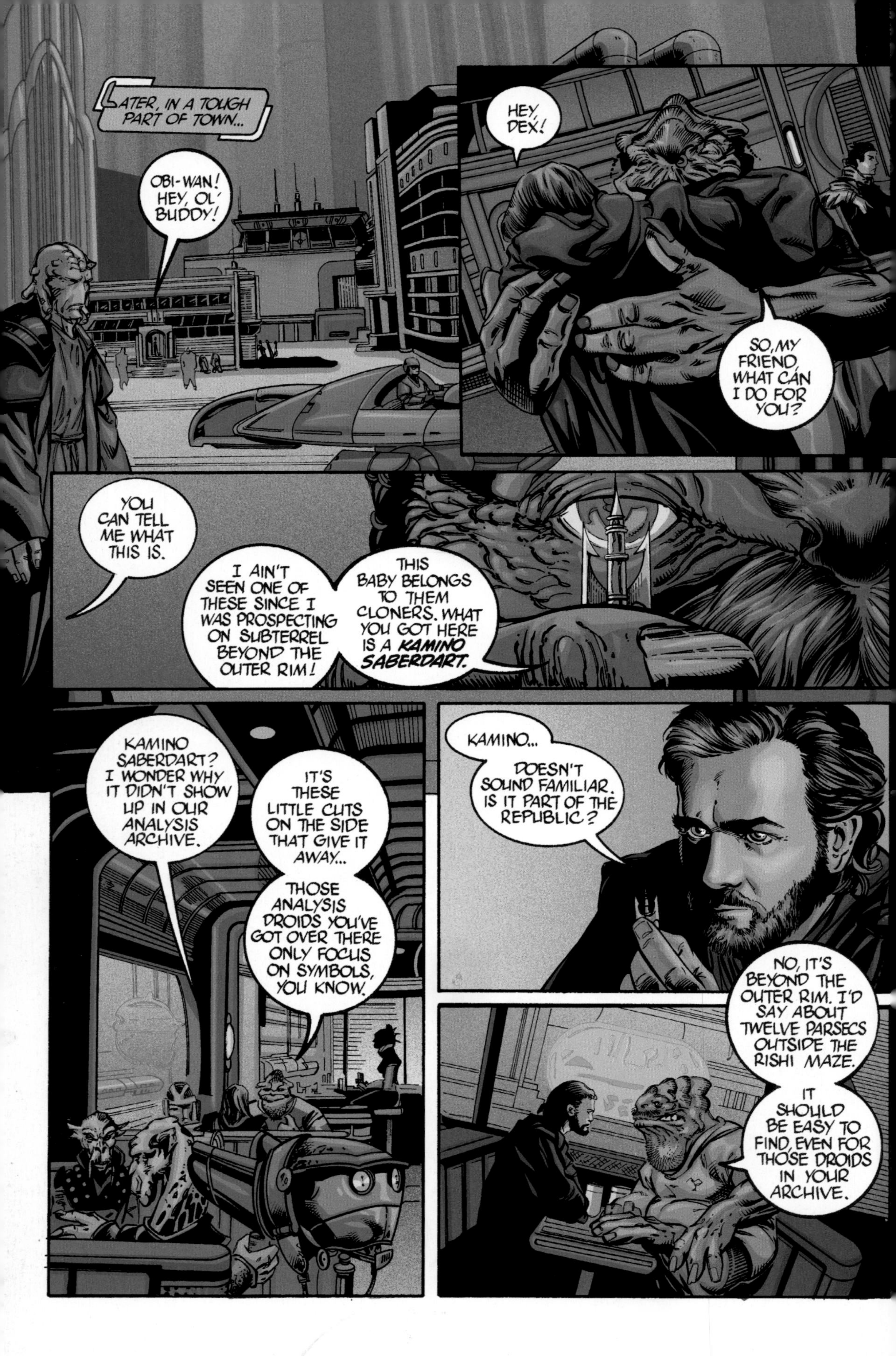
LATER, IN A TOUGH PART OF TOWN...
OBI-WAN! HEY, OL' BUDDY!
HEY, DEX!
SO, MY FRIEND, WHAT CAN I DO FOR YOU?
YOU CAN TELL ME WHAT THIS IS.
I AIN'T SEEN ONE OF THESE SINCE I WAS PROSPECTING ON SUBTERREL BEYOND THE OUTER RIM!
THIS BABY BELONGS TO THEM CLONERS. WHAT YOU GOT HERE IS A KAMINO SABERDART.
KAMINO SABERDART? I WONDER WHY IT DIDN'T SHOW UP IN OUR ANALYSIS ARCHIVE.
IT'S THESE LITTLE CUTS ON THE SIDE THAT GIVE IT AWAY...
THOSE ANALYSIS DROIDS YOU'VE GOT OVER THERE ONLY FOCUS ON SYMBOLS, YOU KNOW.
KAMINO...
DOESN'T SOUND FAMILIAR. IS IT PART OF THE REPUBLIC?
NO, IT'S BEYOND THE OUTER RIM. I'D SAY ABOUT TWELVE PARSECS OUTSIDE THE RISHI MAZE.
IT SHOULD BE EASY TO FIND, EVEN FOR THOSE DROIDS IN YOUR ARCHIVE.

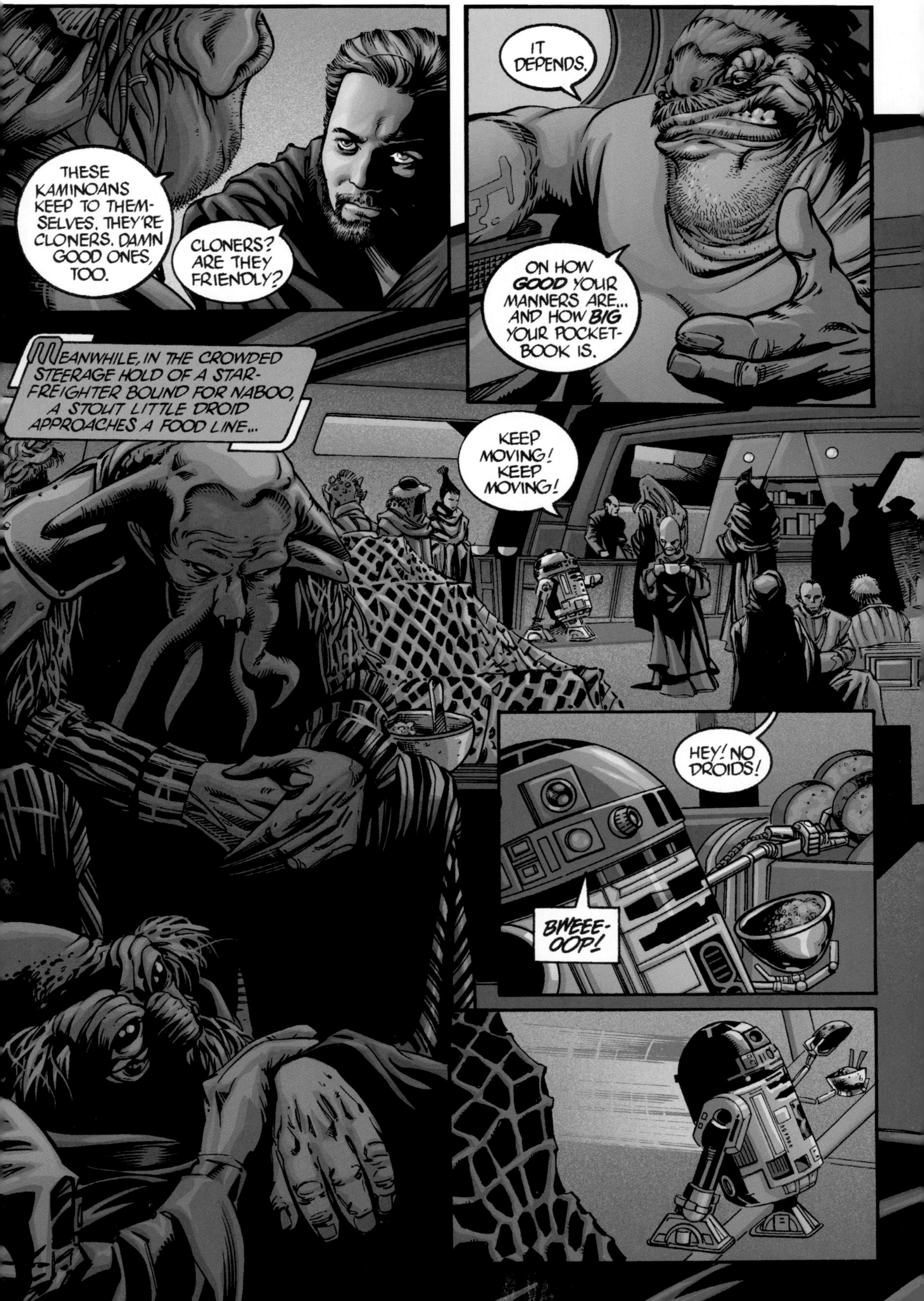
THESE KAMINOANS KEEP TO THEMSELVES. THEY'RE CLONERS. DAMN GOOD ONES, TOO.
CLONERS? ARE THEY FRIENDLY?
IT DEPENDS.
ON HOW GOOD YOUR MANNERS ARE... AND HOW BIG YOUR POCKETBOOK IS.
MEANWHILE, IN THE CROWDED STEERAGE HOLD OF A STAR-FREIGHTER BOUND FOR NABOO, A STOUT LITTLE DROID APPROACHES A FOOD LINE...
KEEP MOVING! KEEP MOVING!
HEY! NO DROIDS!
BWEEE-OOP!

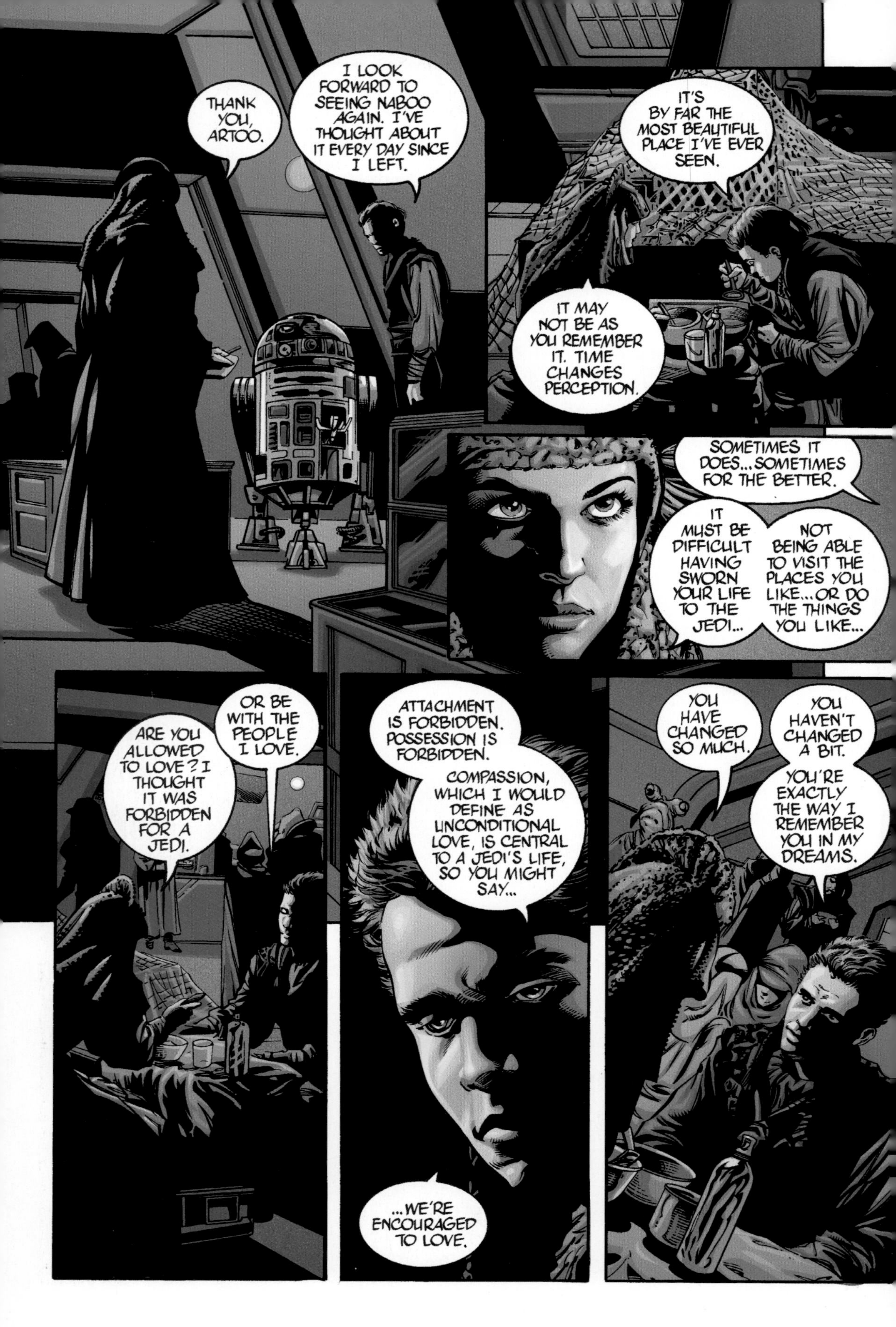
THANK YOU, ARTOO.
I LOOK FORWARD TO SEEING NABOO AGAIN. I'VE THOUGHT ABOUT IT EVERY DAY SINCE I LEFT.
IT'S BY FAR THE MOST BEAUTIFUL PLACE I'VE EVER SEEN.
IT MAY NOT BE AS YOU REMEMBER IT. TIME CHANGES PERCEPTION.
SOMETIMES IT DOES... SOMETIMES FOR THE BETTER.
IT MUST BE DIFFICULT HAVING SWORN YOUR LIFE TO THE JEDI...
NOT BEING ABLE TO VISIT THE PLACES YOU LIKE... OR DO THE THINGS YOU LIKE...
OR BE WITH THE PEOPLE I LOVE.
ARE YOU ALLOWED TO LOVE? I THOUGHT IT WAS FORBIDDEN FOR A JEDI.
ATTACHMENT IS FORBIDDEN. POSSESSION IS FORBIDDEN.
COMPASSION, WHICH I WOULD DEFINE AS UNCONDITIONAL LOVE, IS CENTRAL TO A JEDI'S LIFE, SO YOU MIGHT SAY...
...WE'RE ENCOURAGED TO LOVE.
YOU HAVE CHANGED SO MUCH.
YOU HAVEN'T CHANGED A BIT.
YOU'RE EXACTLY THE WAY I REMEMBER YOU IN MY DREAMS.

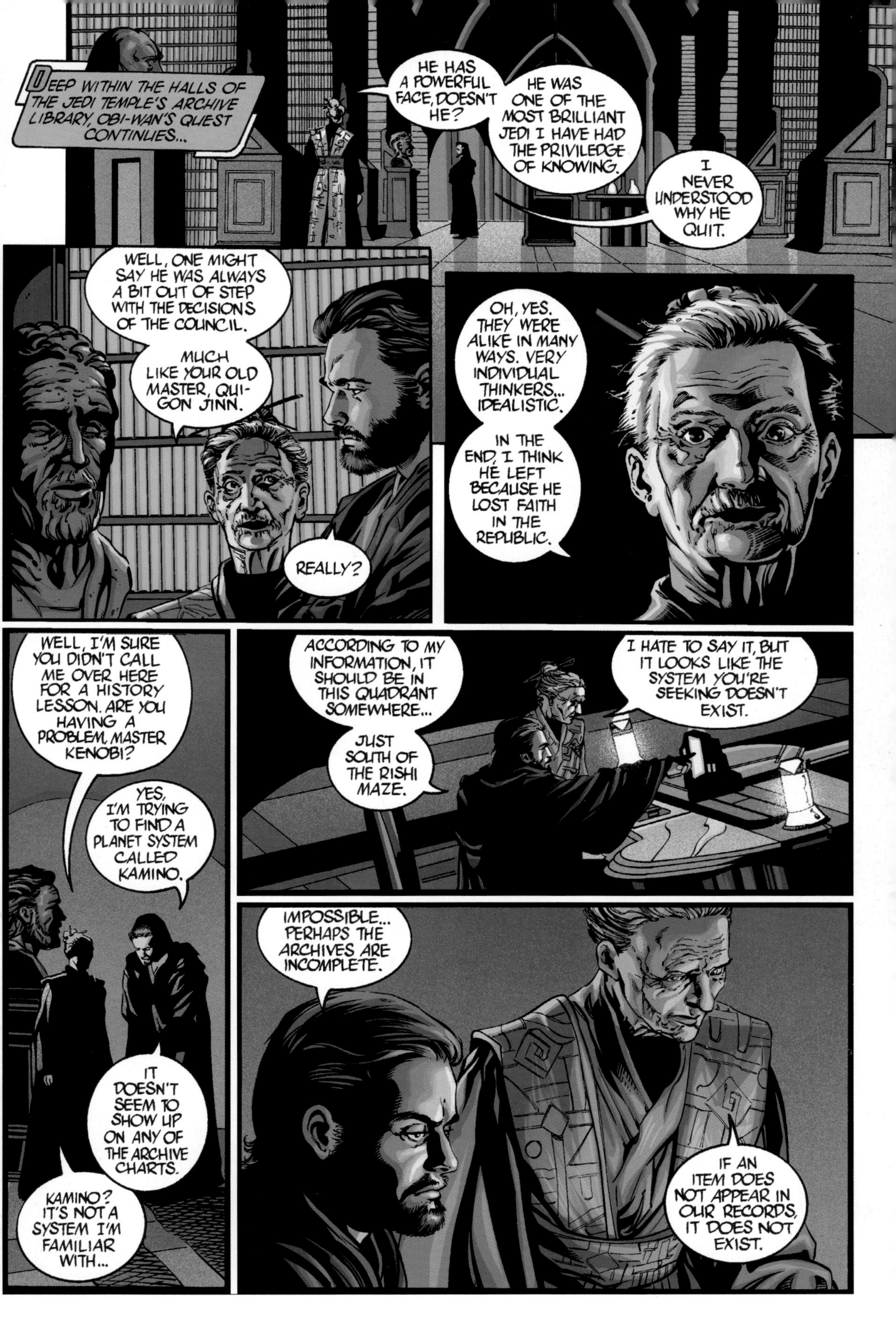
DEEP WITHIN THE HALLS OF THE JEDI TEMPLE'S ARCHIVE LIBRARY, OBI-WAN'S QUEST CONTINUES...
HE HAS A POWERFUL FACE, DOESN'T HE?
HE WAS ONE OF THE MOST BRILLIANT JEDI I HAVE HAD THE PRIVILEDGE OF KNOWING.
I NEVER UNDERSTOOD WHY HE QUIT.
WELL, ONE MIGHT SAY HE WAS ALWAYS A BIT OUT OF STEP WITH THE DECISIONS OF THE COUNCIL.
MUCH LIKE YOUR OLD MASTER, QUI-GON JINN.
REALLY?
OH, YES. THEY WERE ALIKE IN MANY WAYS. VERY INDIVIDUAL THINKERS... IDEALISTIC.
IN THE END, I THINK HE LEFT BECAUSE HE LOST FAITH IN THE REPUBLIC.
WELL, I'M SURE YOU DIDN'T CALL ME OVER HERE FOR A HISTORY LESSON. ARE YOU HAVING A PROBLEM, MASTER KENOBI?
YES, I'M TRYING TO FIND A PLANET SYSTEM CALLED KAMINO.
IT DOESN'T SEEM TO SHOW UP ON ANY OF THE ARCHIVE CHARTS.
KAMINO? IT'S NOT A SYSTEM I'M FAMILIAR WITH...
ACCORDING TO MY INFORMATION, IT SHOULD BE IN THIS QUADRANT SOMEWHERE...
JUST SOUTH OF THE RISHI MAZE.
I HATE TO SAY IT, BUT IT LOOKS LIKE THE SYSTEM YOU'RE SEEKING DOESN'T EXIST.
IMPOSSIBLE... PERHAPS THE ARCHIVES ARE INCOMPLETE.
IF AN ITEM DOES NOT APPEAR IN OUR RECORDS, IT DOES NOT EXIST.

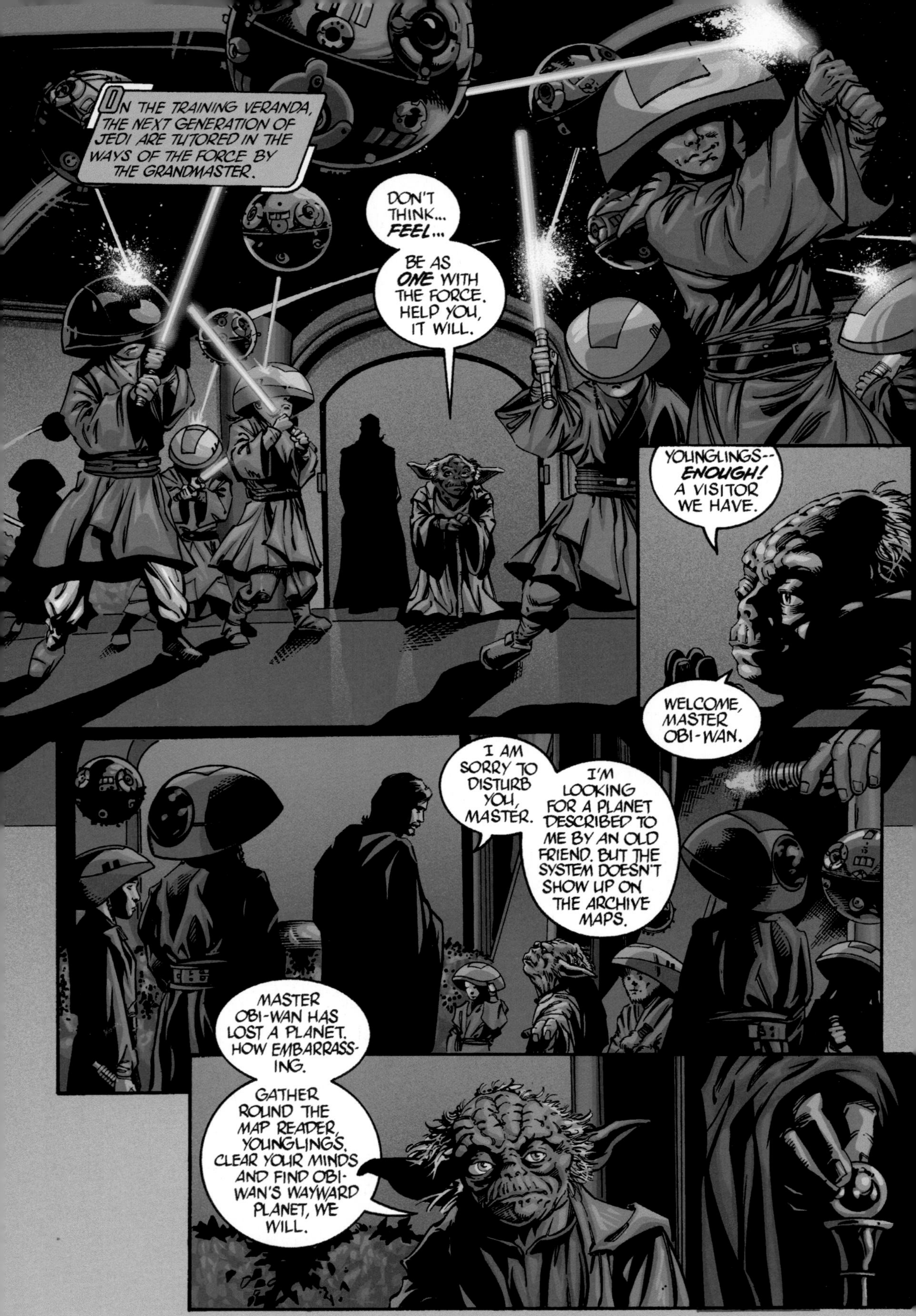
ON THE TRAINING VERANDA, THE NEXT GENERATION OF JEDI ARE TUTORED IN THE WAYS OF THE FORCE BY THE GRANDMASTER.
DON'T THINK... FEEL...
BE AS ONE WITH THE FORCE. HELP YOU, IT WILL.
YOUNGLINGS-- ENOUGH! A VISITOR WE HAVE.
WELCOME, MASTER OBI-WAN.
I AM SORRY TO DISTURB YOU, MASTER.
I'M LOOKING FOR A PLANET DESCRIBED TO ME BY AN OLD FRIEND. BUT THE SYSTEM DOESN'T SHOW UP ON THE ARCHIVE MAPS.
MASTER OBI-WAN HAS LOST A PLANET. HOW EMBARRASS-ING.
GATHER ROUND THE MAP READER, YOUNGLINGS. CLEAR YOUR MINDS AND FIND OBI-WAN'S WAYWARD PLANET, WE WILL.

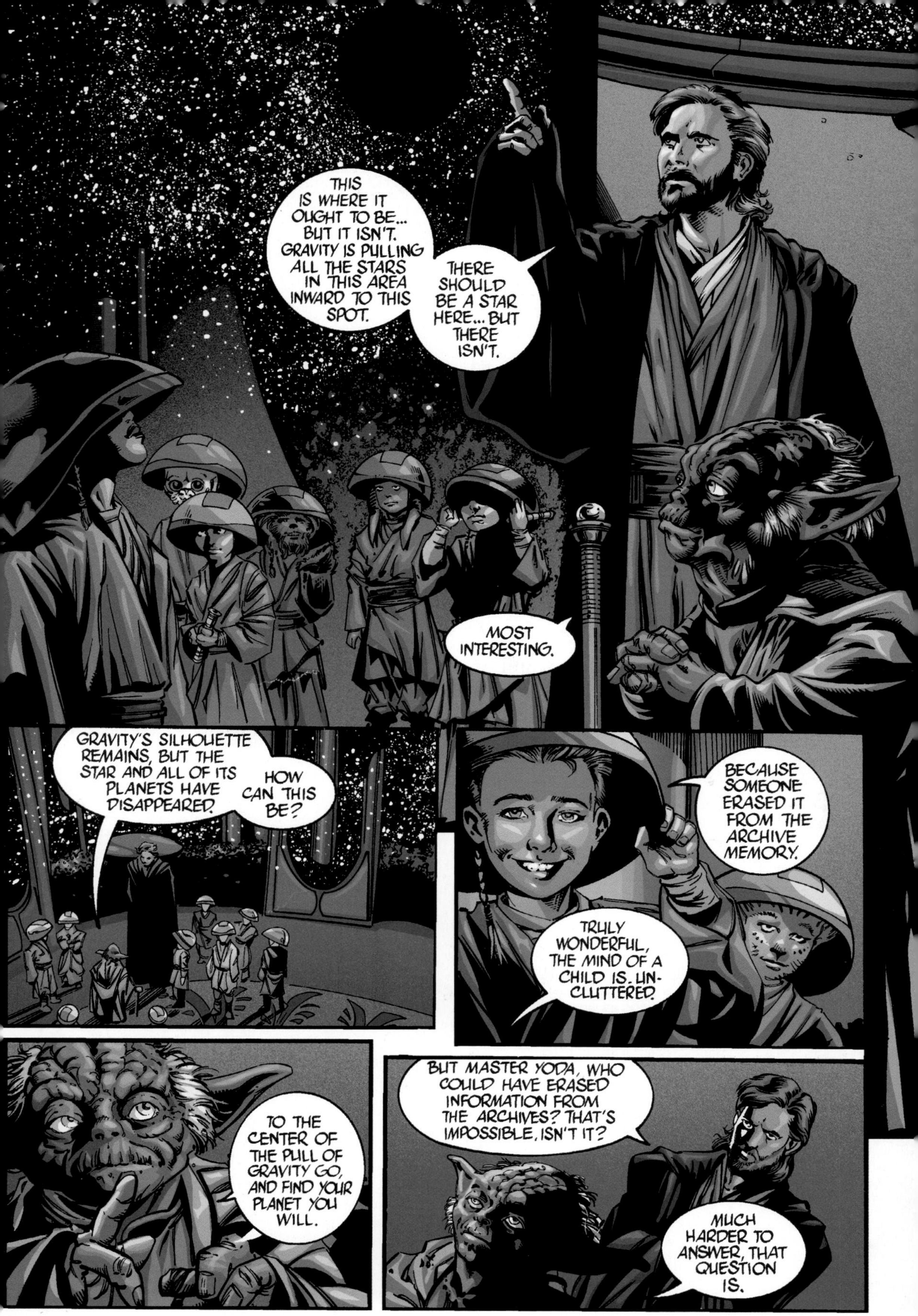
THIS IS WHERE IT OUGHT TO BE... BUT IT ISN'T. GRAVITY IS PULLING ALL THE STARS IN THIS AREA INWARD TO THIS SPOT.
THERE SHOULD BE A STAR HERE... BUT THERE ISN'T.
MOST INTERESTING.
GRAVITY'S SILHOUETTE REMAINS, BUT THE STAR AND ALL OF ITS PLANETS HAVE DISAPPEARED.
HOW CAN THIS BE?
BECAUSE SOMEONE ERASED IT FROM THE ARCHIVE MEMORY.
TRULY WONDERFUL, THE MIND OF A CHILD IS. UNCLUTTERED.
TO THE CENTER OF THE PULL OF GRAVITY GO, AND FIND YOUR PLANET YOU WILL.
BUT MASTER YODA, WHO COULD HAVE ERASED INFORMATION FROM THE ARCHIVES? THAT'S IMPOSSIBLE, ISN'T IT?
MUCH HARDER TO ANSWER, THAT QUESTION IS.

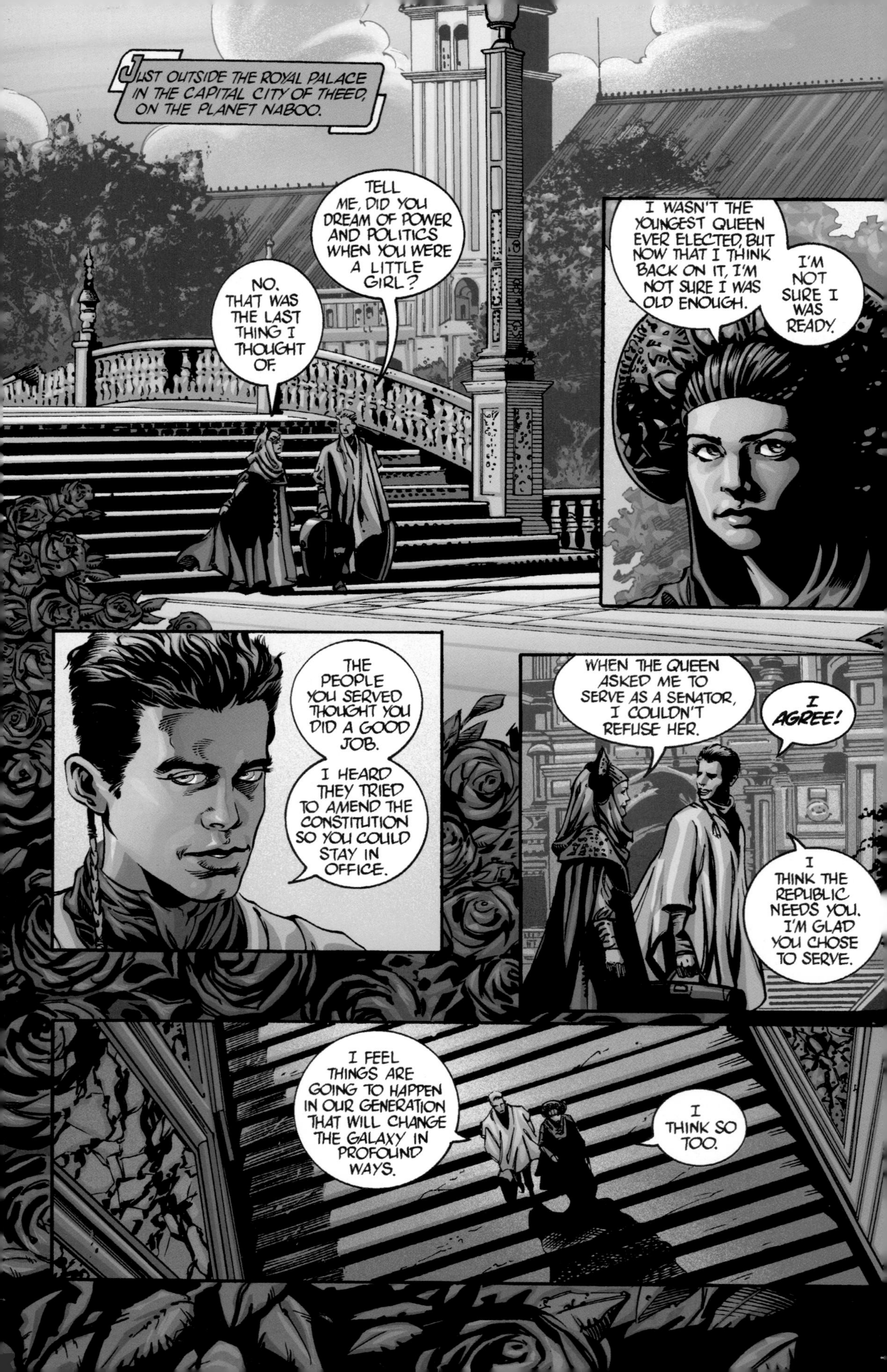
JUST OUTSIDE THE ROYAL PALACE IN THE CAPITAL CITY OF THEED, ON THE PLANET NABOO.
TELL ME, DID YOU DREAM OF POWER AND POLITICS WHEN YOU WERE A LITTLE GIRL?
NO. THAT WAS THE LAST THING I THOUGHT OF.
I WASN'T THE YOUNGEST QUEEN EVER ELECTED, BUT NOW THAT I THINK BACK ON IT, I'M NOT SURE I WAS OLD ENOUGH.
I'M NOT SURE I WAS READY.
THE PEOPLE YOU SERVED THOUGHT YOU DID A GOOD JOB.
I HEARD THEY TRIED TO AMEND THE CONSTITUTION SO YOU COULD STAY IN OFFICE.
WHEN THE QUEEN ASKED ME TO SERVE AS A SENATOR, I COULDN'T REFUSE HER.
I AGREE!
I THINK THE REPUBLIC NEEDS YOU. I'M GLAD YOU CHOSE TO SERVE.
I FEEL THINGS ARE GOING TO HAPPEN IN OUR GENERATION THAT WILL CHANGE THE GALAXY IN PROFOUND WAYS.
I THINK SO TOO.

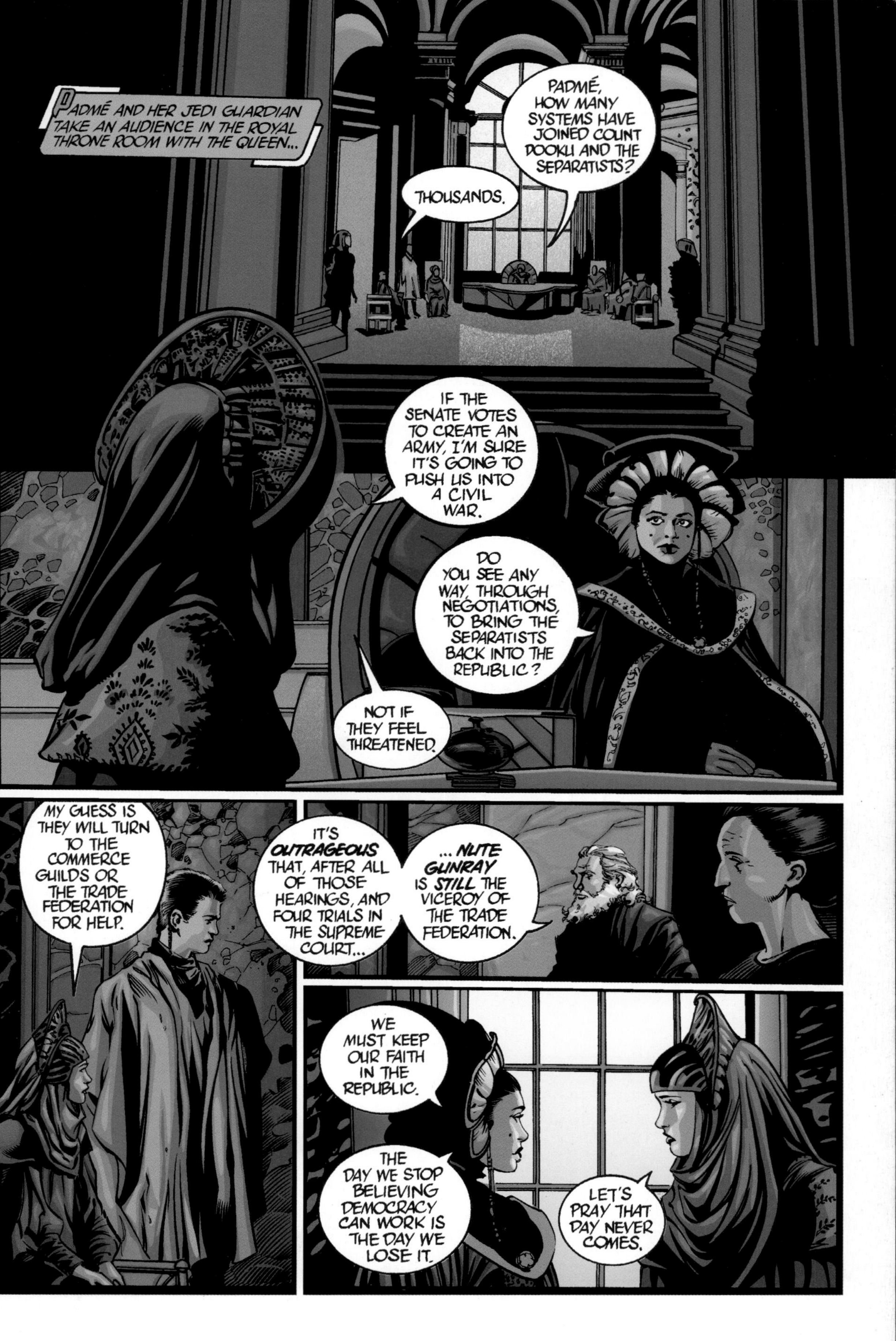
PADMÉ AND HER JEDI GUARDIAN TAKE AN AUDIENCE IN THE ROYAL THRONE ROOM WITH THE QUEEN...
PADMÉ, HOW MANY SYSTEMS HAVE JOINED COUNT DOOKU AND THE SEPARATISTS?
THOUSANDS.
IF THE SENATE VOTES TO CREATE AN ARMY, I'M SURE IT'S GOING TO PUSH US INTO A CIVIL WAR.
DO YOU SEE ANY WAY, THROUGH NEGOTIATIONS, TO BRING THE SEPARATISTS BACK INTO THE REPUBLIC?
NOT IF THEY FEEL THREATENED.
MY GUESS IS THEY WILL TURN TO THE COMMERCE GUILDS OR THE TRADE FEDERATION FOR HELP.
IT'S OUTRAGEOUS THAT, AFTER ALL OF THOSE HEARINGS, AND FOUR TRIALS IN THE SUPREME COURT...
...NUTE GUNRAY IS STILL THE VICEROY OF THE TRADE FEDERATION.
WE MUST KEEP OUR FAITH IN THE REPUBLIC.
THE DAY WE STOP BELIEVING DEMOCRACY CAN WORK IS THE DAY WE LOSE IT.
LET'S PRAY THAT DAY NEVER COMES.

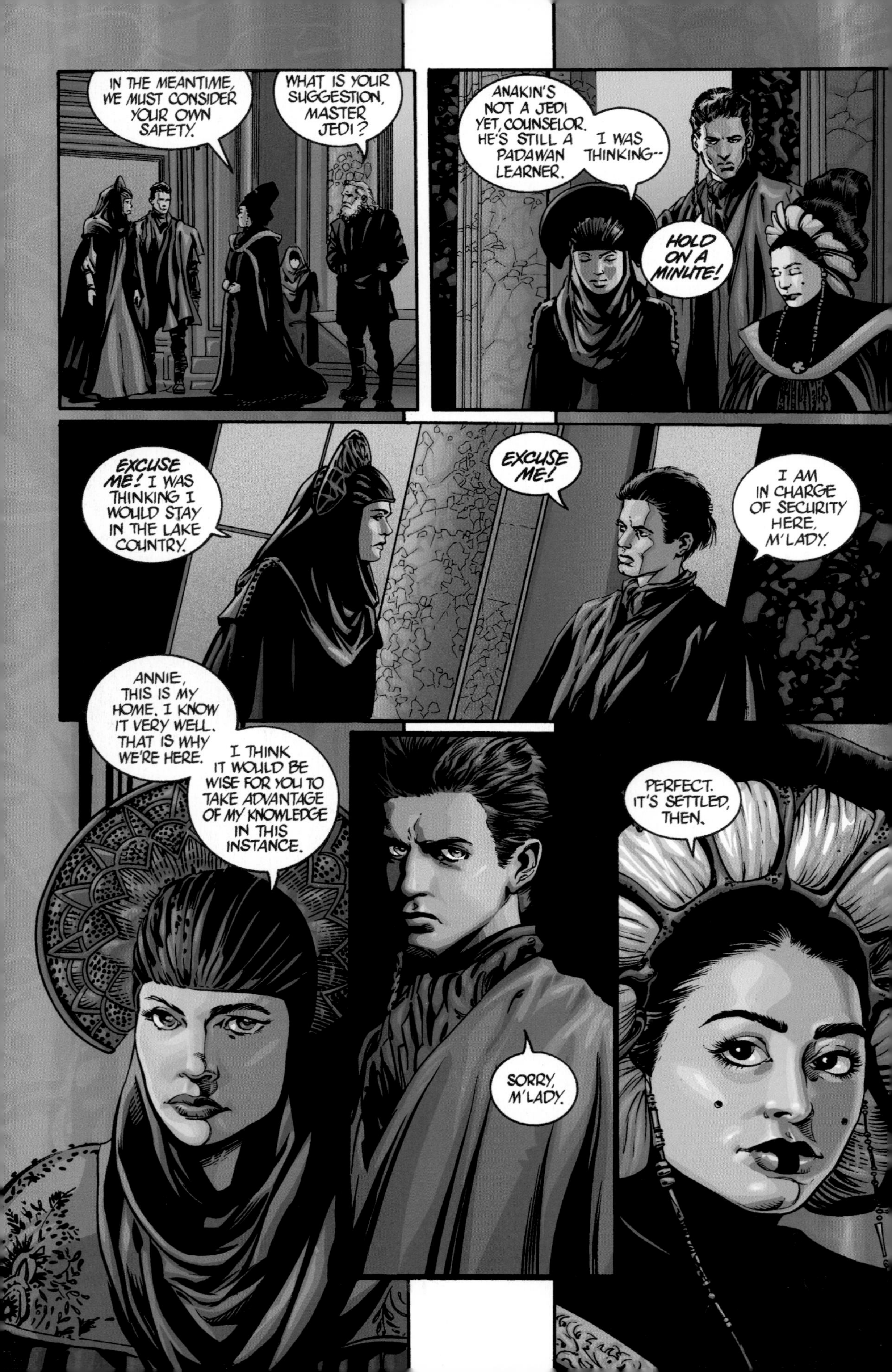
IN THE MEANTIME, WE MUST CONSIDER YOUR OWN SAFETY.
WHAT IS YOUR SUGGESTION, MASTER JEDI?
ANAKIN'S NOT A JEDI YET, COUNSELOR. HE'S STILL A PADAWAN LEARNER.
I WAS THINKING--
HOLD ON A MINUTE!
EXCUSE ME! I WAS THINKING I WOULD STAY IN THE LAKE COUNTRY.
EXCUSE ME!
I AM IN CHARGE OF SECURITY HERE, M'LADY.
ANNIE, THIS IS MY HOME. I KNOW IT VERY WELL. THAT IS WHY WE'RE HERE.
I THINK IT WOULD BE WISE FOR YOU TO TAKE ADVANTAGE OF MY KNOWLEDGE IN THIS INSTANCE.
SORRY, M'LADY.
PERFECT. IT'S SETTLED, THEN.

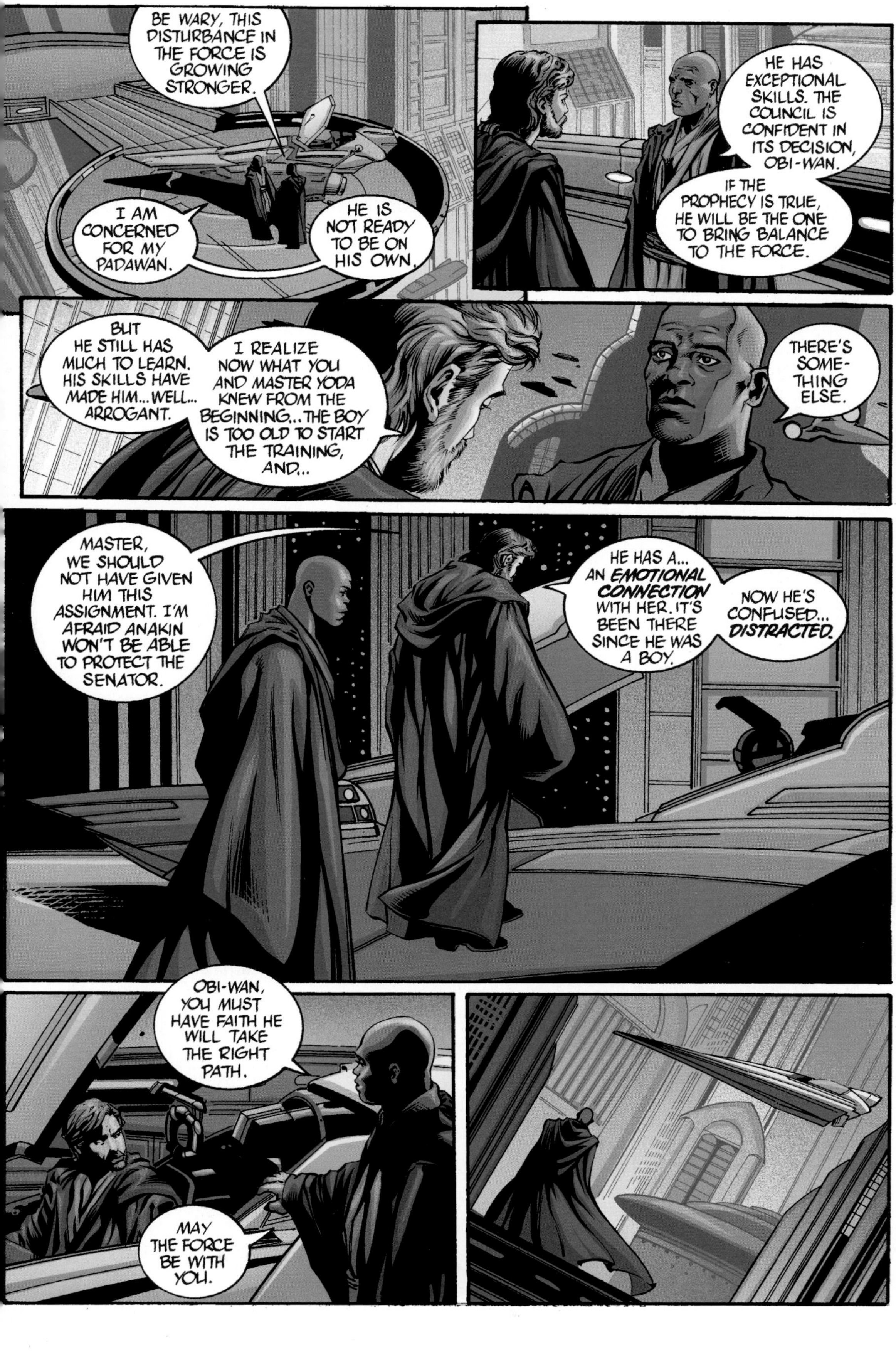
BE WARY, THIS DISTURBANCE IN THE FORCE IS GROWING STRONGER.
I AM CONCERNED FOR MY PADAWAN.
HE IS NOT READY TO BE ON HIS OWN.
HE HAS EXCEPTIONAL SKILLS. THE COUNCIL IS CONFIDENT IN ITS DECISION, OBI-WAN.
IF THE PROPHECY IS TRUE, HE WILL BE THE ONE TO BRING BALANCE TO THE FORCE.
BUT HE STILL HAS MUCH TO LEARN. HIS SKILLS HAVE MADE HIM... WELL... ARROGANT.
I REALIZE NOW WHAT YOU AND MASTER YODA KNEW FROM THE BEGINNING... THE BOY IS TOO OLD TO START THE TRAINING, AND...
THERE'S SOME-THING ELSE.
MASTER, WE SHOULD NOT HAVE GIVEN HIM THIS ASSIGNMENT. I'M AFRAID ANAKIN WON'T BE ABLE TO PROTECT THE SENATOR.
HE HAS A... AN EMOTIONAL CONNECTION WITH HER. IT'S BEEN THERE SINCE HE WAS A BOY.
NOW HE'S CONFUSED... DISTRACTED.
OBI-WAN, YOU MUST HAVE FAITH HE WILL TAKE THE RIGHT PATH.
MAY THE FORCE BE WITH YOU.

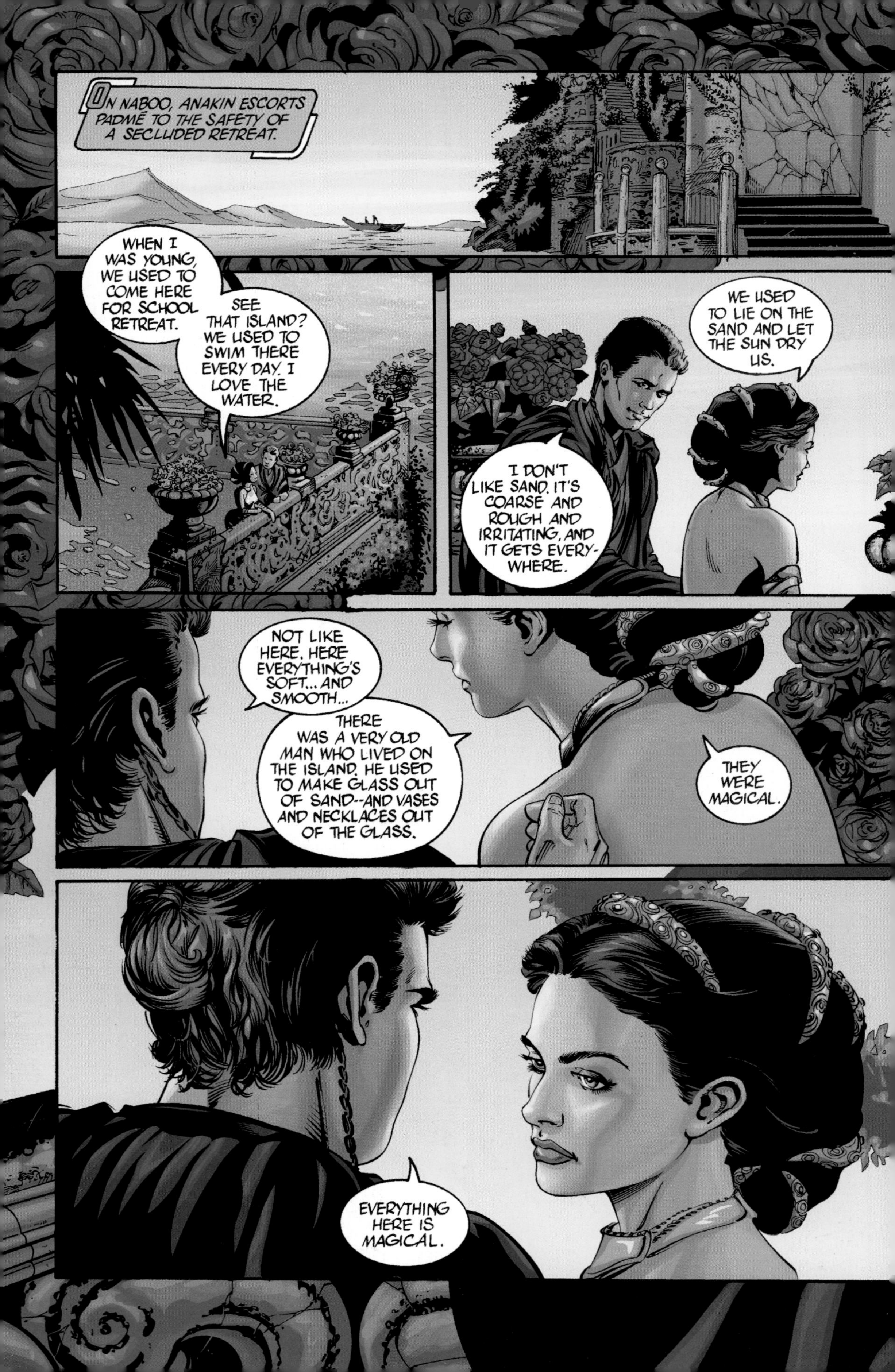
ON NABOO, ANAKIN ESCORTS PADMÉ TO THE SAFETY OF A SECLUDED RETREAT.
WHEN I WAS YOUNG, WE USED TO COME HERE FOR SCHOOL RETREAT.
SEE THAT ISLAND? WE USED TO SWIM THERE EVERY DAY. I LOVE THE WATER.
WE USED TO LIE ON THE SAND AND LET THE SUN DRY US.
I DON'T LIKE SAND. IT'S COARSE AND ROUGH AND IRRITATING, AND IT GETS EVERYWHERE.
NOT LIKE HERE. HERE EVERYTHING'S SOFT... AND SMOOTH...
THERE WAS A VERY OLD MAN WHO LIVED ON THE ISLAND. HE USED TO MAKE GLASS OUT OF SAND--AND VASES AND NECKLACES OUT OF THE GLASS.
THEY WERE MAGICAL.
EVERYTHING HERE IS MAGICAL.

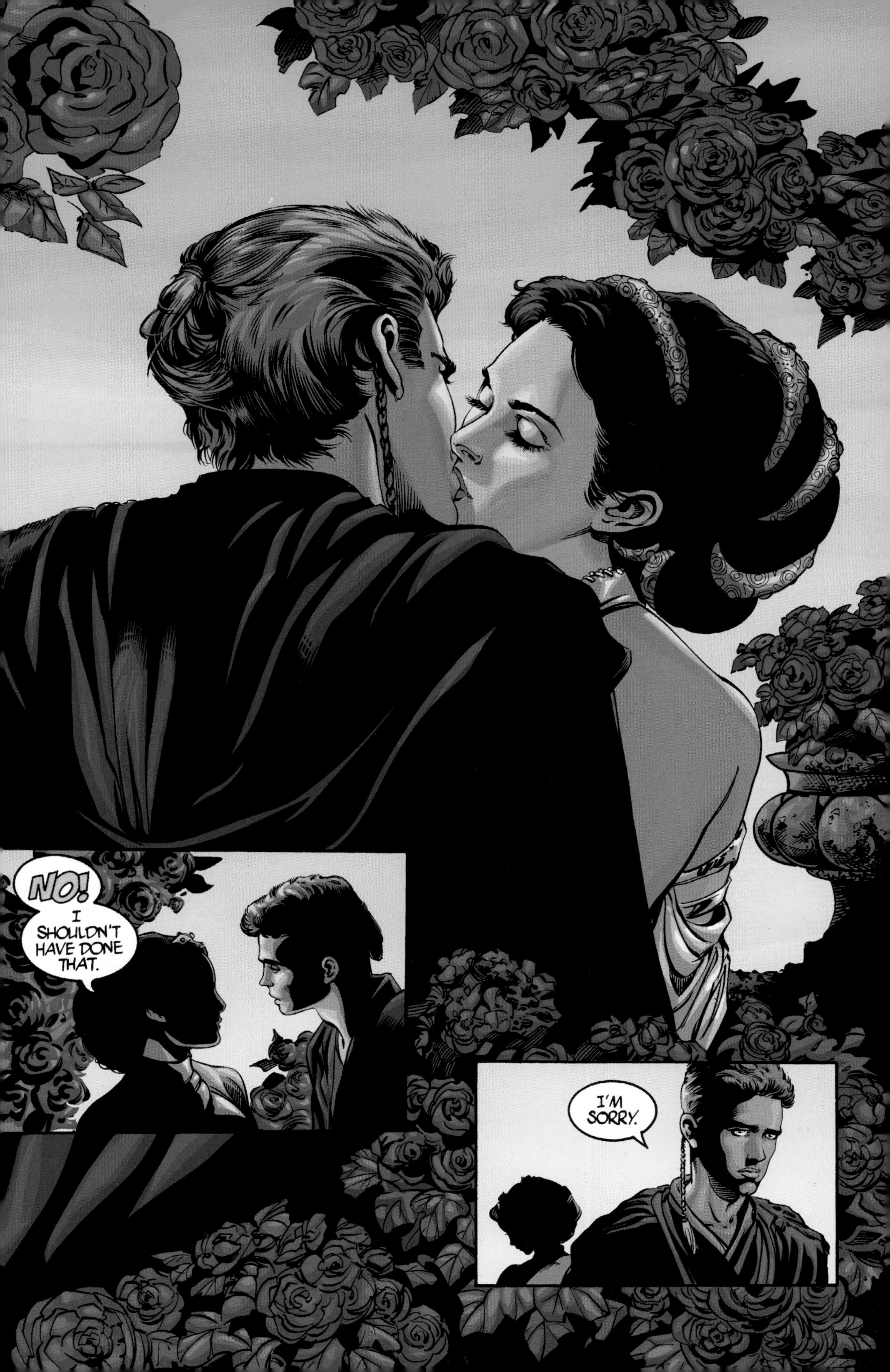
NO! I SHOULDN'T HAVE DONE THAT.
I'M SORRY.

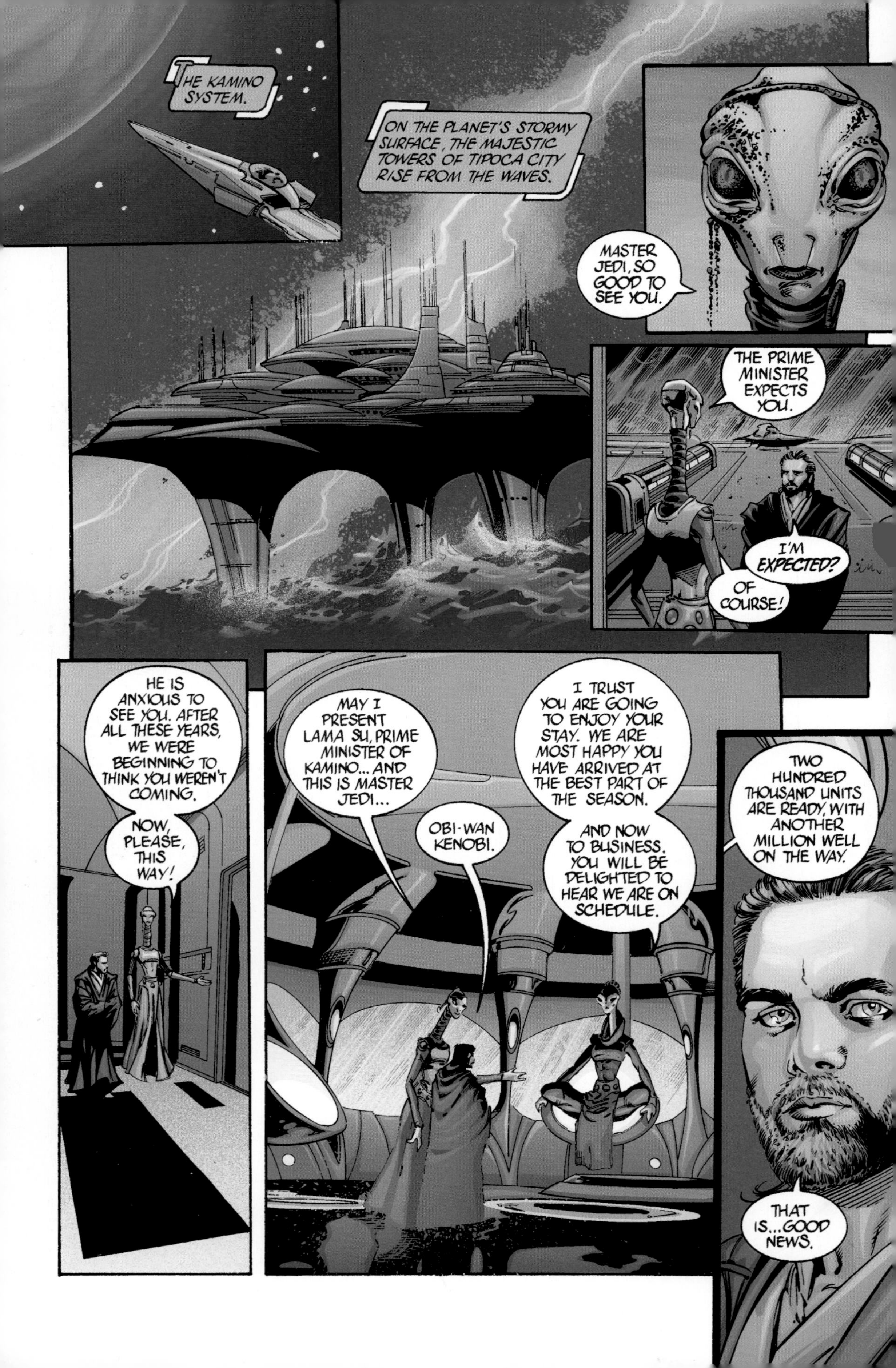
THE KAMINO SYSTEM.
ON THE PLANET'S STORMY SURFACE, THE MAJESTIC TOWERS OF TIPOCA CITY RISE FROM THE WAVES.
MASTER JEDI, SO GOOD TO SEE YOU.
THE PRIME MINISTER EXPECTS YOU.
I'M EXPECTED?
OF COURSE!
HE IS ANXIOUS TO SEE YOU. AFTER ALL THESE YEARS, WE WERE BEGINNING TO THINK YOU WEREN'T COMING.
NOW, PLEASE, THIS WAY!
MAY I PRESENT LAMA SU, PRIME MINISTER OF KAMINO... AND THIS IS MASTER JEDI...
OBI-WAN KENOBI.
I TRUST YOU ARE GOING TO ENJOY YOUR STAY. WE ARE MOST HAPPY YOU HAVE ARRIVED AT THE BEST PART OF THE SEASON.
AND NOW TO BUSINESS. YOU WILL BE DELIGHTED TO HEAR WE ARE ON SCHEDULE.
TWO HUNDRED THOUSAND UNITS ARE READY, WITH ANOTHER MILLION WELL ON THE WAY.
THAT IS...GOOD NEWS.

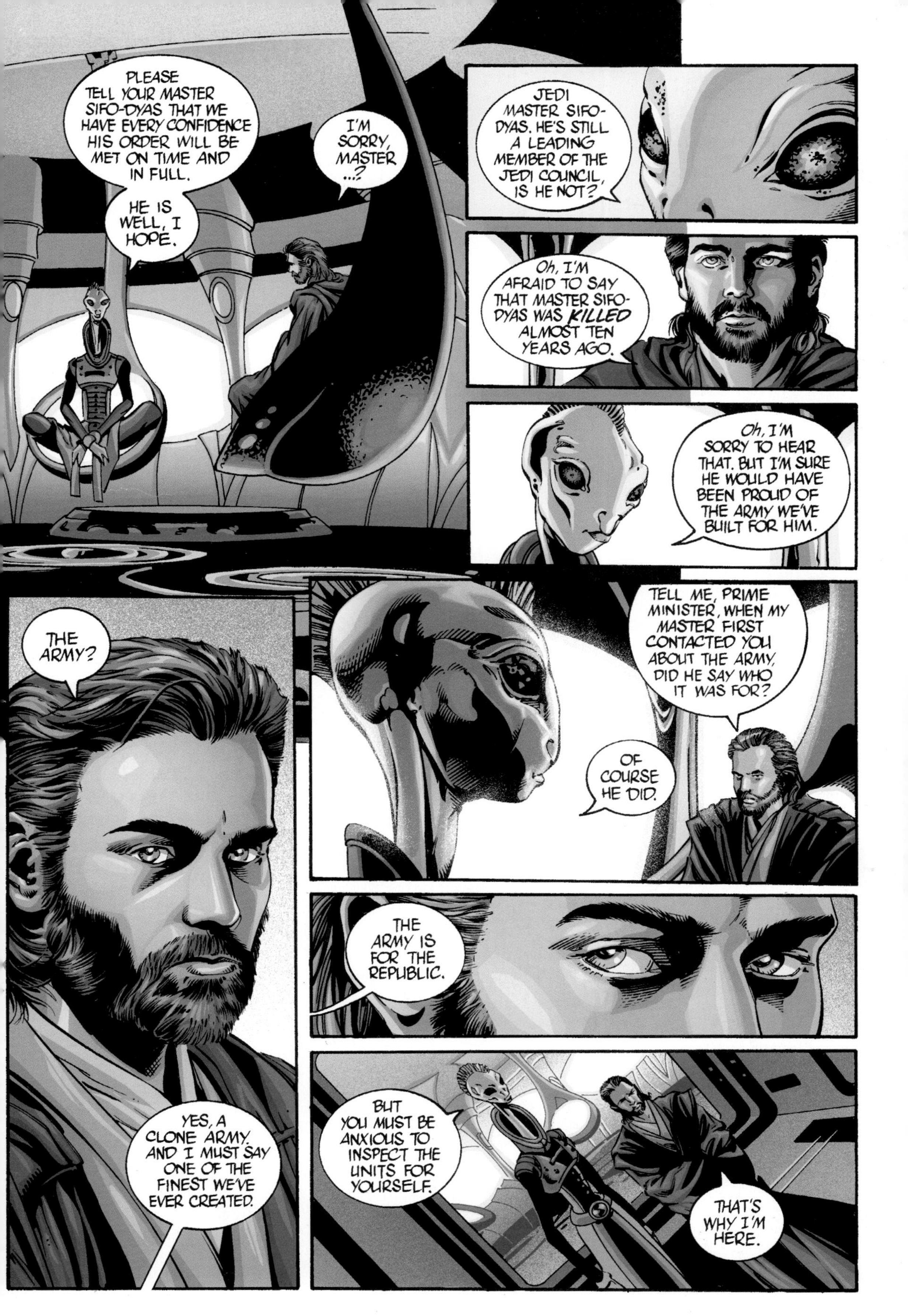

PLEASE TELL YOUR MASTER SIFO-DYAS THAT WE HAVE EVERY CONFIDENCE HIS ORDER WILL BE MET ON TIME AND IN FULL.
HE IS WELL, I HOPE.
I'M SORRY, MASTER ...?
JEDI MASTER SIFO-DYAS. HE'S STILL A LEADING MEMBER OF THE JEDI COUNCIL, IS HE NOT?
Oh, I'M AFRAID TO SAY THAT MASTER SIFO-DYAS WAS KILLED ALMOST TEN YEARS AGO.
Oh, I'M SORRY TO HEAR THAT. BUT I'M SURE HE WOULD HAVE BEEN PROUD OF THE ARMY WE'VE BUILT FOR HIM.
THE ARMY?
YES, A CLONE ARMY. AND I MUST SAY ONE OF THE FINEST WE'VE EVER CREATED.
TELL ME, PRIME MINISTER, WHEN MY MASTER FIRST CONTACTED YOU ABOUT THE ARMY, DID HE SAY WHO IT WAS FOR?
OF COURSE HE DID.
THE ARMY IS FOR THE REPUBLIC.
BUT YOU MUST BE ANXIOUS TO INSPECT THE UNITS FOR YOURSELF.
THAT'S WHY I'M HERE.

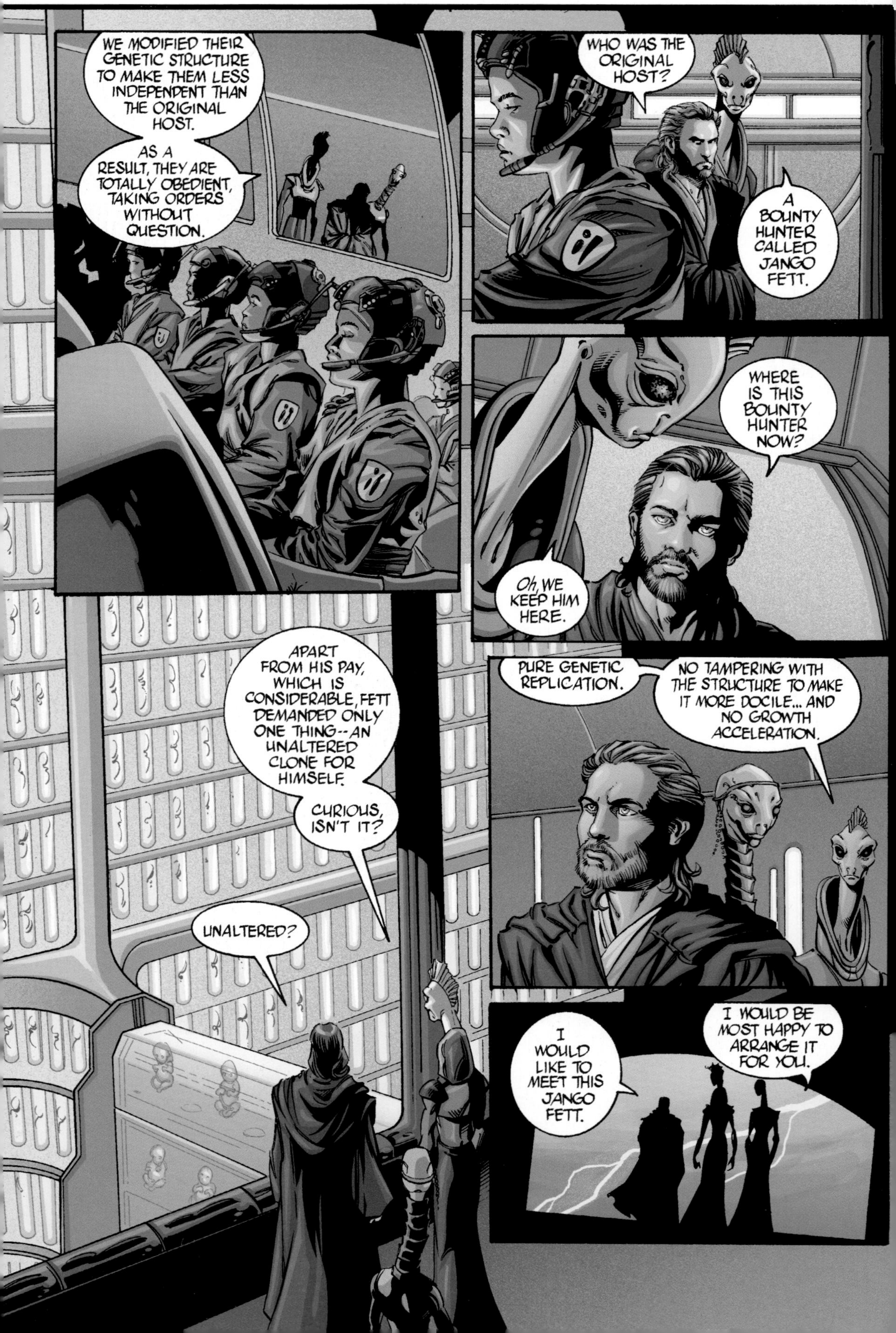
WE MODIFIED THEIR GENETIC STRUCTURE TO MAKE THEM LESS INDEPENDENT THAN THE ORIGINAL HOST.
AS A RESULT, THEY ARE TOTALLY OBEDIENT, TAKING ORDERS WITHOUT QUESTION.
WHO WAS THE ORIGINAL HOST?
A BOUNTY HUNTER CALLED JANGO FETT.
WHERE IS THIS BOUNTY HUNTER NOW?
Oh, WE KEEP HIM HERE.
APART FROM HIS PAY, WHICH IS CONSIDERABLE, FETT DEMANDED ONLY ONE THING--AN UNALTERED CLONE FOR HIMSELF.
CURIOUS, ISN'T IT?
UNALTERED?
PURE GENETIC REPLICATION.
NO TAMPERING WITH THE STRUCTURE TO MAKE IT MORE DOCILE... AND NO GROWTH ACCELERATION.
I WOULD LIKE TO MEET THIS JANGO FETT.
I WOULD BE MOST HAPPY TO ARRANGE IT FOR YOU.

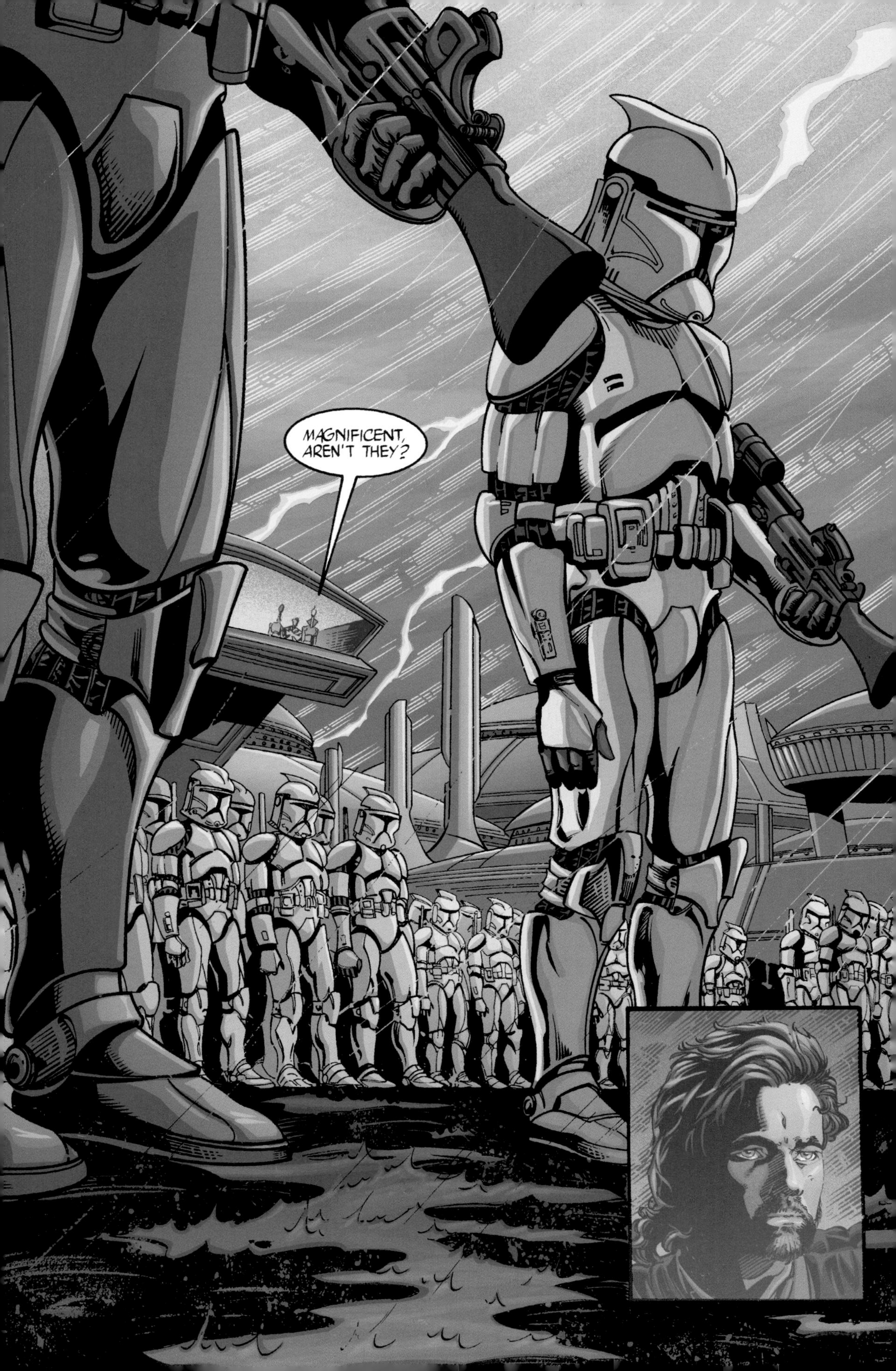
MAGNIFICENT, AREN'T THEY?

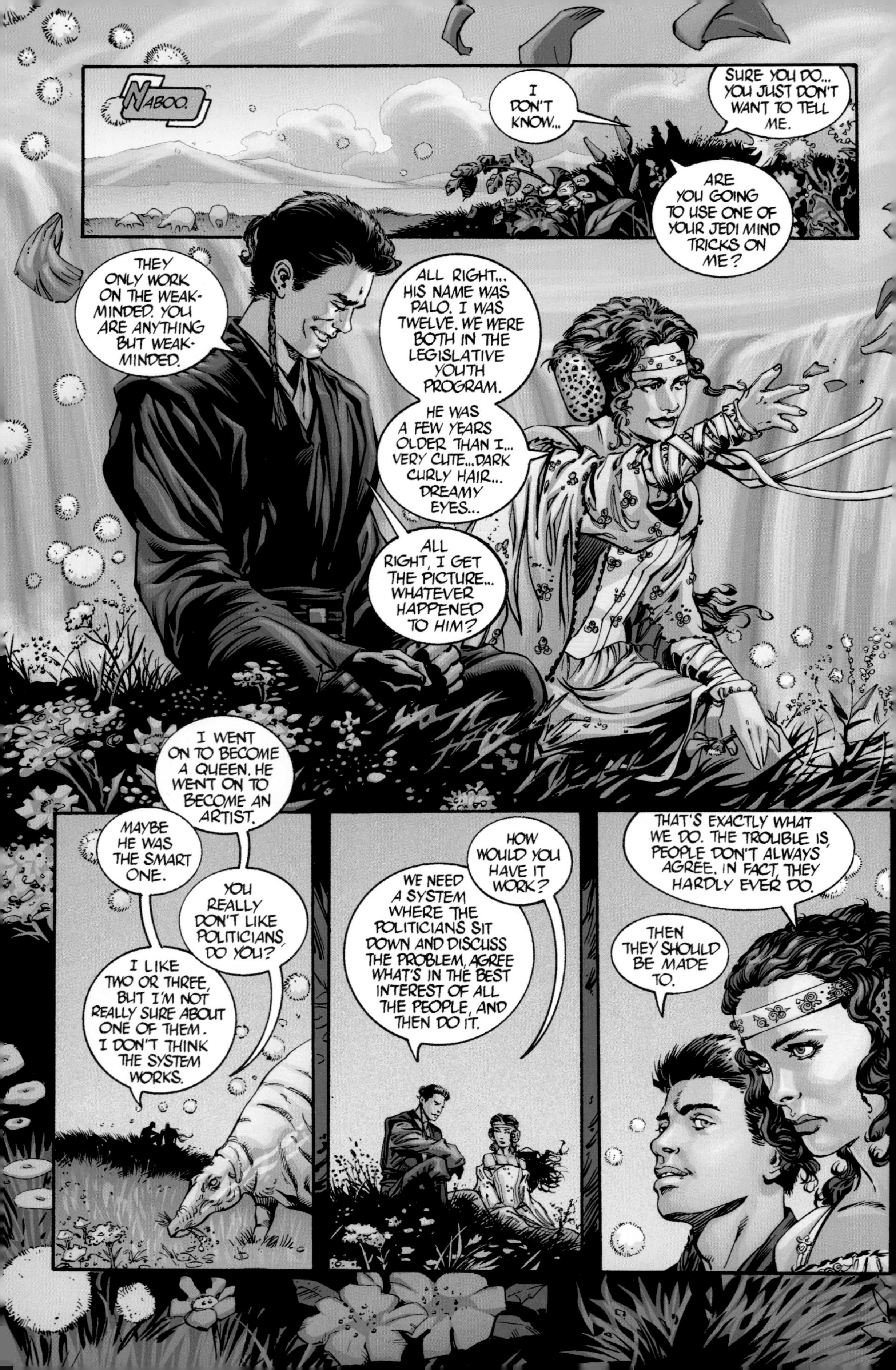
NABOO.
I DON'T KNOW...
SURE YOU DO... YOU JUST DON'T WANT TO TELL ME.
ARE YOU GOING TO USE ONE OF YOUR JEDI MIND TRICKS ON ME?
THEY ONLY WORK ON THE WEAK-MINDED. YOU ARE ANYTHING BUT WEAK-MINDED.
ALL RIGHT... HIS NAME WAS PALO. I WAS TWELVE. WE WERE BOTH IN THE LEGISLATIVE YOUTH PROGRAM.
HE WAS A FEW YEARS OLDER THAN I... VERY CUTE...DARK CURLY HAIR... DREAMY EYES...
ALL RIGHT, I GET THE PICTURE... WHATEVER HAPPENED TO HIM?
I WENT ON TO BECOME A QUEEN. HE WENT ON TO BECOME AN ARTIST.
MAYBE HE WAS THE SMART ONE.
YOU REALLY DON'T LIKE POLITICIANS, DO YOU?
I LIKE TWO OR THREE, BUT I'M NOT REALLY SURE ABOUT ONE OF THEM. I DON'T THINK THE SYSTEM WORKS.
HOW WOULD YOU HAVE IT WORK?
WE NEED A SYSTEM WHERE THE POLITICIANS SIT DOWN AND DISCUSS THE PROBLEM, AGREE WHAT'S IN THE BEST INTEREST OF ALL THE PEOPLE, AND THEN DO IT.
THAT'S EXACTLY WHAT WE DO. THE TROUBLE IS, PEOPLE DON'T ALWAYS AGREE. IN FACT, THEY HARDLY EVER DO.
THEN THEY SHOULD BE MADE TO.

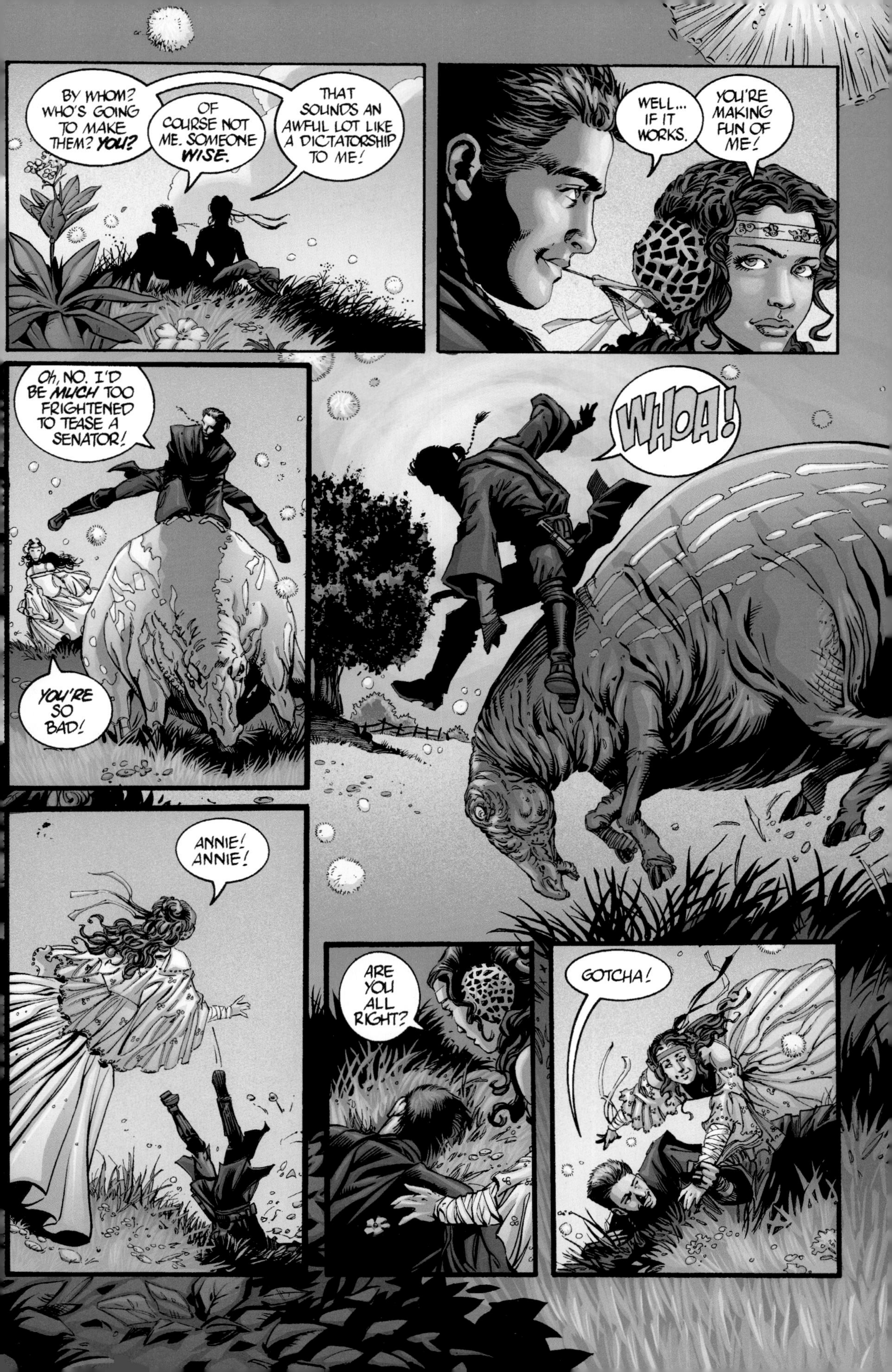
BY WHOM? WHO'S GOING TO MAKE THEM? YOU?
OF COURSE NOT ME. SOMEONE WISE.
THAT SOUNDS AN AWFUL LOT LIKE A DICTATORSHIP TO ME!
YOU'RE MAKING FUN OF ME!
WELL... IF IT WORKS.
Oh, NO. I'D BE MUCH TOO FRIGHTENED TO TEASE A SENATOR!
YOU'RE SO BAD!
WHOA!
ANNIE! ANNIE!
ARE YOU ALL RIGHT?
GOTCHA!

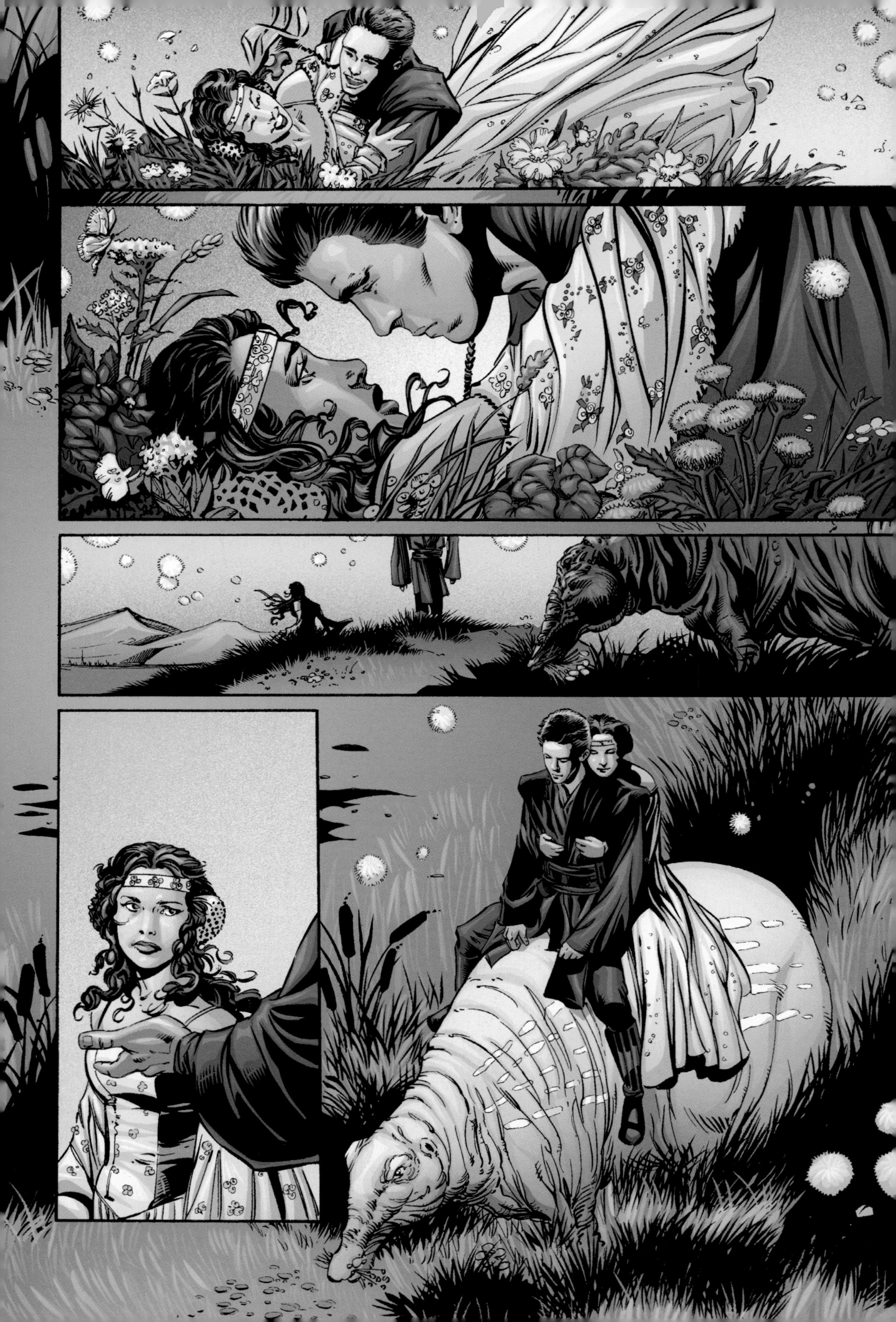

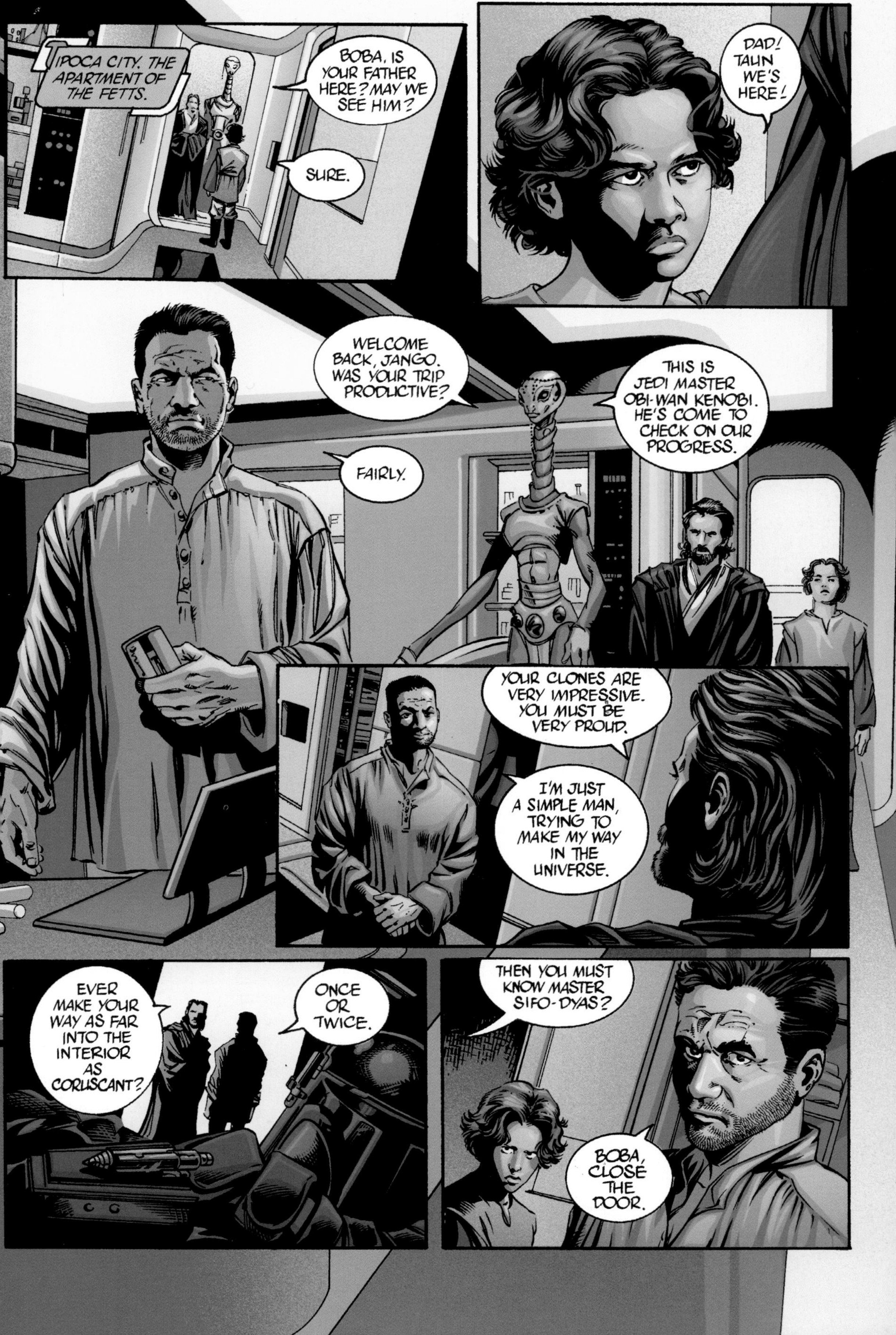
TIPOCA CITY. THE APARTMENT OF THE FETTS.
BOBA, IS YOUR FATHER HERE? MAY WE SEE HIM?
SURE.
DAD! TAUN WE'S HERE!
WELCOME BACK, JANGO. WAS YOUR TRIP PRODUCTIVE?
FAIRLY.
THIS IS JEDI MASTER OBI-WAN KENOBI. HE'S COME TO CHECK ON OUR PROGRESS.
YOUR CLONES ARE VERY IMPRESSIVE. YOU MUST BE VERY PROUD.
I'M JUST A SIMPLE MAN, TRYING TO MAKE MY WAY IN THE UNIVERSE.
EVER MAKE YOUR WAY AS FAR INTO THE INTERIOR AS CORUSCANT?
ONCE OR TWICE.
THEN YOU MUST KNOW MASTER SIFO-DYAS?
BOBA, CLOSE THE DOOR.

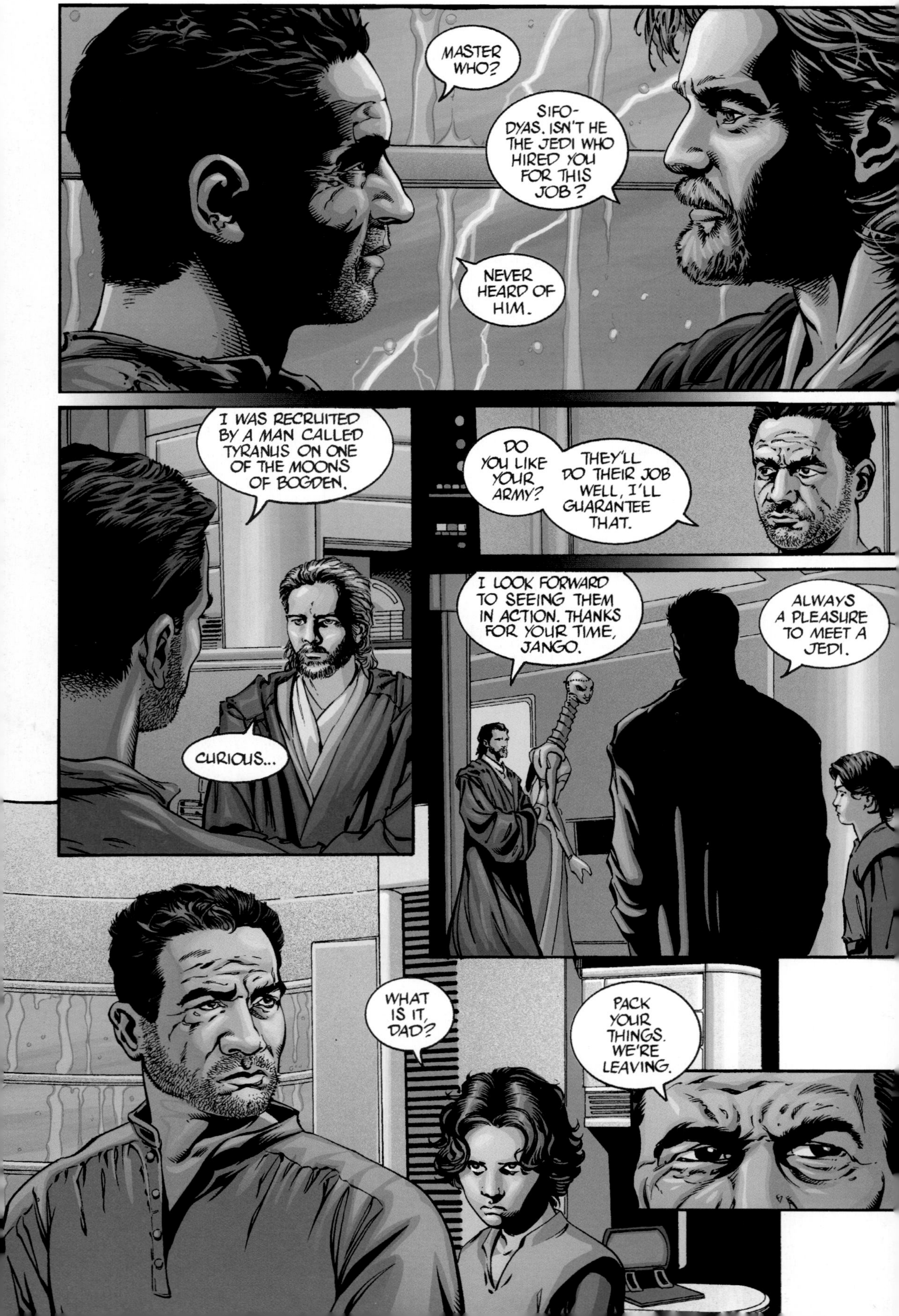
MASTER WHO?
SIFO-DYAS. ISN'T HE THE JEDI WHO HIRED YOU FOR THIS JOB?
NEVER HEARD OF HIM.
I WAS RECRUITED BY A MAN CALLED TYRANUS ON ONE OF THE MOONS OF BOGDEN.
CURIOUS...
DO YOU LIKE YOUR ARMY?
THEY'LL DO THEIR JOB WELL, I'LL GUARANTEE THAT.
I LOOK FORWARD TO SEEING THEM IN ACTION. THANKS FOR YOUR TIME, JANGO.
ALWAYS A PLEASURE TO MEET A JEDI.
WHAT IS IT, DAD?
PACK YOUR THINGS. WE'RE LEAVING.

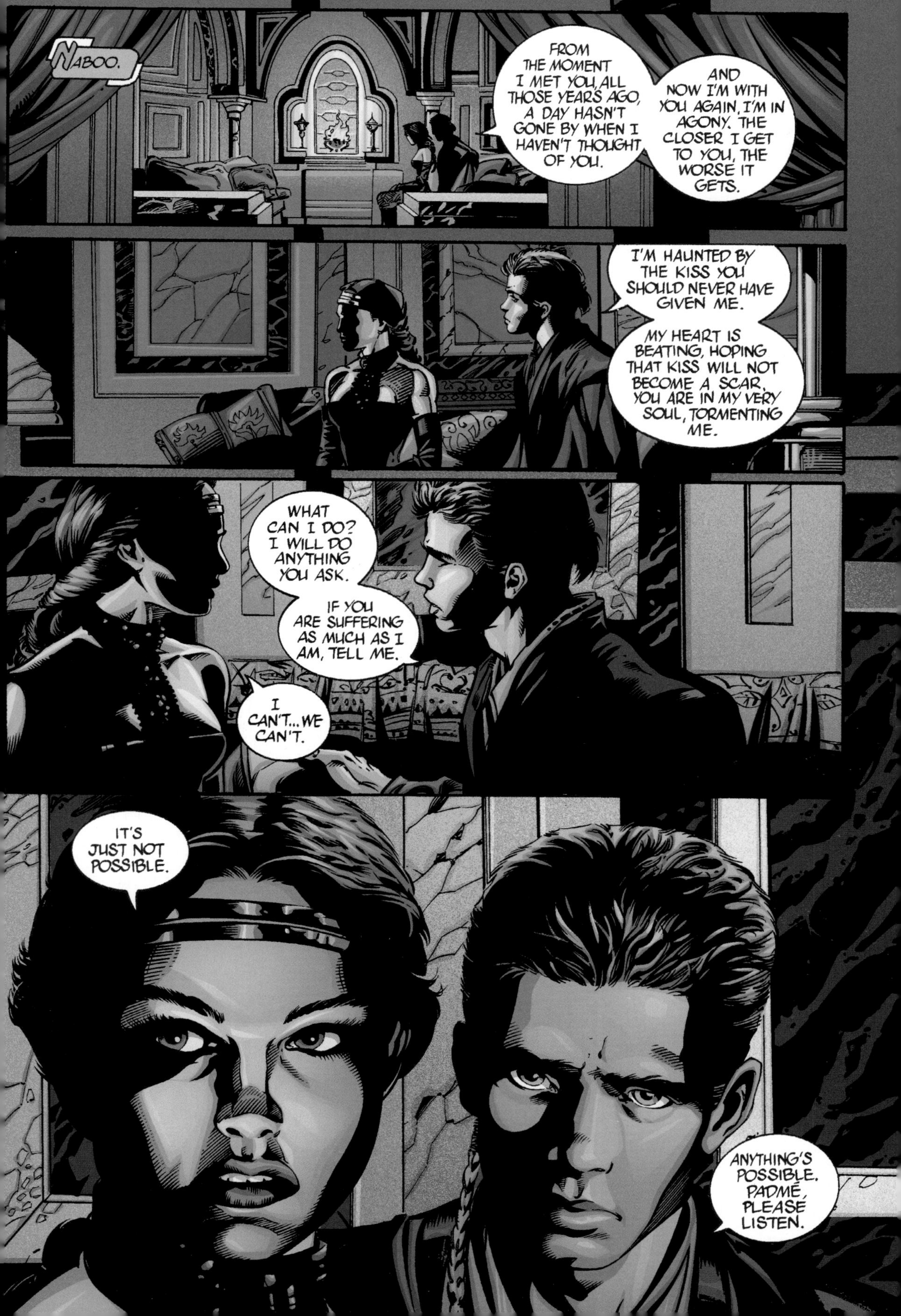
NABOO.
FROM THE MOMENT I MET YOU, ALL THOSE YEARS AGO, A DAY HASN'T GONE BY WHEN I HAVEN'T THOUGHT OF YOU.
AND NOW I'M WITH YOU AGAIN, I'M IN AGONY. THE CLOSER I GET TO YOU, THE WORSE IT GETS.
I'M HAUNTED BY THE KISS YOU SHOULD NEVER HAVE GIVEN ME.
MY HEART IS BEATING, HOPING THAT KISS WILL NOT BECOME A SCAR. YOU ARE IN MY VERY SOUL, TORMENTING ME.
WHAT CAN I DO? I WILL DO ANYTHING YOU ASK.
IF YOU ARE SUFFERING AS MUCH AS I AM, TELL ME.
I CAN'T...WE CAN'T.
IT'S JUST NOT POSSIBLE.
ANYTHING'S POSSIBLE. PADMÉ, PLEASE LISTEN.

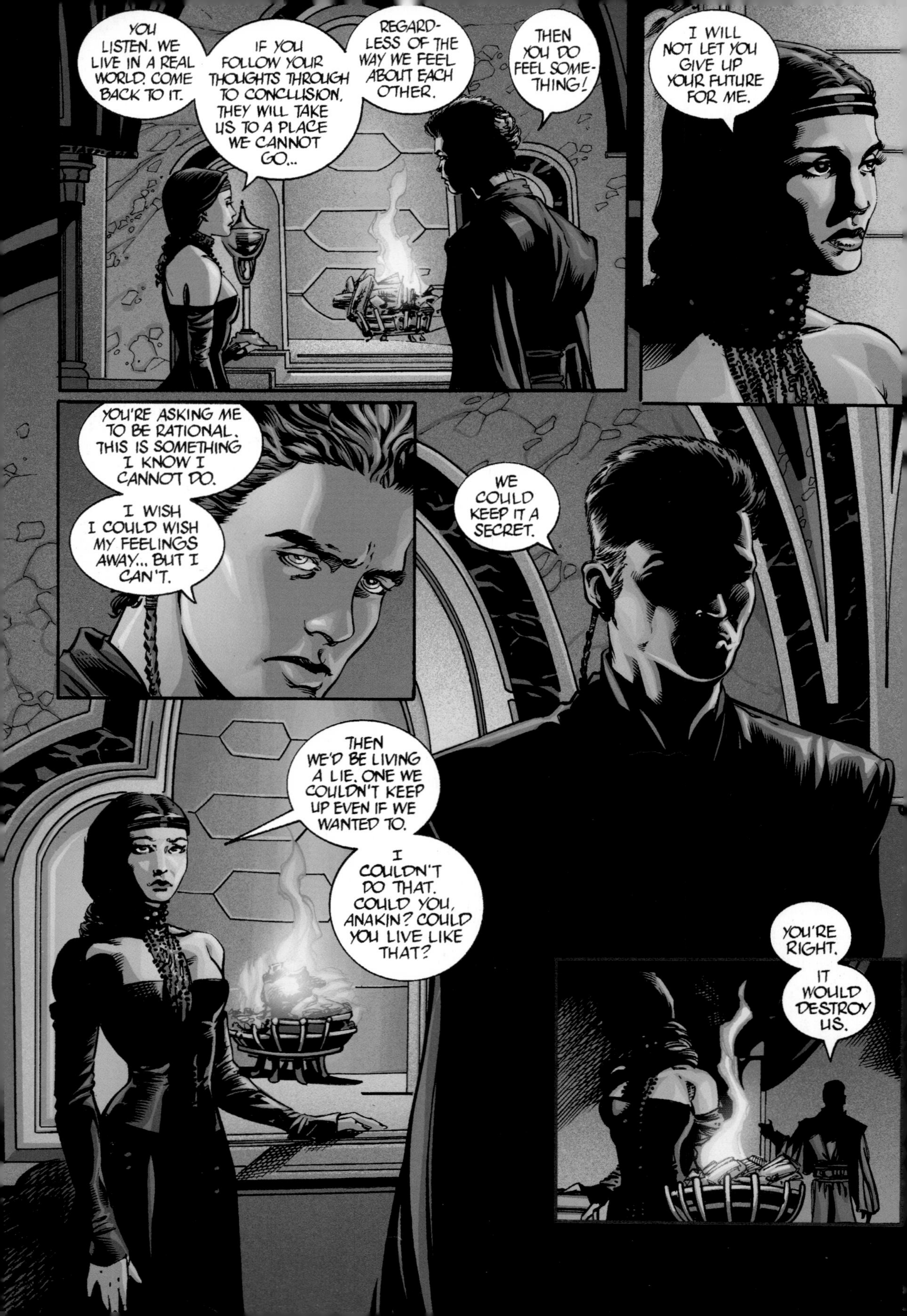
YOU LISTEN. WE LIVE IN A REAL WORLD. COME BACK TO IT.
IF YOU FOLLOW YOUR THOUGHTS THROUGH TO CONCLUSION, THEY WILL TAKE US TO A PLACE WE CANNOT GO...
REGARDLESS OF THE WAY WE FEEL ABOUT EACH OTHER.
THEN YOU DO FEEL SOMETHING!
I WILL NOT LET YOU GIVE UP YOUR FUTURE FOR ME.
YOU'RE ASKING ME TO BE RATIONAL. THIS IS SOMETHING I KNOW I CANNOT DO.
I WISH I COULD WISH MY FEELINGS AWAY... BUT I CAN'T.
WE COULD KEEP IT A SECRET.
THEN WE'D BE LIVING A LIE. ONE WE COULDN'T KEEP UP EVEN IF WE WANTED TO.
I COULDN'T DO THAT. COULD YOU, ANAKIN? COULD YOU LIVE LIKE THAT?
YOU'RE RIGHT.
IT WOULD DESTROY US.

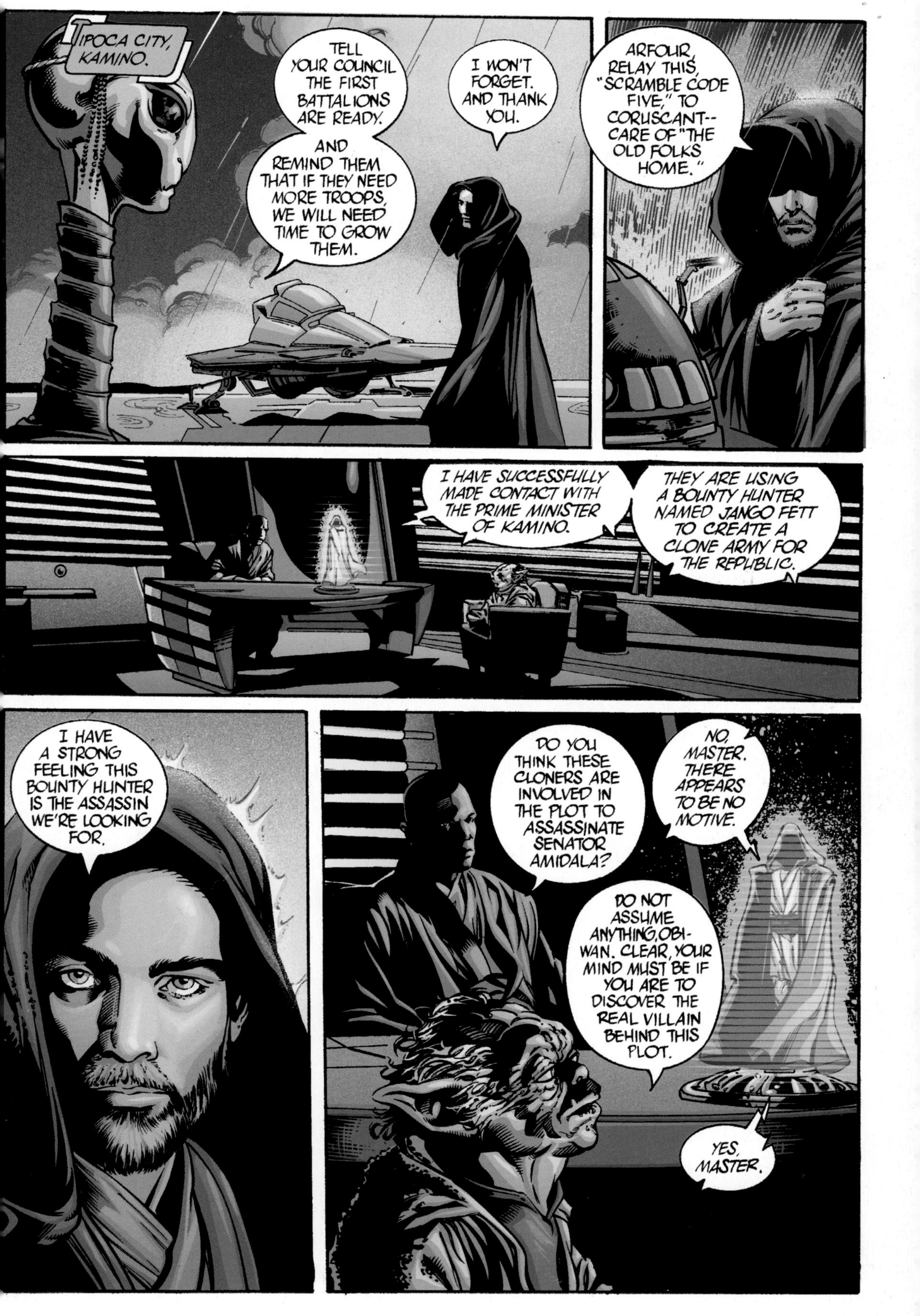

TIPOCA CITY, KAMINO.
TELL YOUR COUNCIL THE FIRST BATTALIONS ARE READY.
AND REMIND THEM THAT IF THEY NEED MORE TROOPS, WE WILL NEED TIME TO GROW THEM.
I WON'T FORGET. AND THANK YOU.
ARFOUR, RELAY THIS, "SCRAMBLE CODE FIVE," TO CORUSCANT-- CARE OF "THE OLD FOLKS HOME."
I HAVE SUCCESSFULLY MADE CONTACT WITH THE PRIME MINISTER OF KAMINO.
THEY ARE USING A BOUNTY HUNTER NAMED JANGO FETT TO CREATE A CLONE ARMY FOR THE REPUBLIC.
I HAVE A STRONG FEELING THIS BOUNTY HUNTER IS THE ASSASSIN WE'RE LOOKING FOR.
DO YOU THINK THESE CLONERS ARE INVOLVED IN THE PLOT TO ASSASSINATE SENATOR AMIDALA?
NO, MASTER. THERE APPEARS TO BE NO MOTIVE.
DO NOT ASSUME ANYTHING, OBI-WAN. CLEAR, YOUR MIND MUST BE IF YOU ARE TO DISCOVER THE REAL VILLAIN BEHIND THIS PLOT.
YES, MASTER.

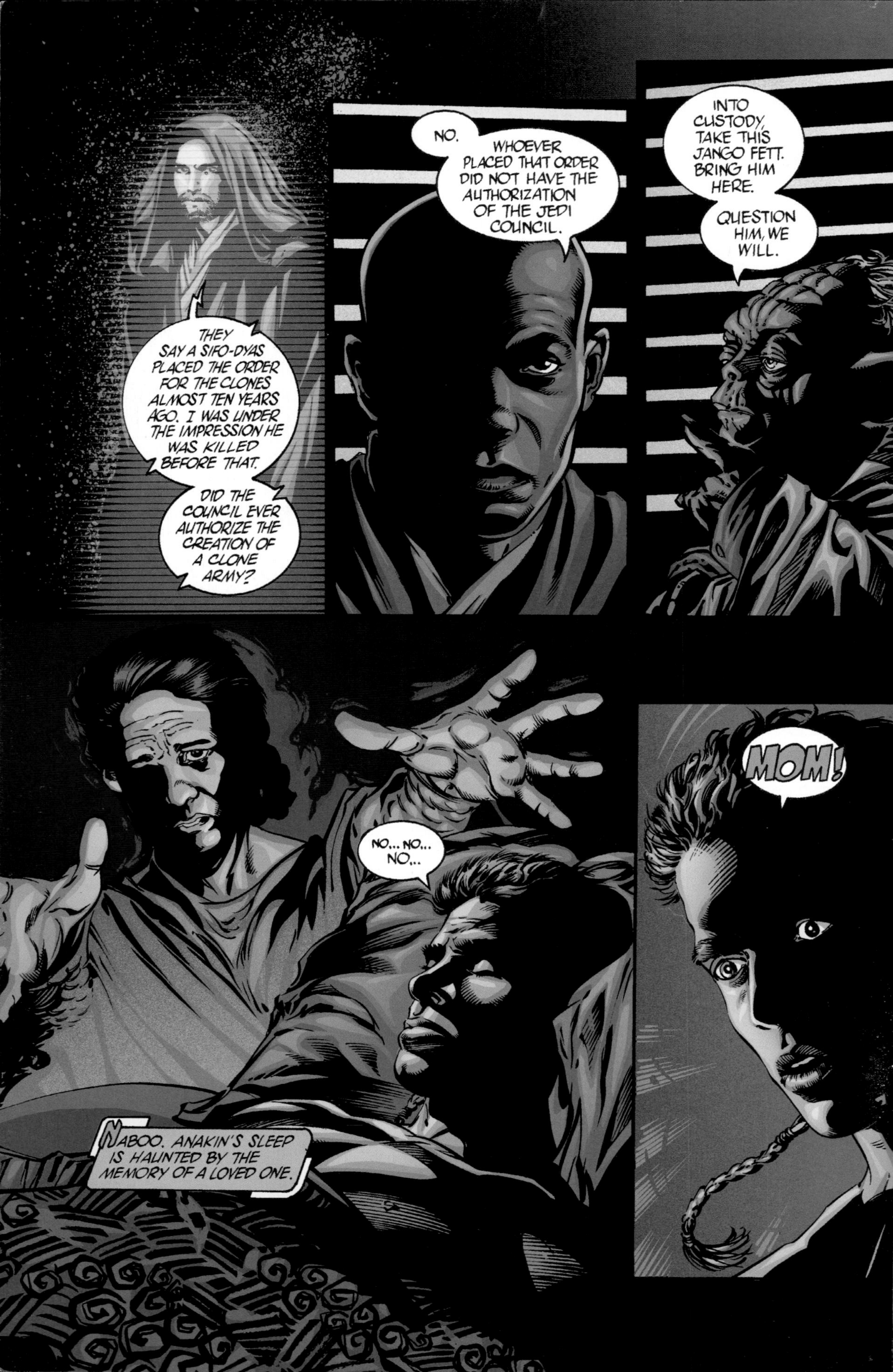
THEY SAY A SIFO-DYAS PLACED THE ORDER FOR THE CLONES ALMOST TEN YEARS AGO. I WAS UNDER THE IMPRESSION HE WAS KILLED BEFORE THAT.
DID THE COUNCIL EVER AUTHORIZE THE CREATION OF A CLONE ARMY?
NO.
WHOEVER PLACED THAT ORDER DID NOT HAVE THE AUTHORIZATION OF THE JEDI COUNCIL.
INTO CUSTODY, TAKE THIS JANGO FETT. BRING HIM HERE.
QUESTION HIM, WE WILL.
NABOO. ANAKIN'S SLEEP IS HAUNTED BY THE MEMORY OF A LOVED ONE.
NO... NO... NO...
MOM!

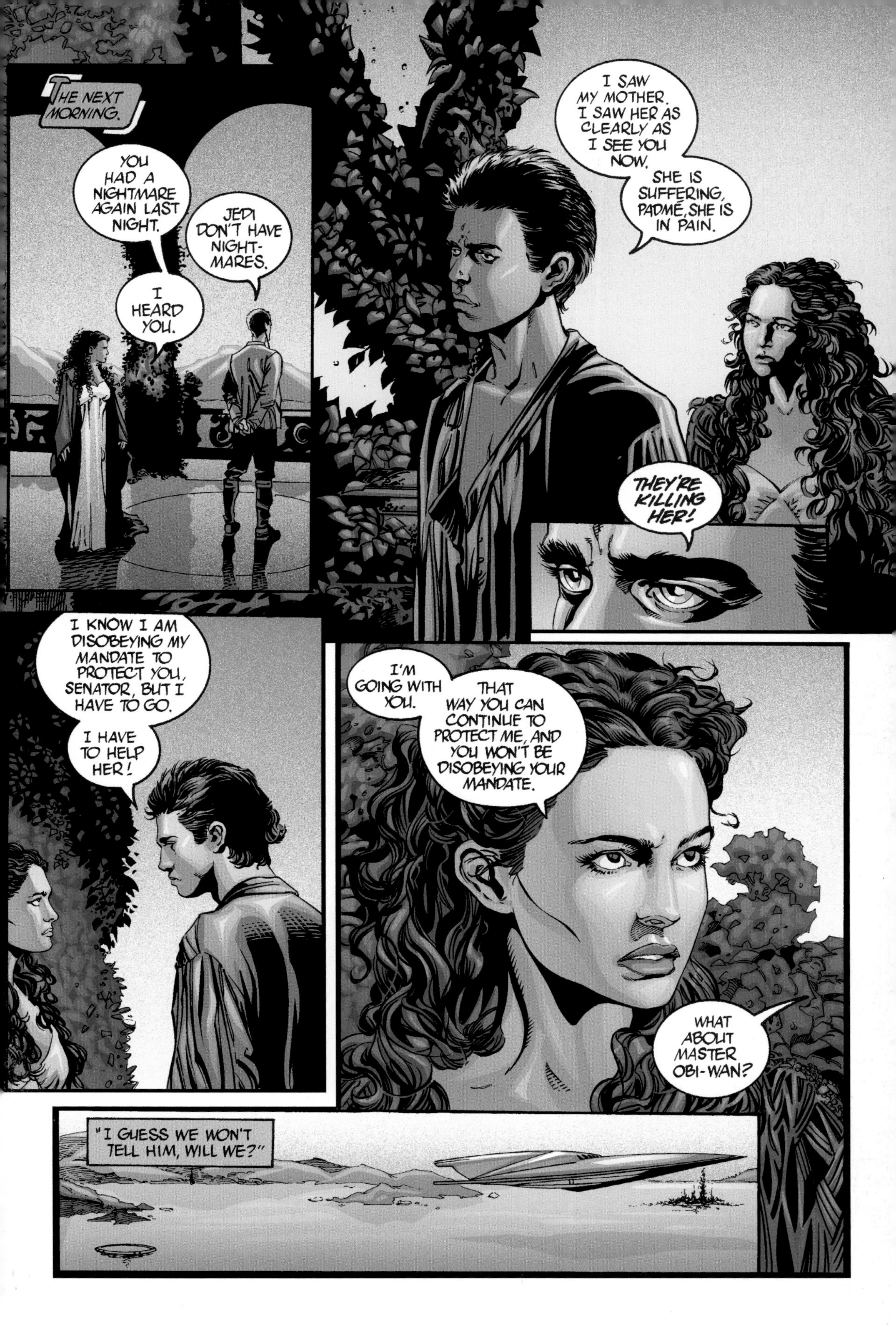
THE NEXT MORNING.
YOU HAD A NIGHTMARE AGAIN LAST NIGHT.
JEDI DON'T HAVE NIGHT-MARES.
I HEARD YOU.
I SAW MY MOTHER. I SAW HER AS CLEARLY AS I SEE YOU NOW.
SHE IS SUFFERING, PADMÉ, SHE IS IN PAIN.
THEY'RE KILLING HER!
I KNOW I AM DISOBEYING MY MANDATE TO PROTECT YOU, SENATOR, BUT I HAVE TO GO.
I HAVE TO HELP HER!
I'M GOING WITH YOU.
THAT WAY YOU CAN CONTINUE TO PROTECT ME, AND YOU WON'T BE DISOBEYING YOUR MANDATE.
WHAT ABOUT MASTER OBI-WAN?
"I GUESS WE WON'T TELL HIM, WILL WE?"

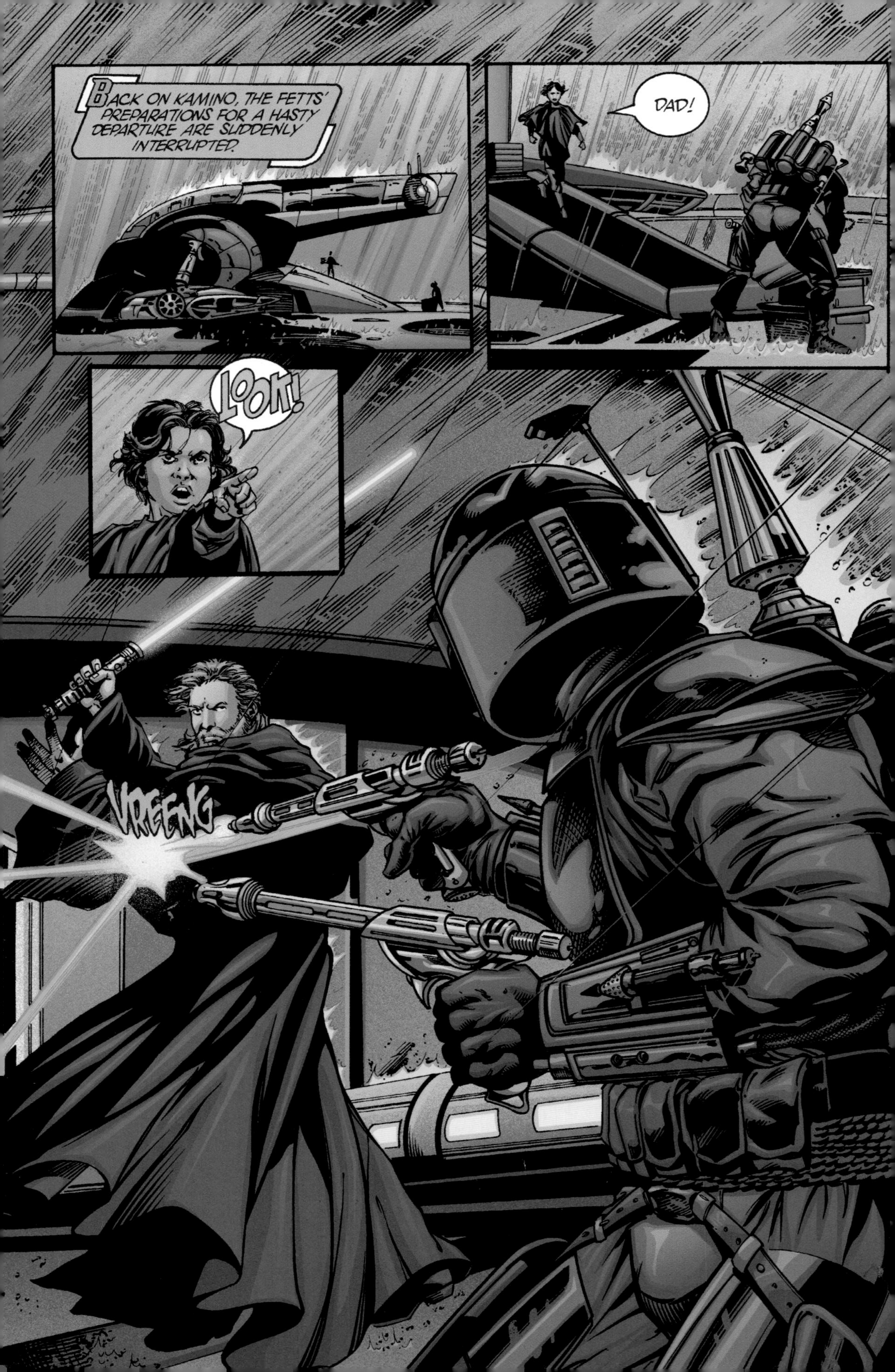
BACK ON KAMINO, THE FETTS' PREPARATIONS FOR A HASTY DEPARTURE ARE SUDDENLY INTERRUPTED.
DAD!
LOOK!
VREENG

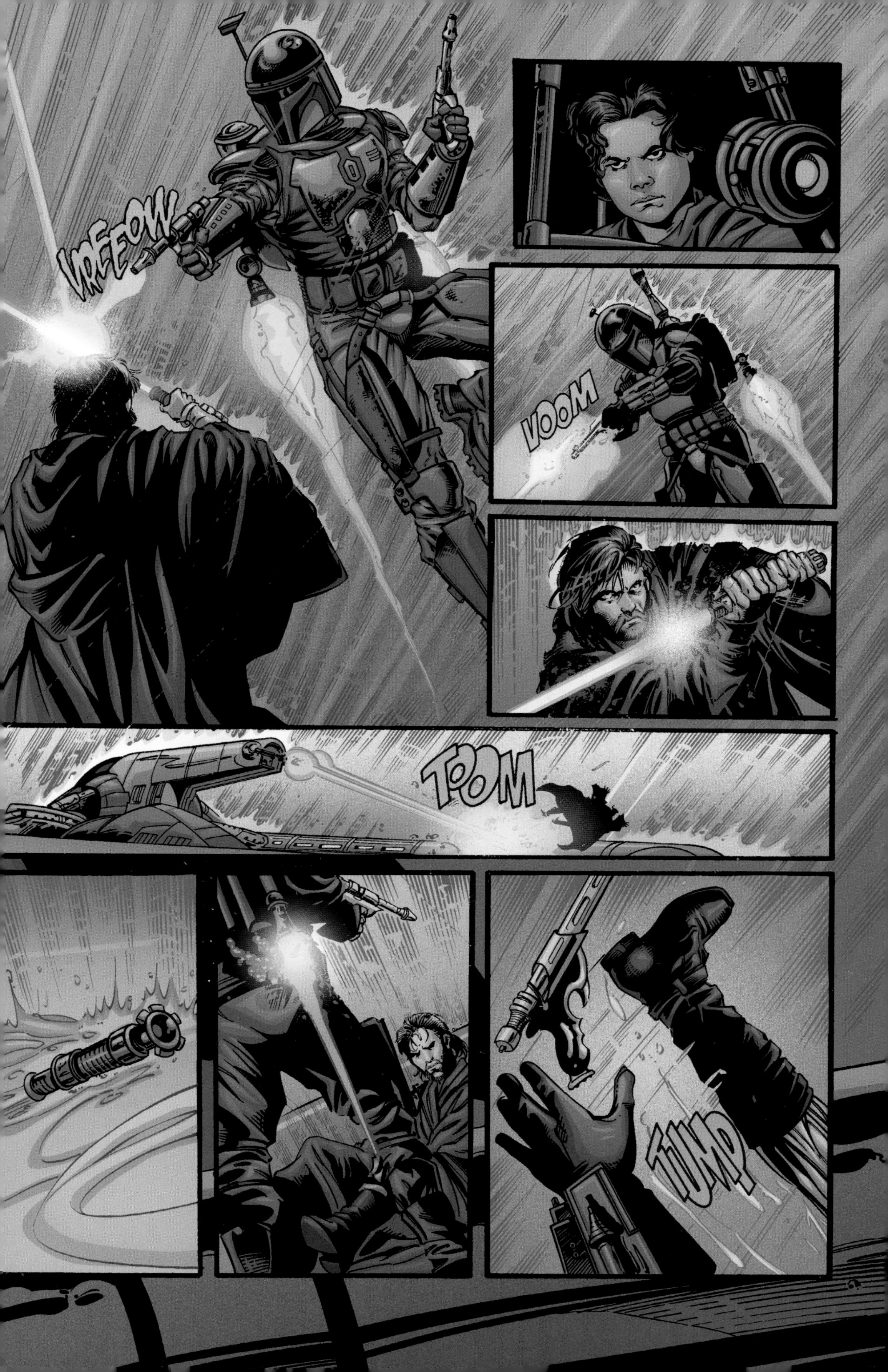
VREEOW
VOOM
TOOM
TUMP!

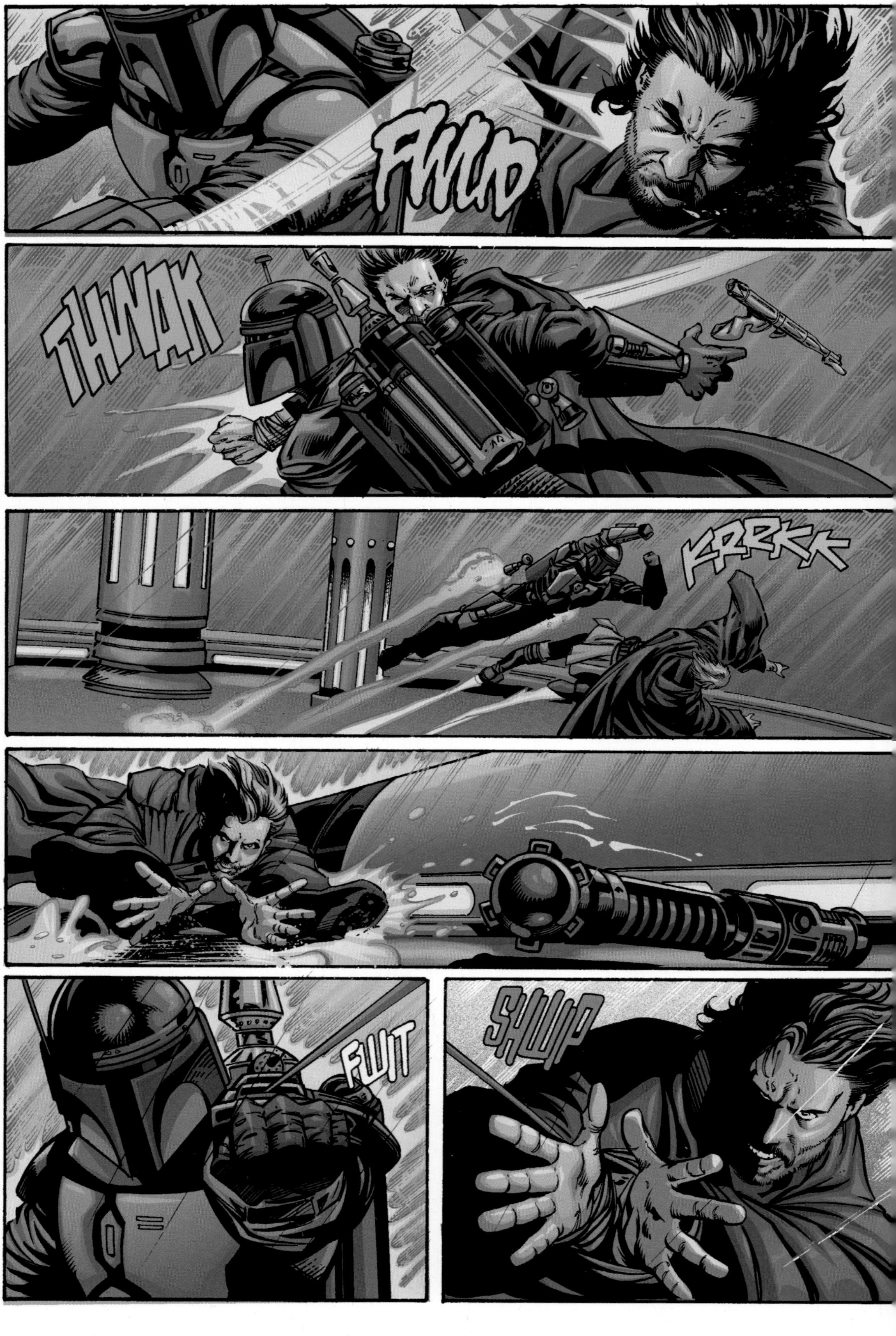
FWUD
THWAK
KRRKK
SHWIP
FWIT

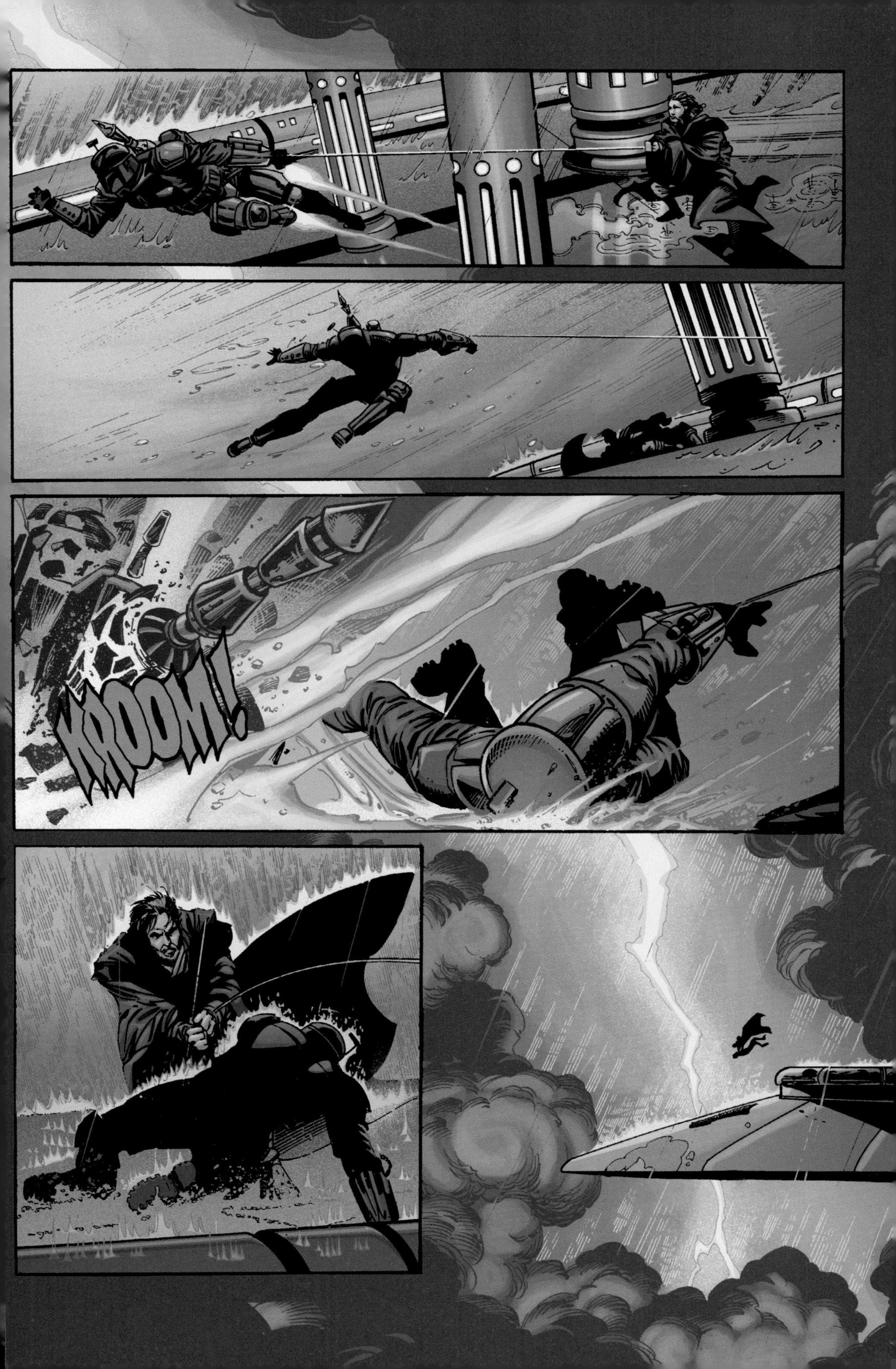
KROOM!

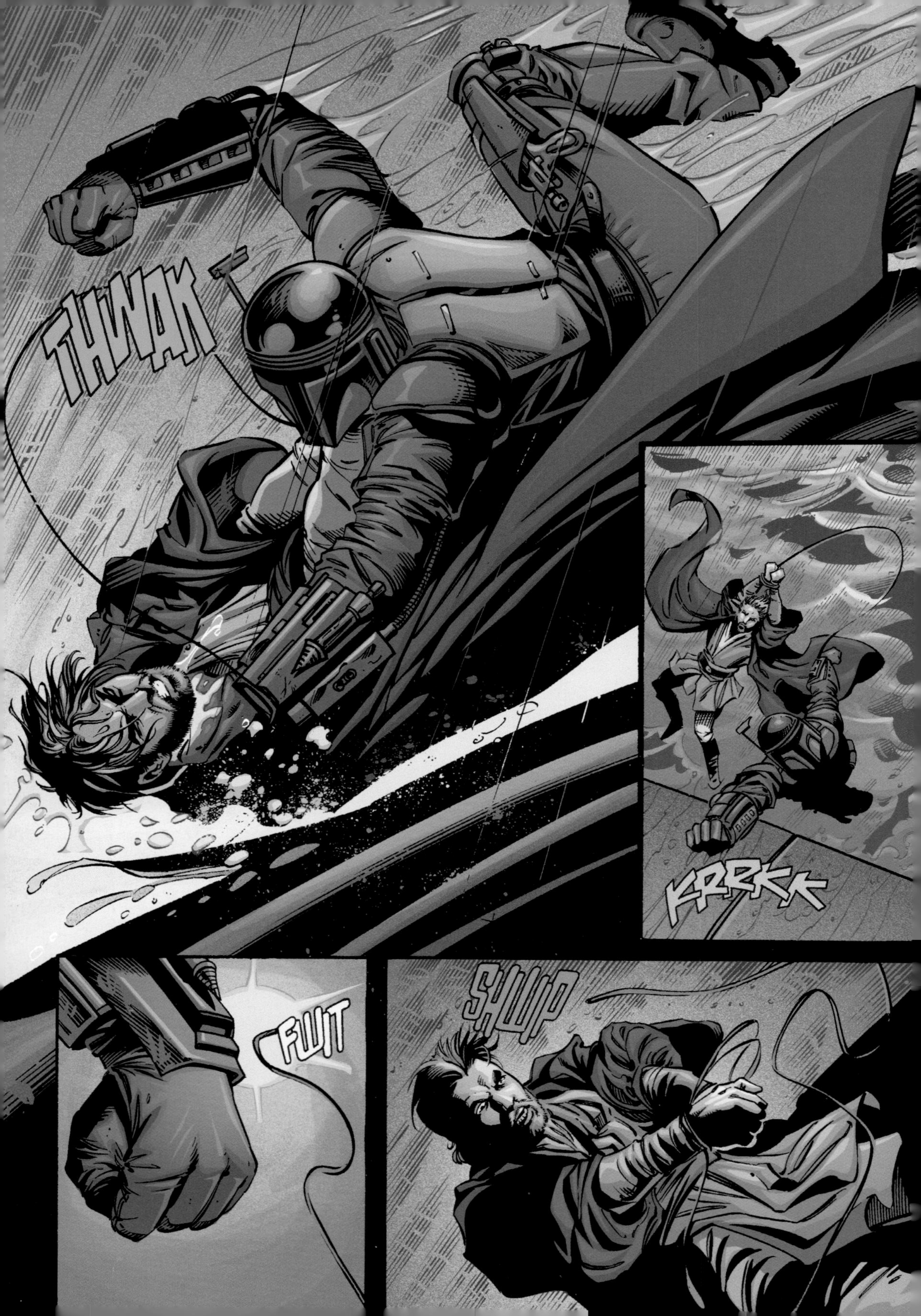
THWAK
KRRKK
FWIT
SHWIP

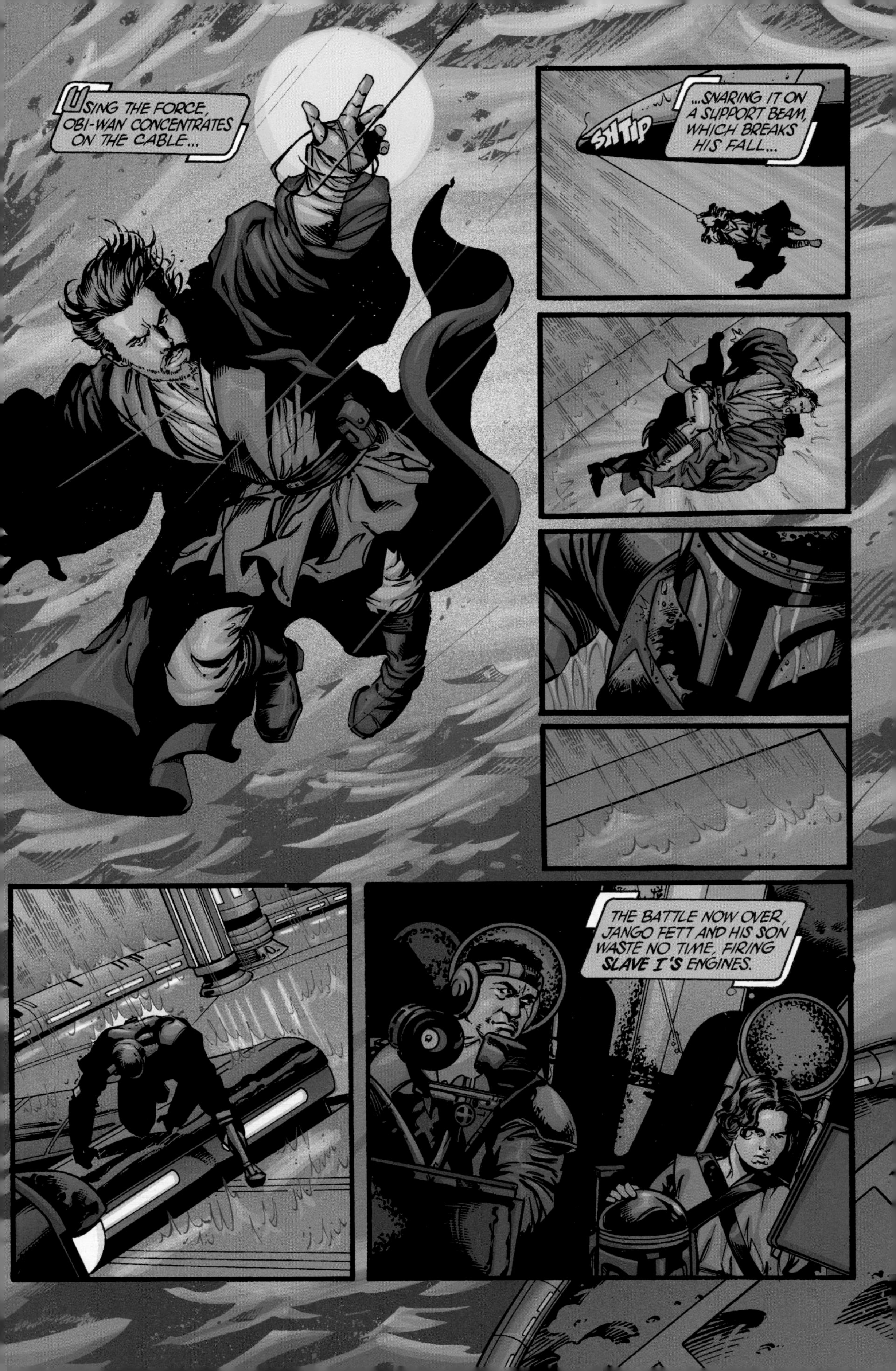
USING THE FORCE, OBI-WAN CONCENTRATES ON THE CABLE...
SHTIP
...SNARING IT ON A SUPPORT BEAM, WHICH BREAKS HIS FALL...
THE BATTLE NOW OVER, JANGO FETT AND HIS SON WASTE NO TIME, FIRING SLAVE I'S ENGINES.

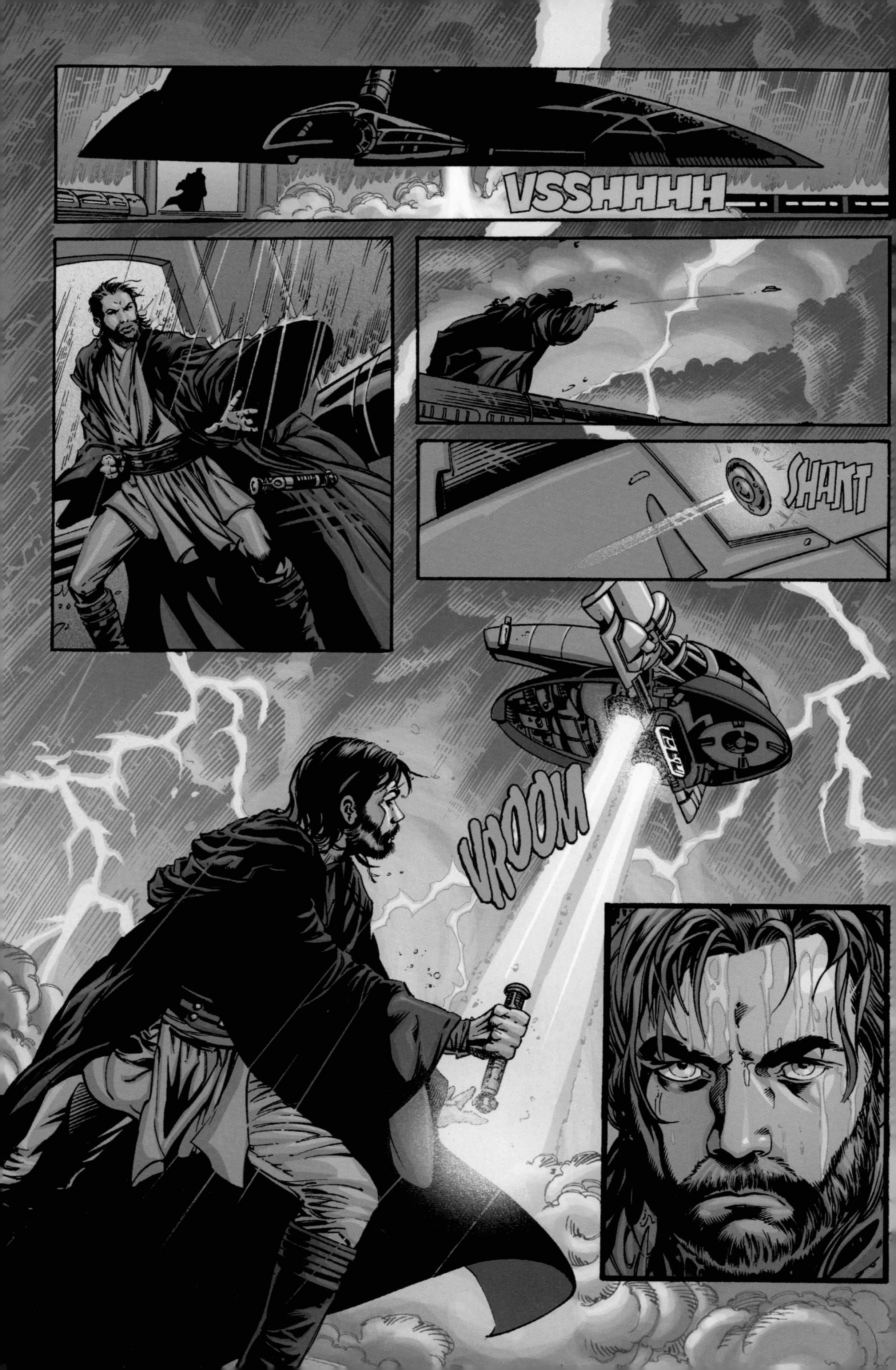
VSSHHHH
SHAKT
VROOM

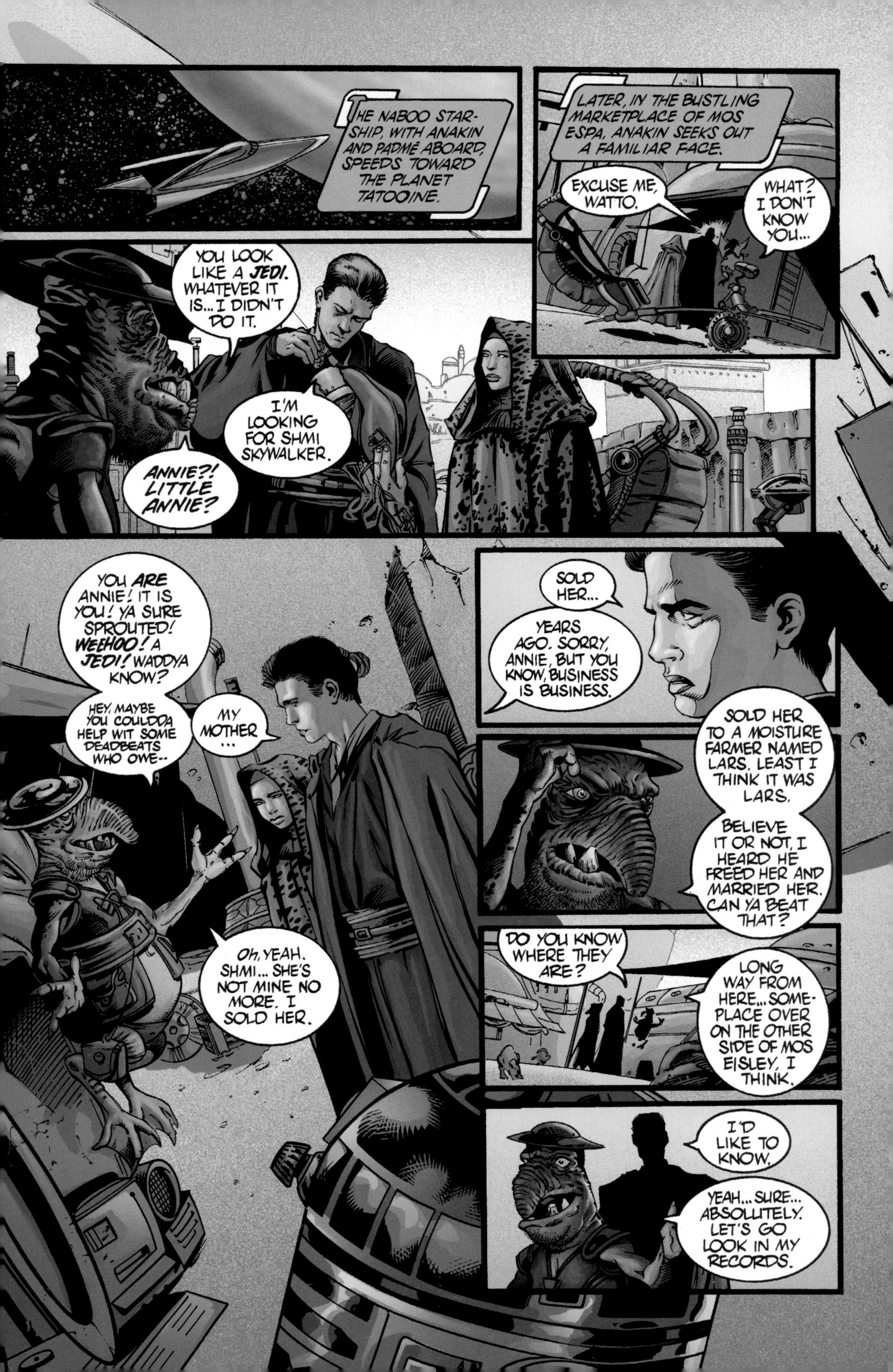

THE NABOO STARSHIP, WITH ANAKIN AND PADMÉ ABOARD, SPEEDS TOWARD THE PLANET TATOOINE.
LATER, IN THE BUSTLING MARKETPLACE OF MOS ESPA, ANAKIN SEEKS OUT A FAMILIAR FACE.
EXCUSE ME, WATTO.
WHAT? I DON'T KNOW YOU...
YOU LOOK LIKE A JEDI. WHATEVER IT IS...I DIDN'T DO IT.
I'M LOOKING FOR SHMI SKYWALKER.
ANNIE?! LITTLE ANNIE?
YOU ARE ANNIE! IT IS YOU! YA SURE SPROUTED! WEEHOO! A JEDI! WADDYA KNOW?
HEY, MAYBE YOU COULDDA HELP WIT SOME DEADBEATS WHO OWE--
MY MOTHER...
Oh, YEAH. SHMI... SHE'S NOT MINE NO MORE. I SOLD HER.
SOLD HER...
YEARS AGO. SORRY, ANNIE, BUT YOU KNOW, BUSINESS IS BUSINESS.
SOLD HER TO A MOISTURE FARMER NAMED LARS. LEAST I THINK IT WAS LARS.
BELIEVE IT OR NOT, I HEARD HE FREED HER AND MARRIED HER. CAN YA BEAT THAT?
DO YOU KNOW WHERE THEY ARE?
LONG WAY FROM HERE... SOMEPLACE OVER ON THE OTHER SIDE OF MOS EISLEY, I THINK.
I'D LIKE TO KNOW.
YEAH... SURE... ABSOLUTELY. LET'S GO LOOK IN MY RECORDS.

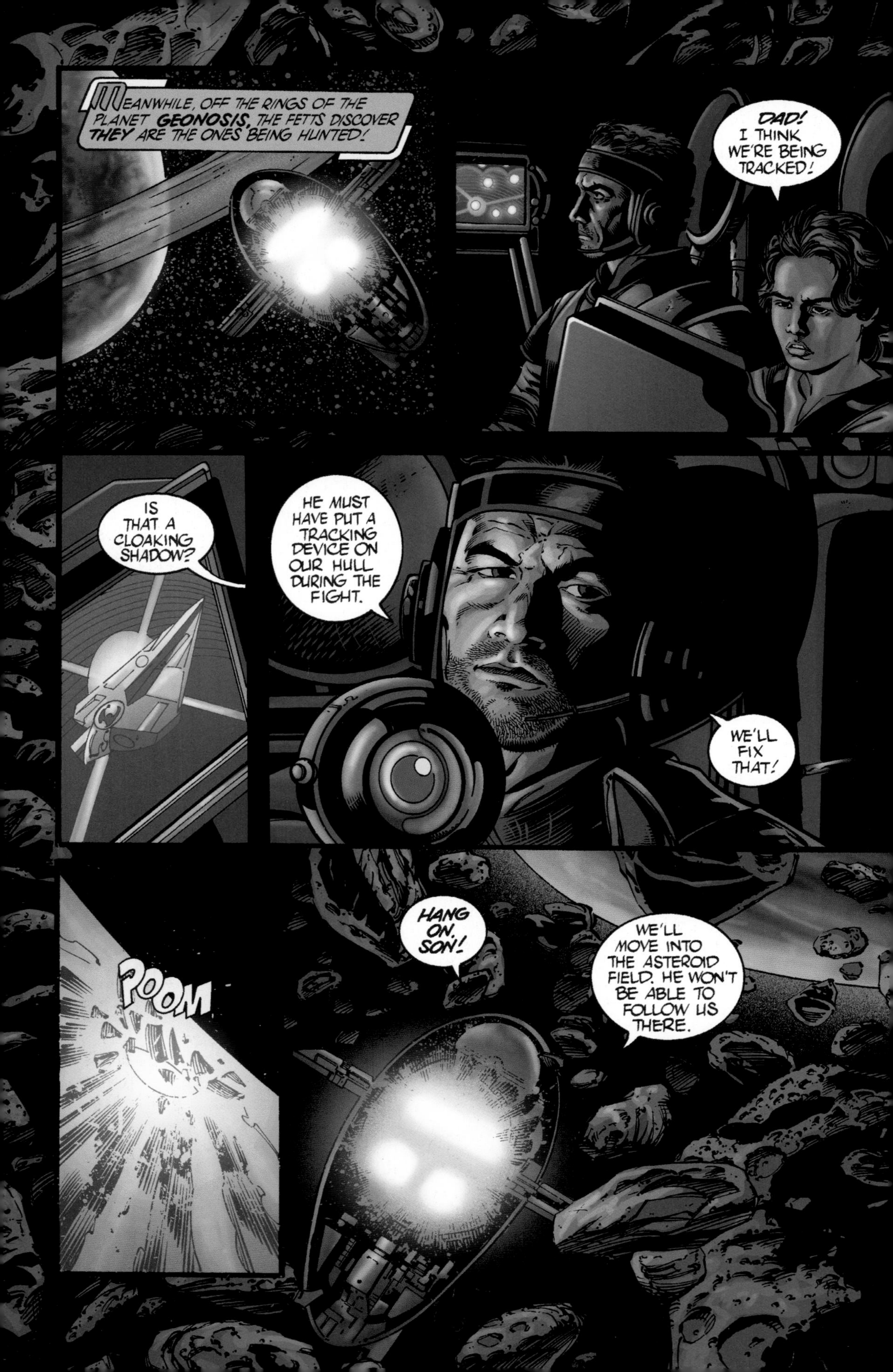
MEANWHILE, OFF THE RINGS OF THE PLANET GEONOSIS, THE FETTS DISCOVER THEY ARE THE ONES BEING HUNTED!
DAD! I THINK WE'RE BEING TRACKED!
IS THAT A CLOAKING SHADOW?
HE MUST HAVE PUT A TRACKING DEVICE ON OUR HULL DURING THE FIGHT.
WE'LL FIX THAT!
POOM
HANG ON, SON!
WE'LL MOVE INTO THE ASTEROID FIELD. HE WON'T BE ABLE TO FOLLOW US THERE.

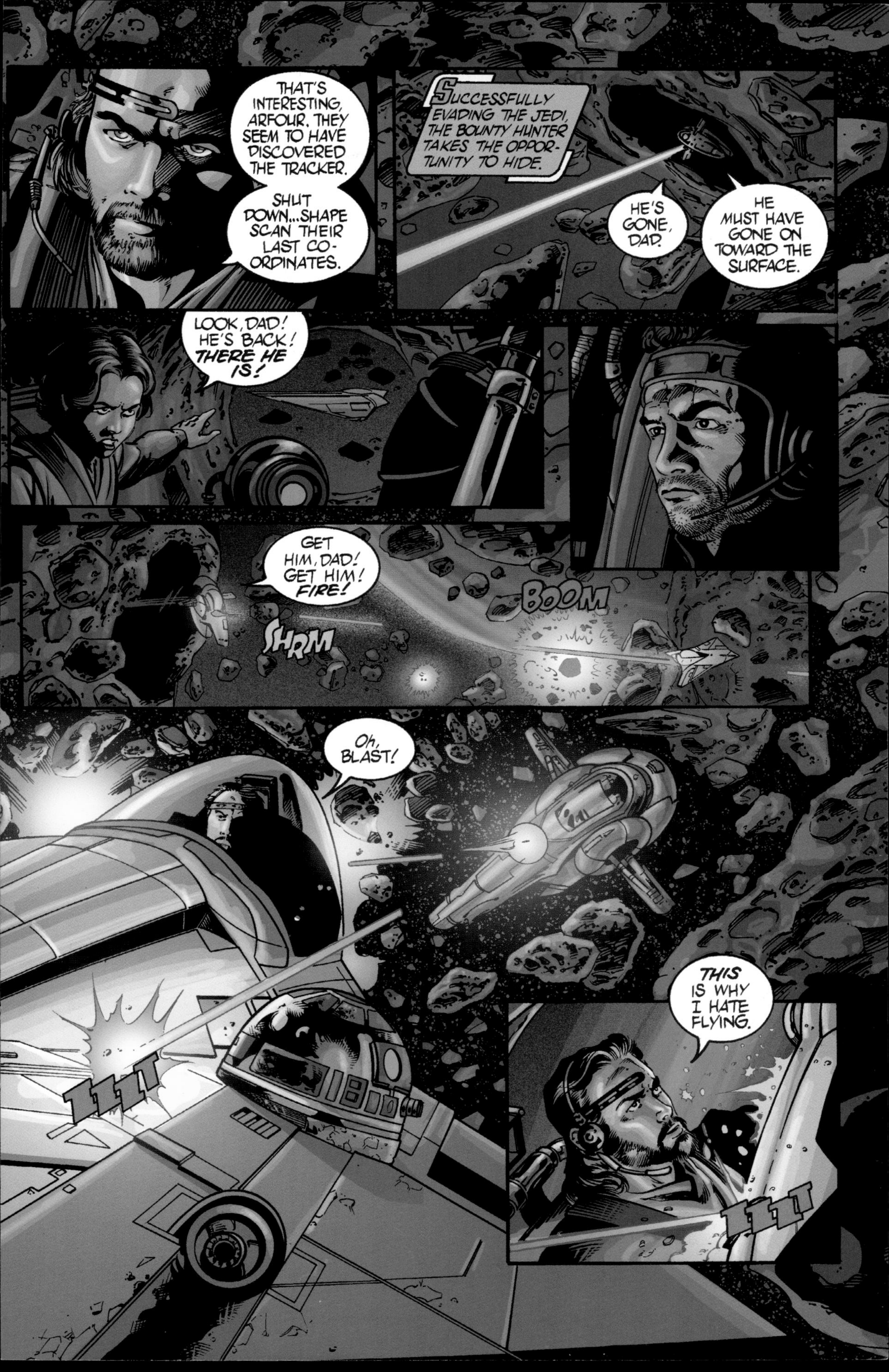

THAT'S INTERESTING, ARFOUR. THEY SEEM TO HAVE DISCOVERED THE TRACKER.
SHUT DOWN...SHAPE SCAN THEIR LAST CO-ORDINATES.
SUCCESSFULLY EVADING THE JEDI, THE BOUNTY HUNTER TAKES THE OPPORTUNITY TO HIDE.
HE'S GONE, DAD.
HE MUST HAVE GONE ON TOWARD THE SURFACE.
LOOK, DAD! HE'S BACK! THERE HE IS!
GET HIM, DAD! GET HIM! FIRE!
BOOM
SHRM
Oh, BLAST!
ZZZT
THIS IS WHY I HATE FLYING.
ZZZT

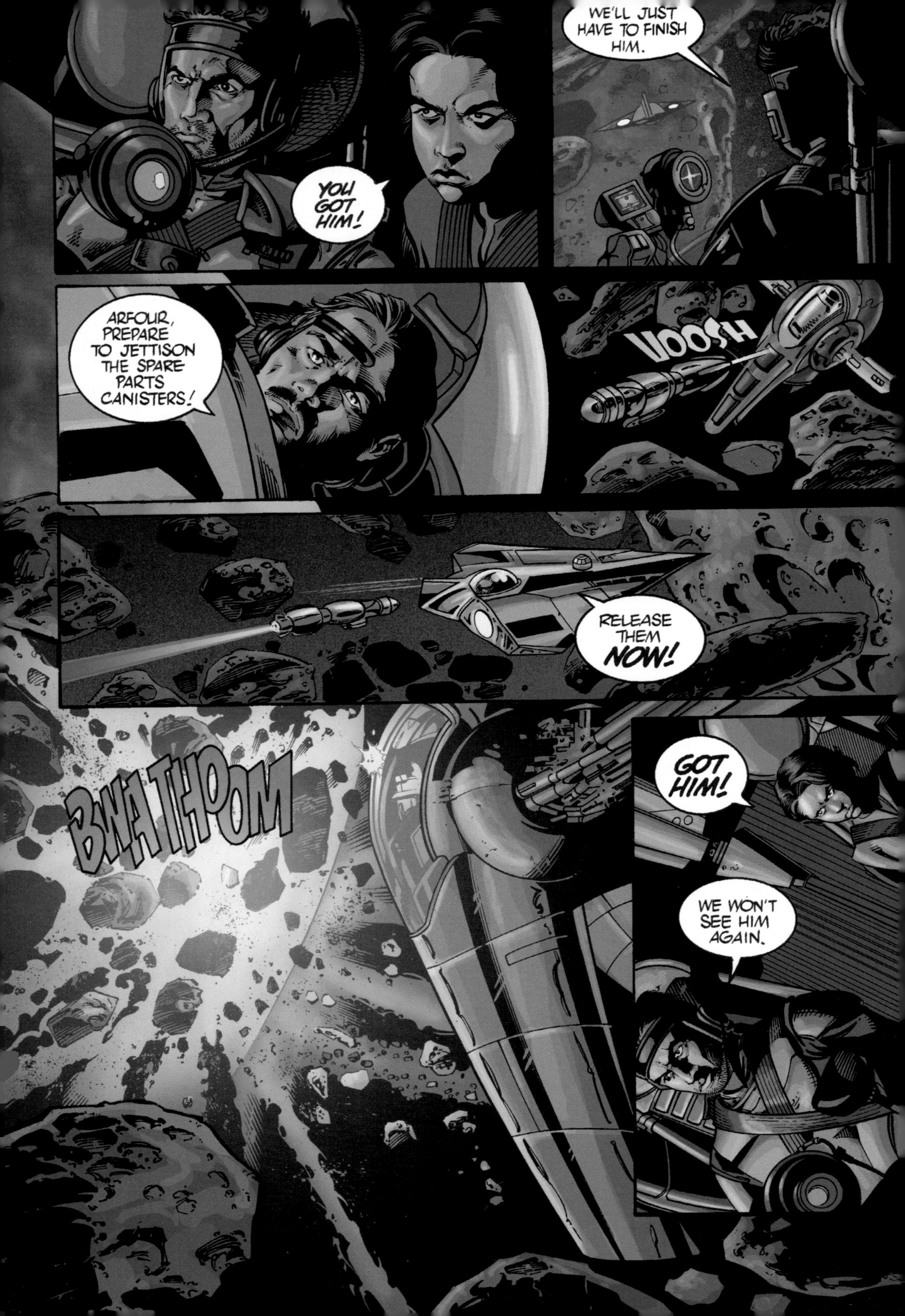
YOU GOT HIM!
WE'LL JUST HAVE TO FINISH HIM.
ARFOUR, PREPARE TO JETTISON THE SPARE PARTS CANISTERS!
VOOSH
RELEASE THEM NOW!
BWATHOOM
GOT HIM!
WE WON'T SEE HIM AGAIN.

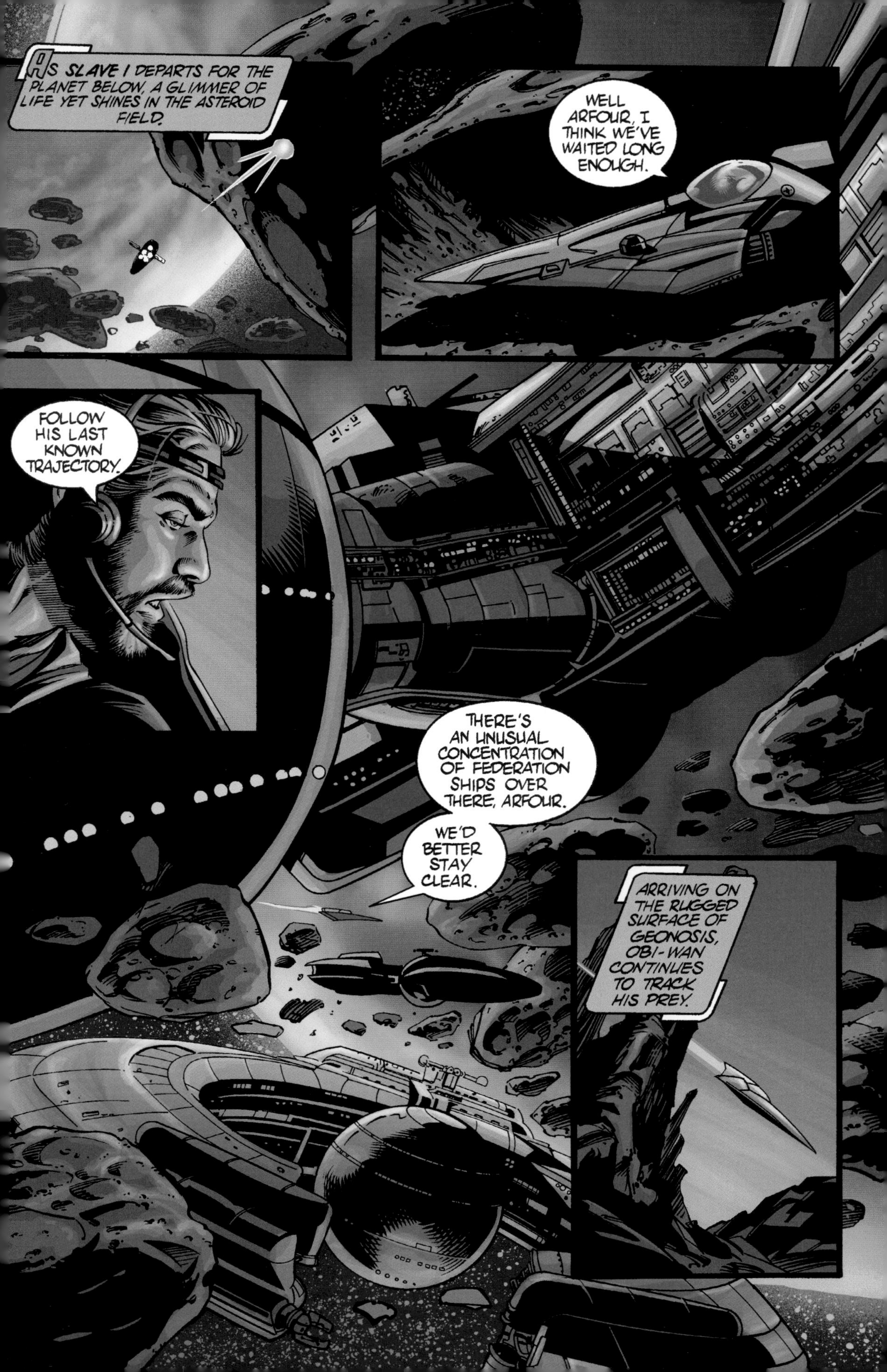
As SLAVE I DEPARTS FOR THE PLANET BELOW, A GLIMMER OF LIFE YET SHINES IN THE ASTEROID FIELD.
WELL ARFOUR, I THINK WE'VE WAITED LONG ENOUGH.
FOLLOW HIS LAST KNOWN TRAJECTORY.
THERE'S AN UNUSUAL CONCENTRATION OF FEDERATION SHIPS OVER THERE, ARFOUR.
WE'D BETTER STAY CLEAR.
ARRIVING ON THE RUGGED SURFACE OF GEONOSIS, OBI-WAN CONTINUES TO TRACK HIS PREY.

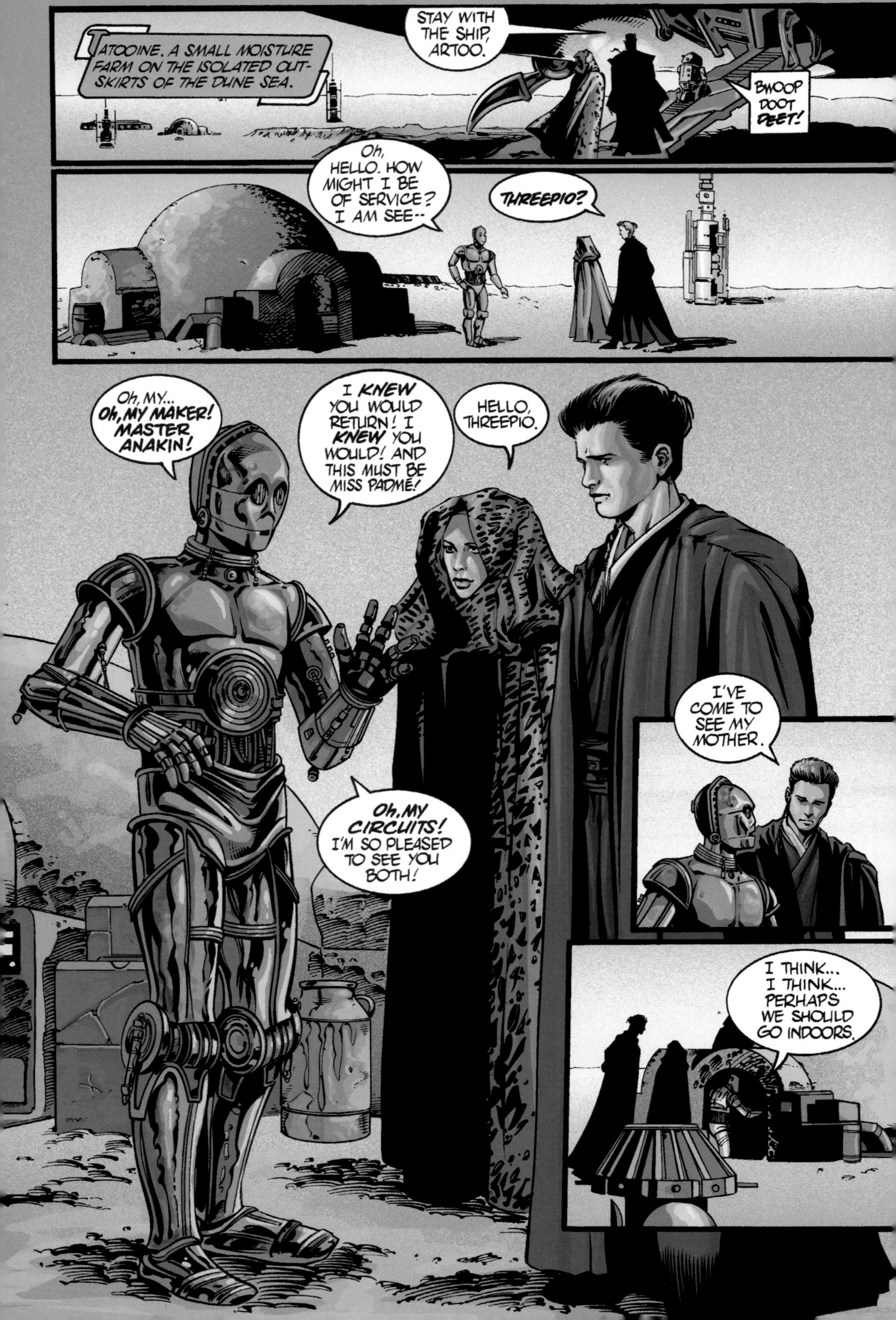
TATOOINE. A SMALL MOISTURE FARM ON THE ISOLATED OUT-SKIRTS OF THE DUNE SEA.
STAY WITH THE SHIP, ARTOO.
BWOOP DOOT DEET!
Oh, HELLO. HOW MIGHT I BE OF SERVICE? I AM SEE--
THREEPIO?
Oh, MY... Oh, MY MAKER! MASTER ANAKIN!
I KNEW YOU WOULD RETURN! I KNEW YOU WOULD! AND THIS MUST BE MISS PADMÉ!
HELLO, THREEPIO.
Oh, MY CIRCUITS! I'M SO PLEASED TO SEE YOU BOTH!
I'VE COME TO SEE MY MOTHER.
I THINK... I THINK... PERHAPS WE SHOULD GO INDOORS.

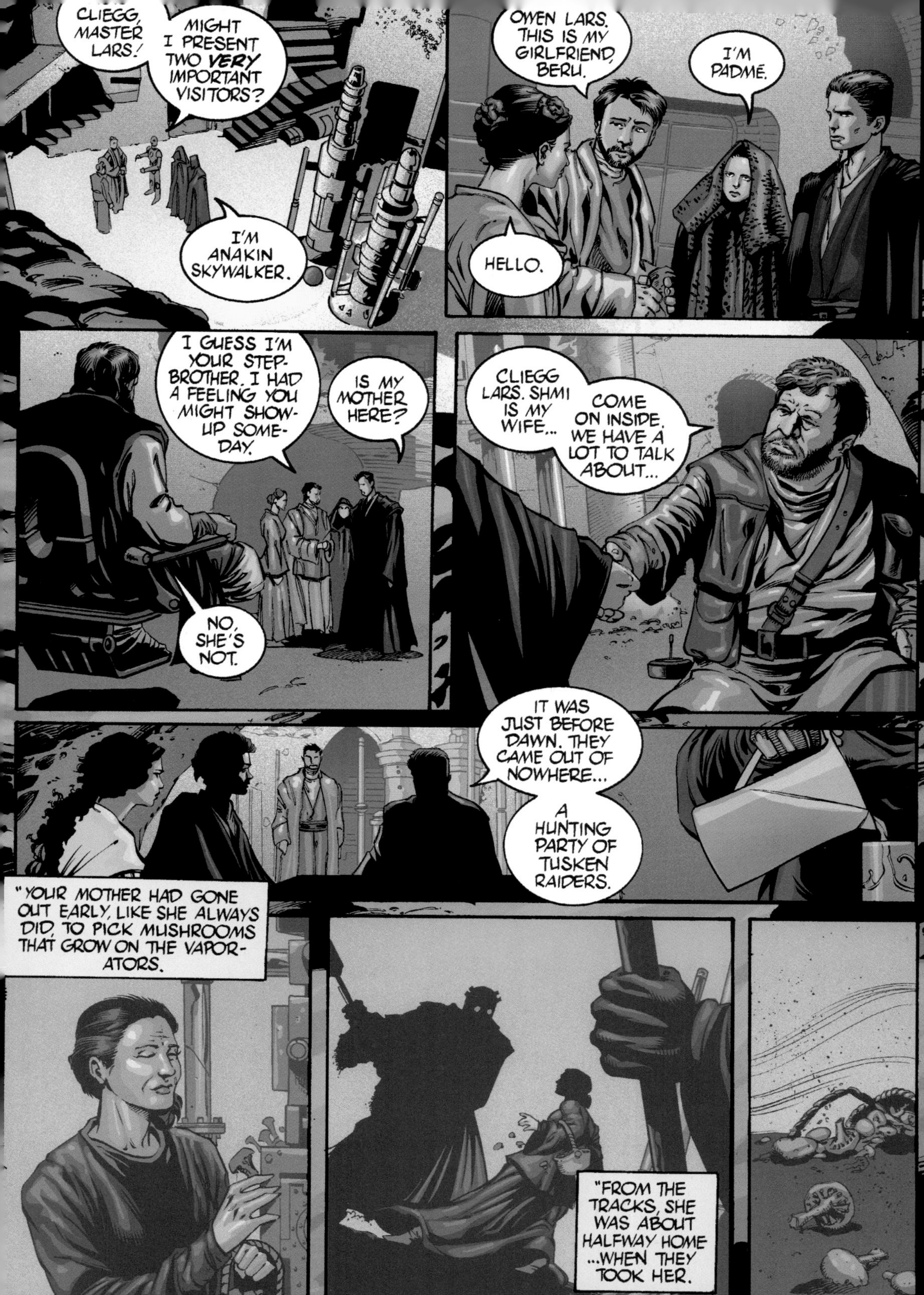
CLIEGG, MASTER LARS!
MIGHT I PRESENT TWO VERY IMPORTANT VISITORS?
I'M ANAKIN SKYWALKER.
OWEN LARS. THIS IS MY GIRLFRIEND, BERU.
I'M PADMÉ.
HELLO.
I GUESS I'M YOUR STEP-BROTHER. I HAD A FEELING YOU MIGHT SHOW-UP SOME-DAY.
IS MY MOTHER HERE?
NO, SHE'S NOT.
CLIEGG LARS. SHMI IS MY WIFE...
COME ON INSIDE. WE HAVE A LOT TO TALK ABOUT...
IT WAS JUST BEFORE DAWN. THEY CAME OUT OF NOWHERE...
A HUNTING PARTY OF TUSKEN RAIDERS.
"YOUR MOTHER HAD GONE OUT EARLY, LIKE SHE ALWAYS DID, TO PICK MUSHROOMS THAT GROW ON THE VAPOR-ATORS.
"FROM THE TRACKS, SHE WAS ABOUT HALFWAY HOME ...WHEN THEY TOOK HER.

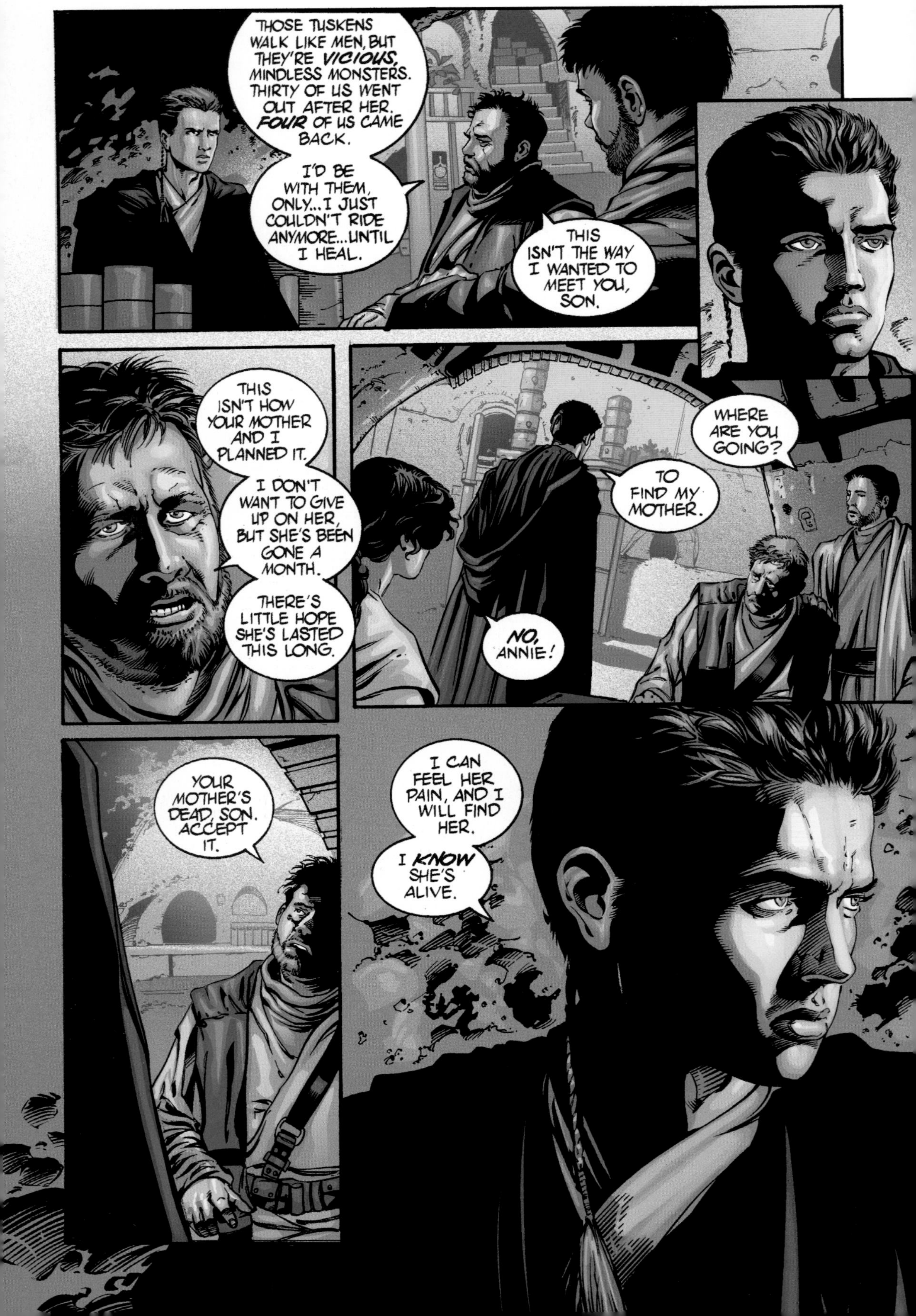
THOSE TUSKENS WALK LIKE MEN, BUT THEY'RE VICIOUS, MINDLESS MONSTERS. THIRTY OF US WENT OUT AFTER HER. FOUR OF US CAME BACK.
I'D BE WITH THEM, ONLY... I JUST COULDN'T RIDE ANYMORE... UNTIL I HEAL.
THIS ISN'T THE WAY I WANTED TO MEET YOU, SON.
THIS ISN'T HOW YOUR MOTHER AND I PLANNED IT.
I DON'T WANT TO GIVE UP ON HER, BUT SHE'S BEEN GONE A MONTH.
THERE'S LITTLE HOPE SHE'S LASTED THIS LONG.
WHERE ARE YOU GOING?
TO FIND MY MOTHER.
NO, ANNIE!
YOUR MOTHER'S DEAD, SON. ACCEPT IT.
I CAN FEEL HER PAIN, AND I WILL FIND HER.
I KNOW SHE'S ALIVE.

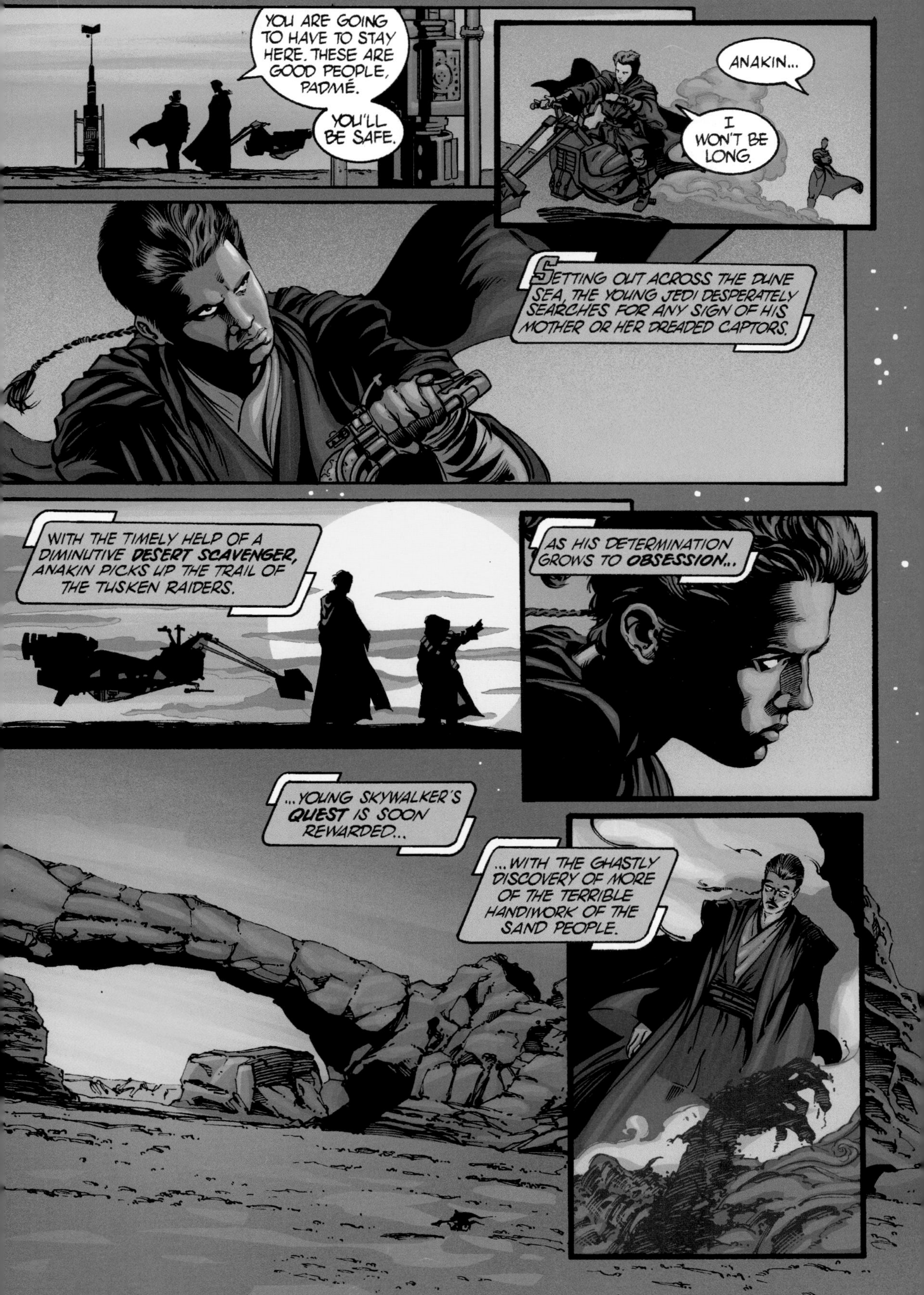
YOU ARE GOING TO HAVE TO STAY HERE. THESE ARE GOOD PEOPLE, PADMÉ.
YOU'LL BE SAFE.
ANAKIN...
I WON'T BE LONG.
SETTING OUT ACROSS THE DUNE SEA, THE YOUNG JEDI DESPERATELY SEARCHES FOR ANY SIGN OF HIS MOTHER OR HER DREADED CAPTORS.
WITH THE TIMELY HELP OF A DIMINUTIVE DESERT SCAVENGER, ANAKIN PICKS UP THE TRAIL OF THE TUSKEN RAIDERS.
AS HIS DETERMINATION GROWS TO OBSESSION...
...YOUNG SKYWALKER'S QUEST IS SOON REWARDED...
...WITH THE GHASTLY DISCOVERY OF MORE OF THE TERRIBLE HANDIWORK OF THE SAND PEOPLE.

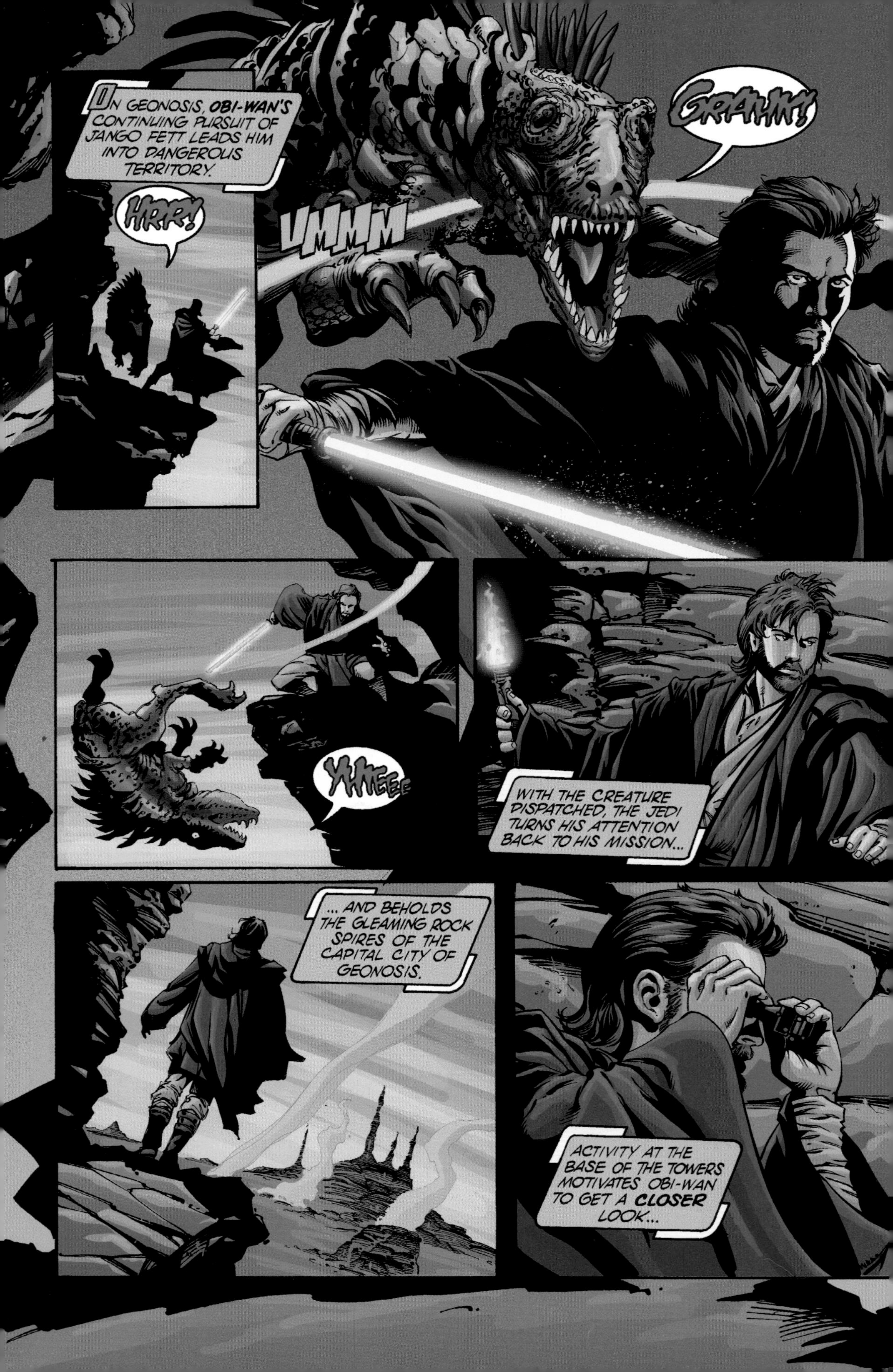

ON GEONOSIS, OBI-WAN'S CONTINUING PURSUIT OF JANGO FETT LEADS HIM INTO DANGEROUS TERRITORY.
HRR!
GRAWK!
UMMM
YHHEEE
WITH THE CREATURE DISPATCHED, THE JEDI TURNS HIS ATTENTION BACK TO HIS MISSION...
... AND BEHOLDS THE GLEAMING ROCK SPIRES OF THE CAPITAL CITY OF GEONOSIS.
ACTIVITY AT THE BASE OF THE TOWERS MOTIVATES OBI-WAN TO GET A CLOSER LOOK...

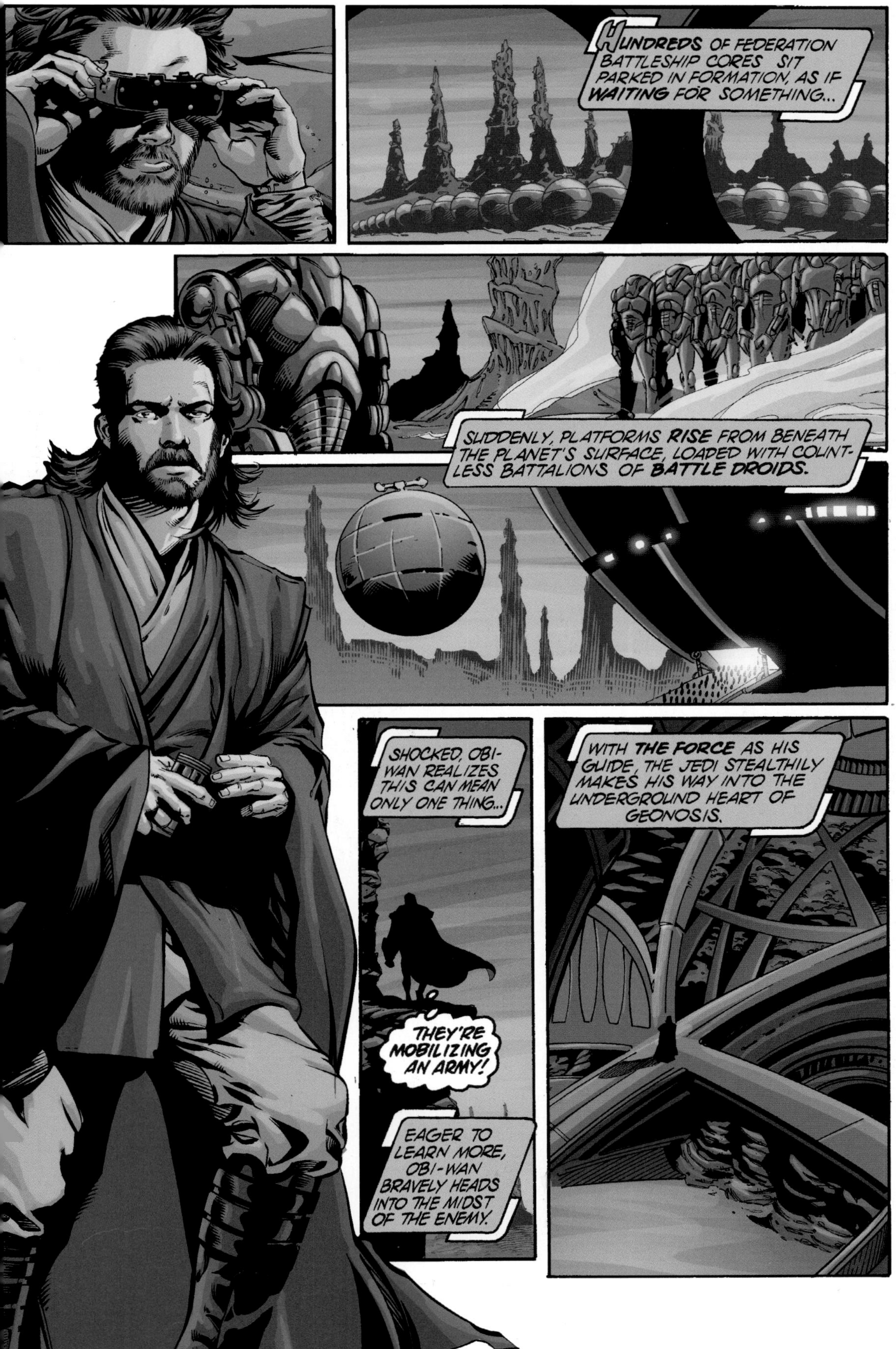
HUNDREDS OF FEDERATION BATTLESHIP CORES SIT PARKED IN FORMATION, AS IF WAITING FOR SOMETHING...
SUDDENLY, PLATFORMS RISE FROM BENEATH THE PLANET'S SURFACE, LOADED WITH COUNTLESS BATTALIONS OF BATTLE DROIDS.
SHOCKED, OBI-WAN REALIZES THIS CAN MEAN ONLY ONE THING...
THEY'RE MOBILIZING AN ARMY!
EAGER TO LEARN MORE, OBI-WAN BRAVELY HEADS INTO THE MIDST OF THE ENEMY.
WITH THE FORCE AS HIS GUIDE, THE JEDI STEALTHILY MAKES HIS WAY INTO THE UNDERGROUND HEART OF GEONOSIS.

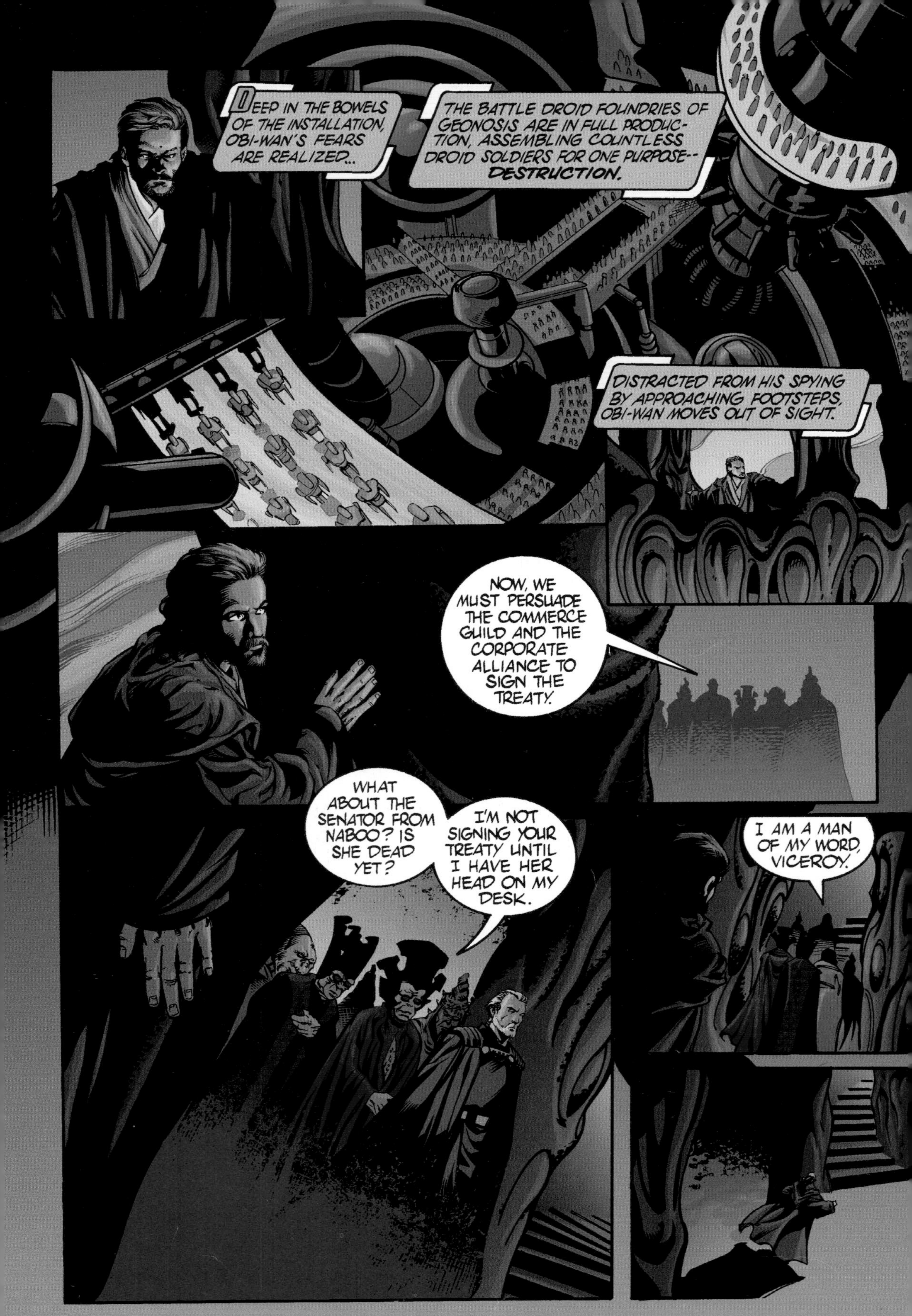
DEEP IN THE BOWELS OF THE INSTALLATION, OBI-WAN'S FEARS ARE REALIZED...
THE BATTLE DROID FOUNDRIES OF GEONOSIS ARE IN FULL PRODUCTION, ASSEMBLING COUNTLESS DROID SOLDIERS FOR ONE PURPOSE-- DESTRUCTION.
DISTRACTED FROM HIS SPYING BY APPROACHING FOOTSTEPS, OBI-WAN MOVES OUT OF SIGHT.
NOW, WE MUST PERSUADE THE COMMERCE GUILD AND THE CORPORATE ALLIANCE TO SIGN THE TREATY.
WHAT ABOUT THE SENATOR FROM NABOO? IS SHE DEAD YET?
I'M NOT SIGNING YOUR TREATY UNTIL I HAVE HER HEAD ON MY DESK.
I AM A MAN OF MY WORD, VICEROY.

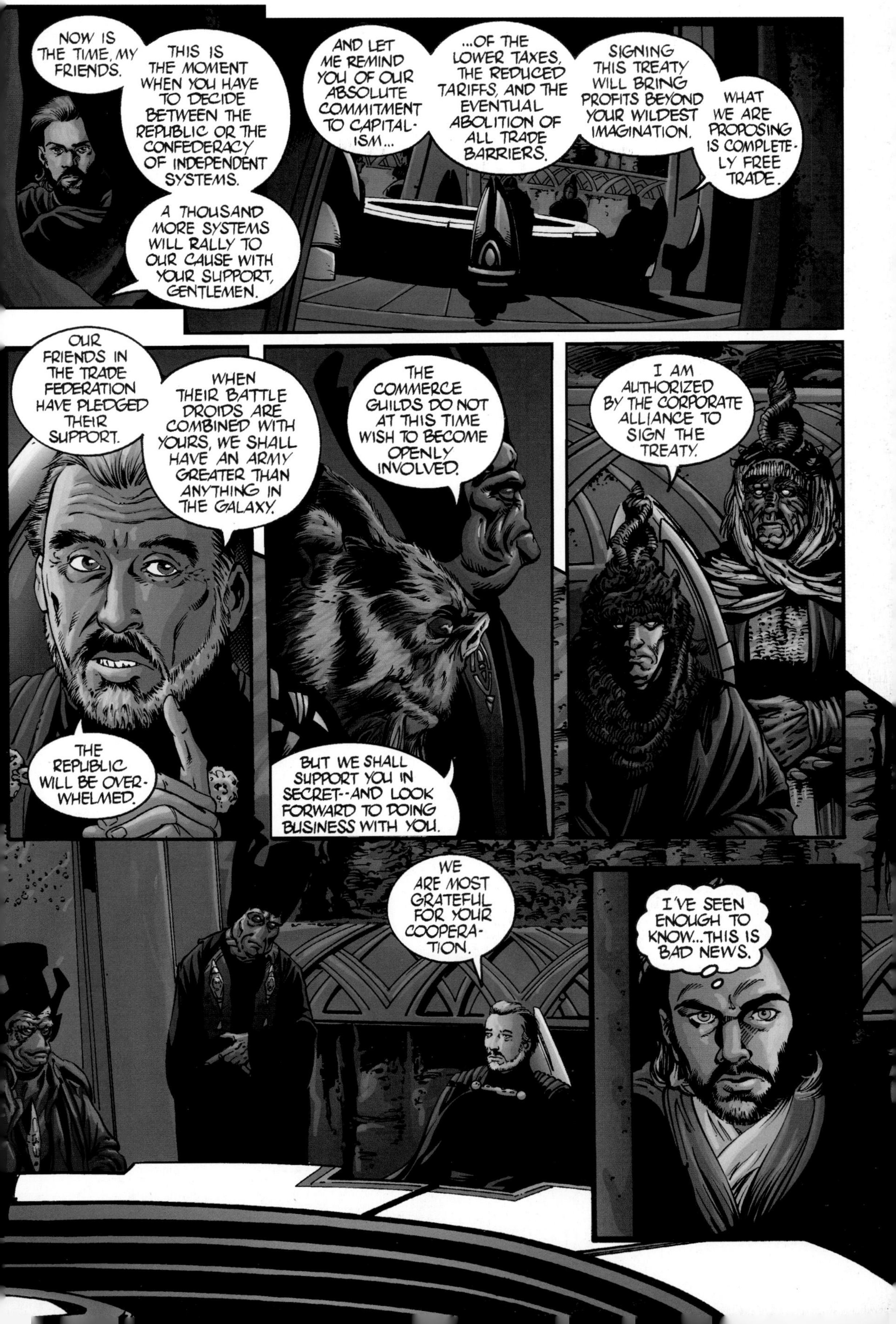
NOW IS THE TIME, MY FRIENDS.
THIS IS THE MOMENT WHEN YOU HAVE TO DECIDE BETWEEN THE REPUBLIC OR THE CONFEDERACY OF INDEPENDENT SYSTEMS.
A THOUSAND MORE SYSTEMS WILL RALLY TO OUR CAUSE WITH YOUR SUPPORT, GENTLEMEN.
AND LET ME REMIND YOU OF OUR ABSOLUTE COMMITMENT TO CAPITAL-ISM...
...OF THE LOWER TAXES, THE REDUCED TARIFFS, AND THE EVENTUAL ABOLITION OF ALL TRADE BARRIERS.
SIGNING THIS TREATY WILL BRING PROFITS BEYOND YOUR WILDEST IMAGINATION.
WHAT WE ARE PROPOSING IS COMPLETE-LY FREE TRADE.
OUR FRIENDS IN THE TRADE FEDERATION HAVE PLEDGED THEIR SUPPORT.
WHEN THEIR BATTLE DROIDS ARE COMBINED WITH YOURS, WE SHALL HAVE AN ARMY GREATER THAN ANYTHING IN THE GALAXY.
THE REPUBLIC WILL BE OVER-WHELMED.
THE COMMERCE GUILDS DO NOT AT THIS TIME WISH TO BECOME OPENLY INVOLVED.
BUT WE SHALL SUPPORT YOU IN SECRET--AND LOOK FORWARD TO DOING BUSINESS WITH YOU.
I AM AUTHORIZED BY THE CORPORATE ALLIANCE TO SIGN THE TREATY.
WE ARE MOST GRATEFUL FOR YOUR COOPERA-TION.
I'VE SEEN ENOUGH TO KNOW...THIS IS BAD NEWS.

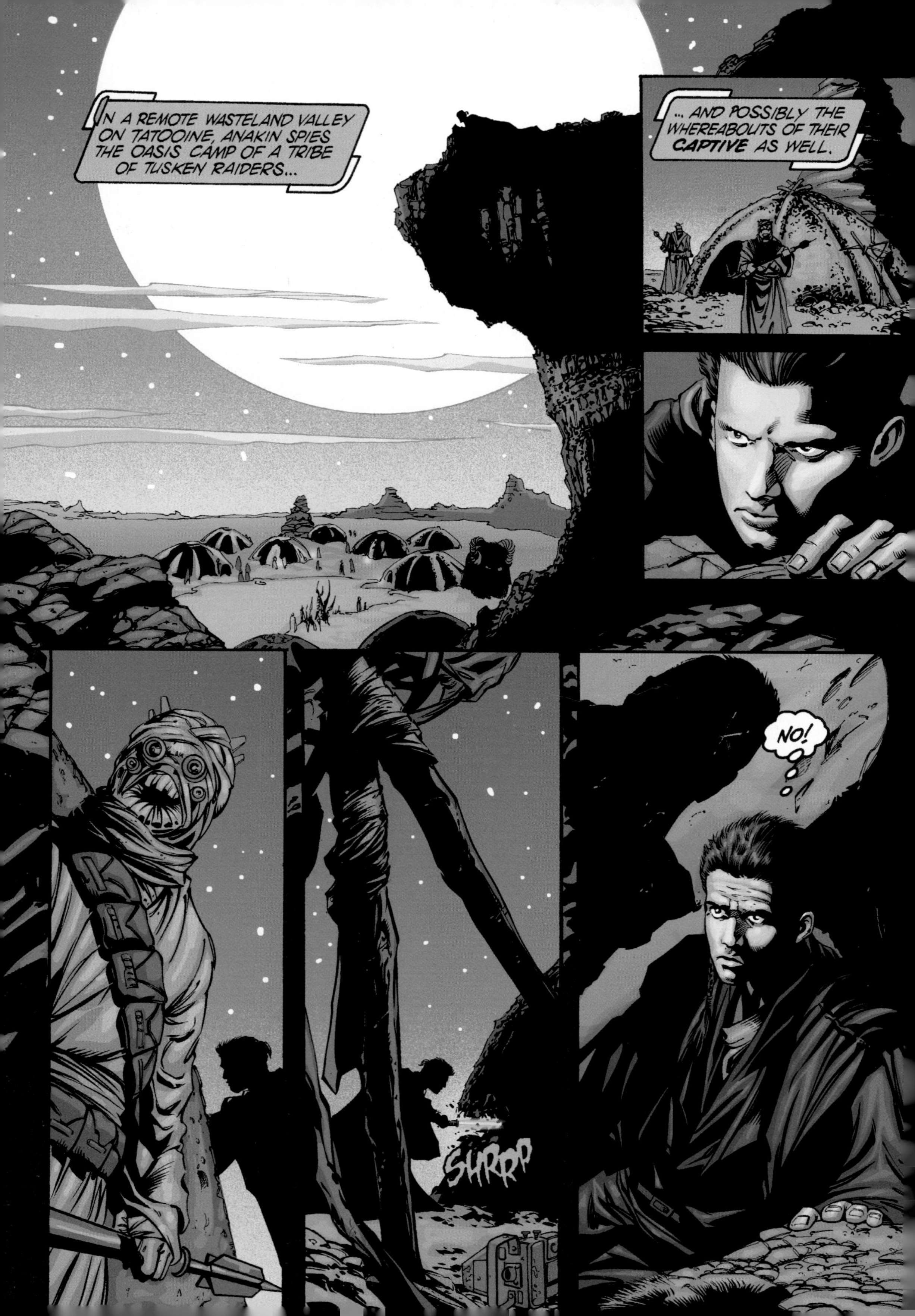
IN A REMOTE WASTELAND VALLEY ON TATOOINE, ANAKIN SPIES THE OASIS CAMP OF A TRIBE OF TUSKEN RAIDERS...
... AND POSSIBLY THE WHEREABOUTS OF THEIR CAPTIVE AS WELL.
SHRRP
NO!

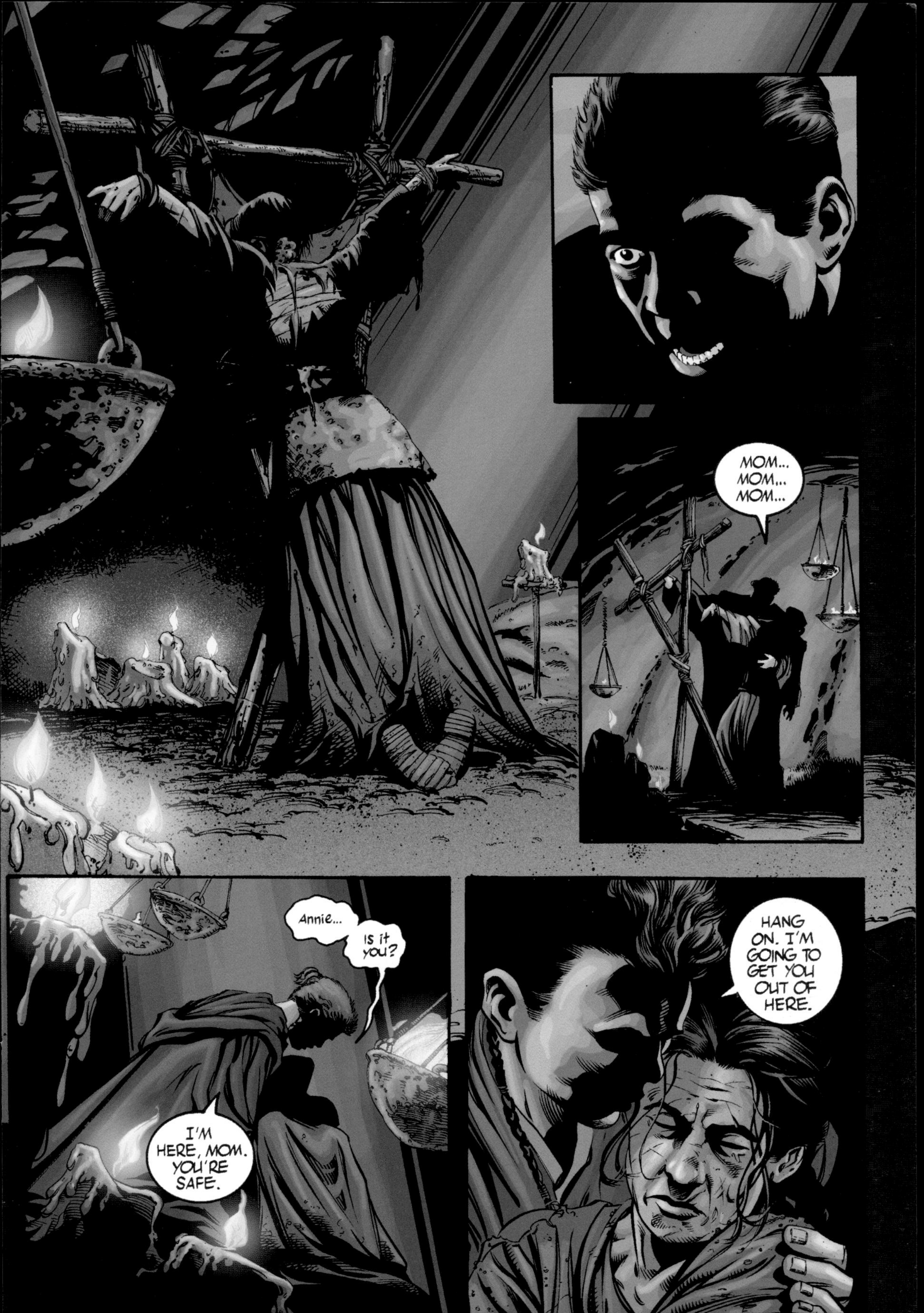
MOM... MOM... MOM...
Annie...
Is it you?
I'M HERE, MOM. YOU'RE SAFE.
HANG ON. I'M GOING TO GET YOU OUT OF HERE.

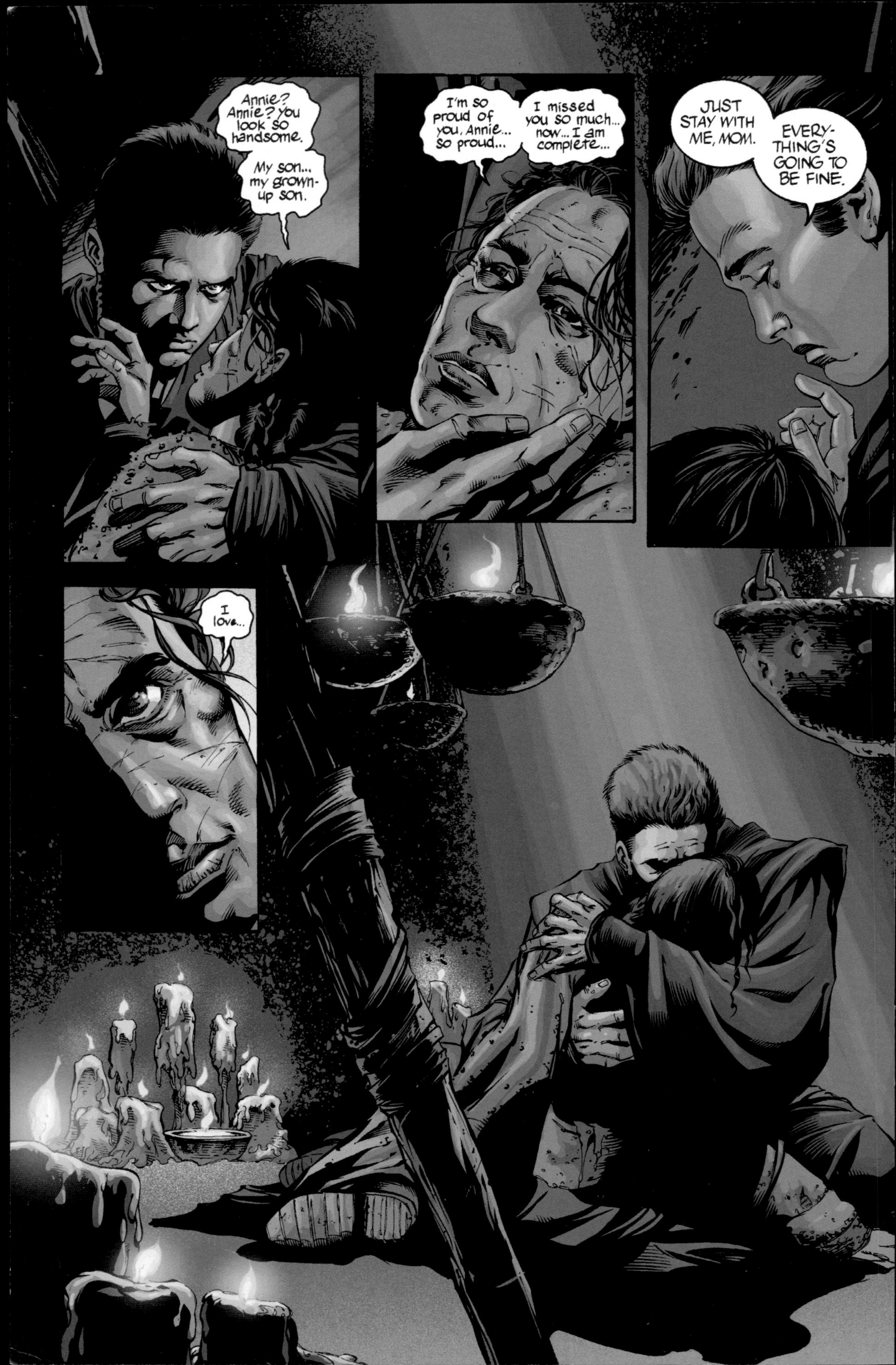
Annie? Annie? you look so handsome.
My son... my grown-up son.
I'm so proud of you, Annie... so proud...
I missed you so much... now... I am complete...
JUST STAY WITH ME, MOM.
EVERY-THING'S GOING TO BE FINE.
I love...

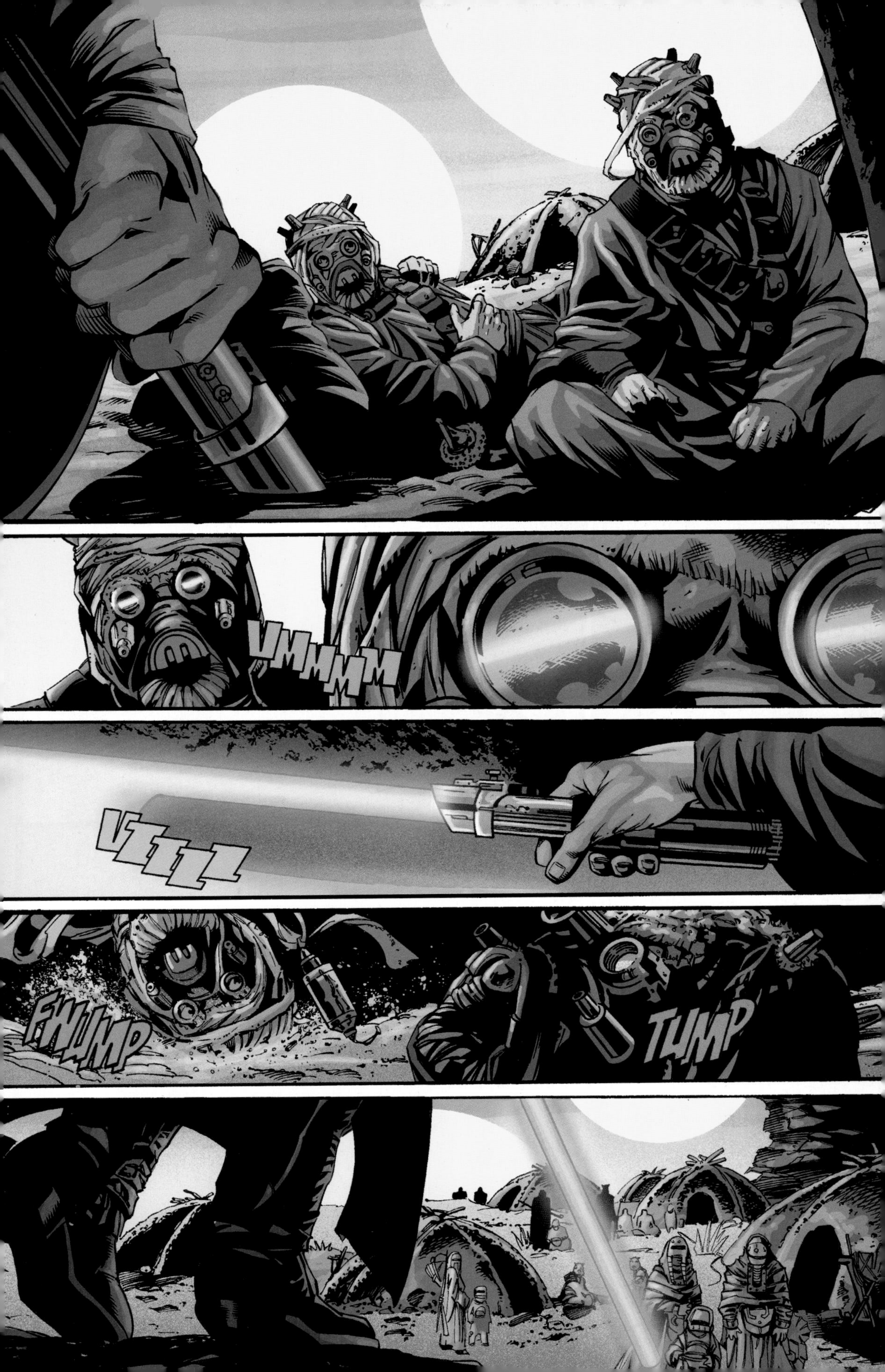
UMMMMM
VZZZZ
FWUMP
TUMP

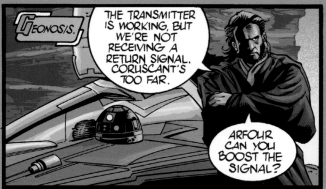
GEONOSIS.

THE TRANSMITTER IS WORKING, BUT WE'RE NOT RECEIVING A RETURN SIGNAL. CORUSCANT'S TOO FAR.

ARFOUR CAN YOU BOOST THE SIGNAL?

VEEP BREOOT!

MAYBE WE CAN CONTACT ANAKIN ON NABOO. IT'S MUCH CLOSER.

HE'S BACK! HE'S BACK!

FEEER

GEONOSIS.

ANAKIN, ANAKIN, DO YOU COPY? THIS IS OBI-WAN KENOBI.

MAYBE HE'S NOT ON NABOO, ARFOUR. WIDEN YOUR SEARCH SIGNAL.

UNFORTUNATELY FOR THE JEDI, HIS LINGERING PRESENCE HAS NOT GONE UNDETECTED.

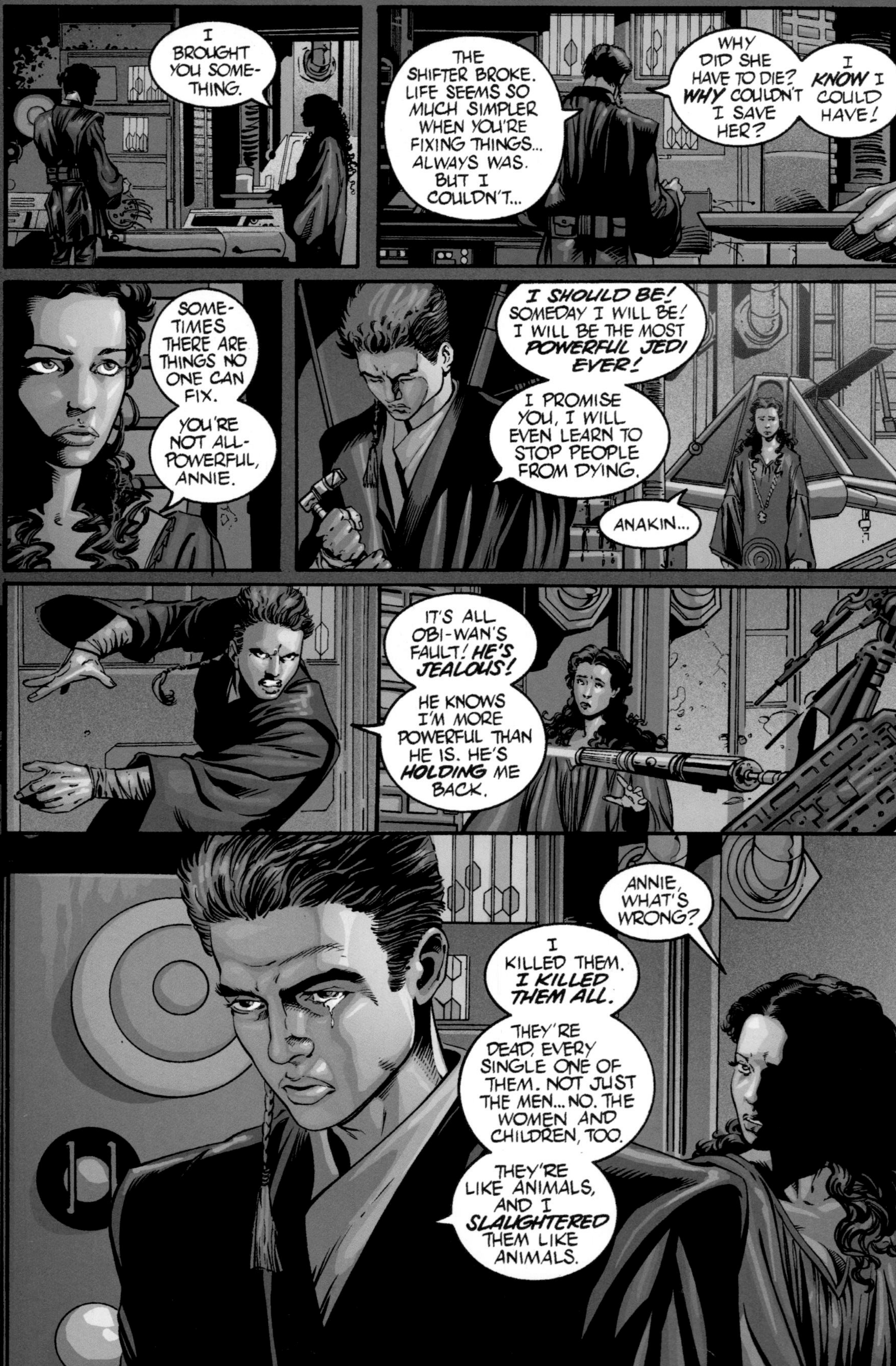
I BROUGHT YOU SOME-THING.
THE SHIFTER BROKE. LIFE SEEMS SO MUCH SIMPLER WHEN YOU'RE FIXING THINGS... ALWAYS WAS. BUT I COULDN'T...
WHY DID SHE HAVE TO DIE? WHY COULDN'T I SAVE HER?
I KNOW I COULD HAVE!
SOME-TIMES THERE ARE THINGS NO ONE CAN FIX.
YOU'RE NOT ALL-POWERFUL, ANNIE.
I SHOULD BE! SOMEDAY I WILL BE! I WILL BE THE MOST POWERFUL JEDI EVER!
I PROMISE YOU, I WILL EVEN LEARN TO STOP PEOPLE FROM DYING.
ANAKIN...
IT'S ALL OBI-WAN'S FAULT! HE'S JEALOUS!
HE KNOWS I'M MORE POWERFUL THAN HE IS. HE'S HOLDING ME BACK.
ANNIE, WHAT'S WRONG?
I KILLED THEM. I KILLED THEM ALL.
THEY'RE DEAD, EVERY SINGLE ONE OF THEM. NOT JUST THE MEN... NO. THE WOMEN AND CHILDREN, TOO.
THEY'RE LIKE ANIMALS, AND I SLAUGHTERED THEM LIKE ANIMALS.

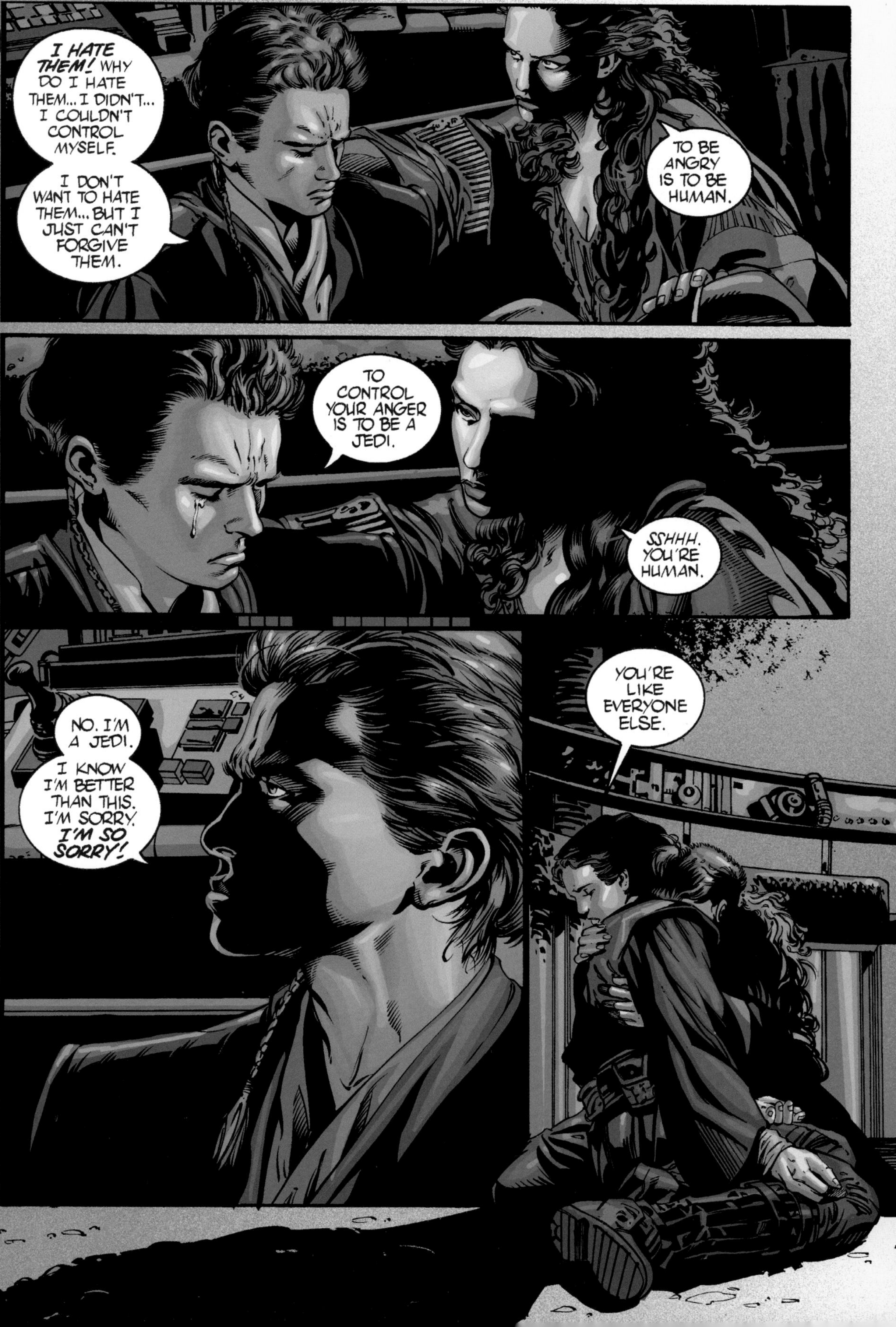
I HATE THEM! WHY DO I HATE THEM... I DIDN'T... I COULDN'T CONTROL MYSELF.
I DON'T WANT TO HATE THEM... BUT I JUST CAN'T FORGIVE THEM.
TO BE ANGRY IS TO BE HUMAN.
TO CONTROL YOUR ANGER IS TO BE A JEDI.
SSHHH. YOU'RE HUMAN.
NO. I'M A JEDI.
I KNOW I'M BETTER THAN THIS. I'M SORRY. I'M SO SORRY!
YOU'RE LIKE EVERYONE ELSE.

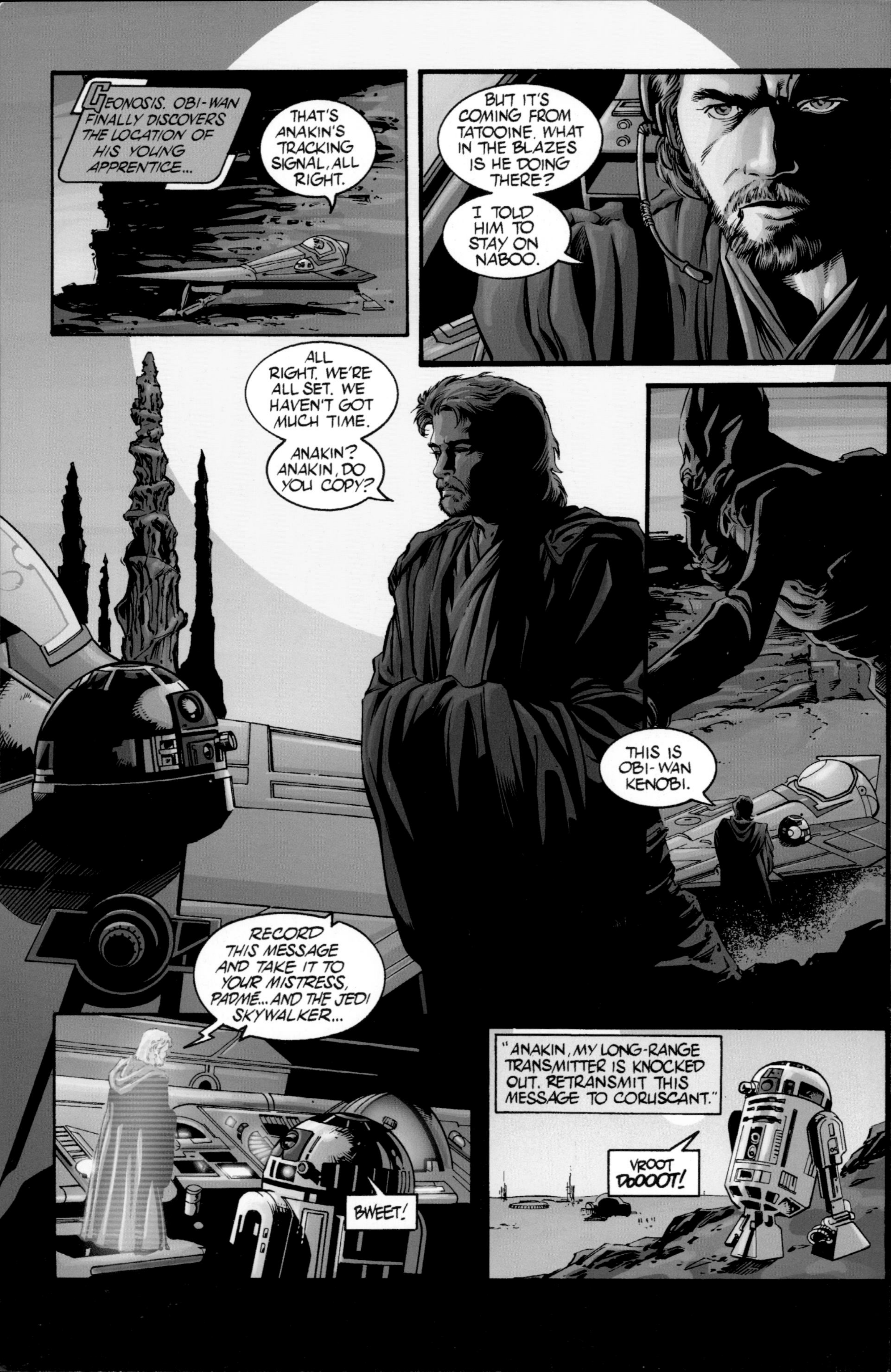
GEONOSIS. OBI-WAN FINALLY DISCOVERS THE LOCATION OF HIS YOUNG APPRENTICE...
THAT'S ANAKIN'S TRACKING SIGNAL, ALL RIGHT.
BUT IT'S COMING FROM TATOOINE. WHAT IN THE BLAZES IS HE DOING THERE?
I TOLD HIM TO STAY ON NABOO.
ALL RIGHT. WE'RE ALL SET. WE HAVEN'T GOT MUCH TIME.
ANAKIN? ANAKIN, DO YOU COPY?
THIS IS OBI-WAN KENOBI.
RECORD THIS MESSAGE AND TAKE IT TO YOUR MISTRESS, PADMÉ... AND THE JEDI SKYWALKER...
BWEET!
"ANAKIN, MY LONG-RANGE TRANSMITTER IS KNOCKED OUT. RETRANSMIT THIS MESSAGE TO CORUSCANT."
VROOT DOOOOT!

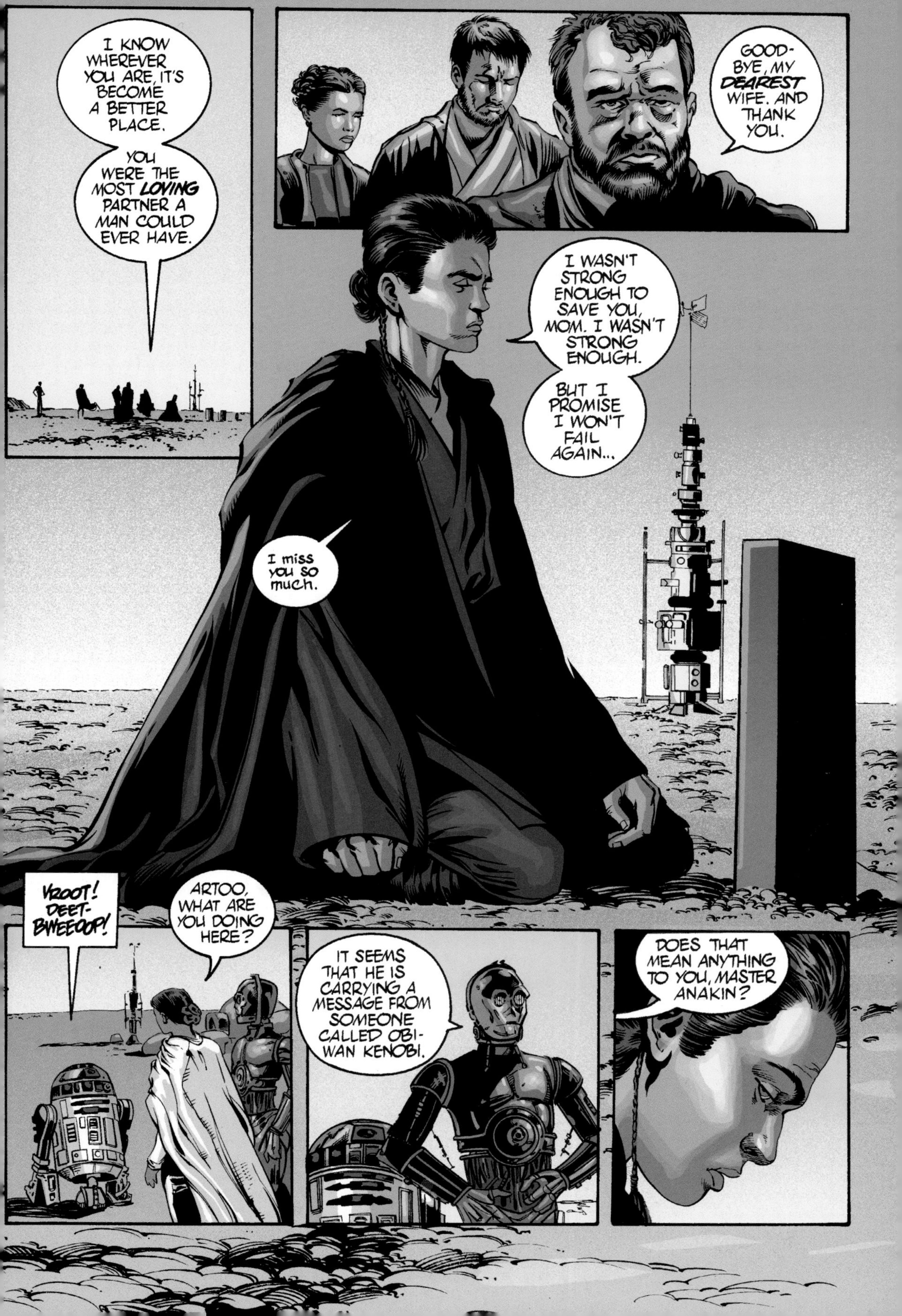

I KNOW WHEREVER YOU ARE, IT'S BECOME A BETTER PLACE.
YOU WERE THE MOST LOVING PARTNER A MAN COULD EVER HAVE.
GOOD-BYE, MY DEAREST WIFE. AND THANK YOU.
I WASN'T STRONG ENOUGH TO SAVE YOU, MOM. I WASN'T STRONG ENOUGH.
BUT I PROMISE I WON'T FAIL AGAIN...
I miss you so much.
VROOT! DEET-BWEEOOP!
ARTOO, WHAT ARE YOU DOING HERE?
IT SEEMS THAT HE IS CARRYING A MESSAGE FROM SOMEONE CALLED OBI-WAN KENOBI.
DOES THAT MEAN ANYTHING TO YOU, MASTER ANAKIN?

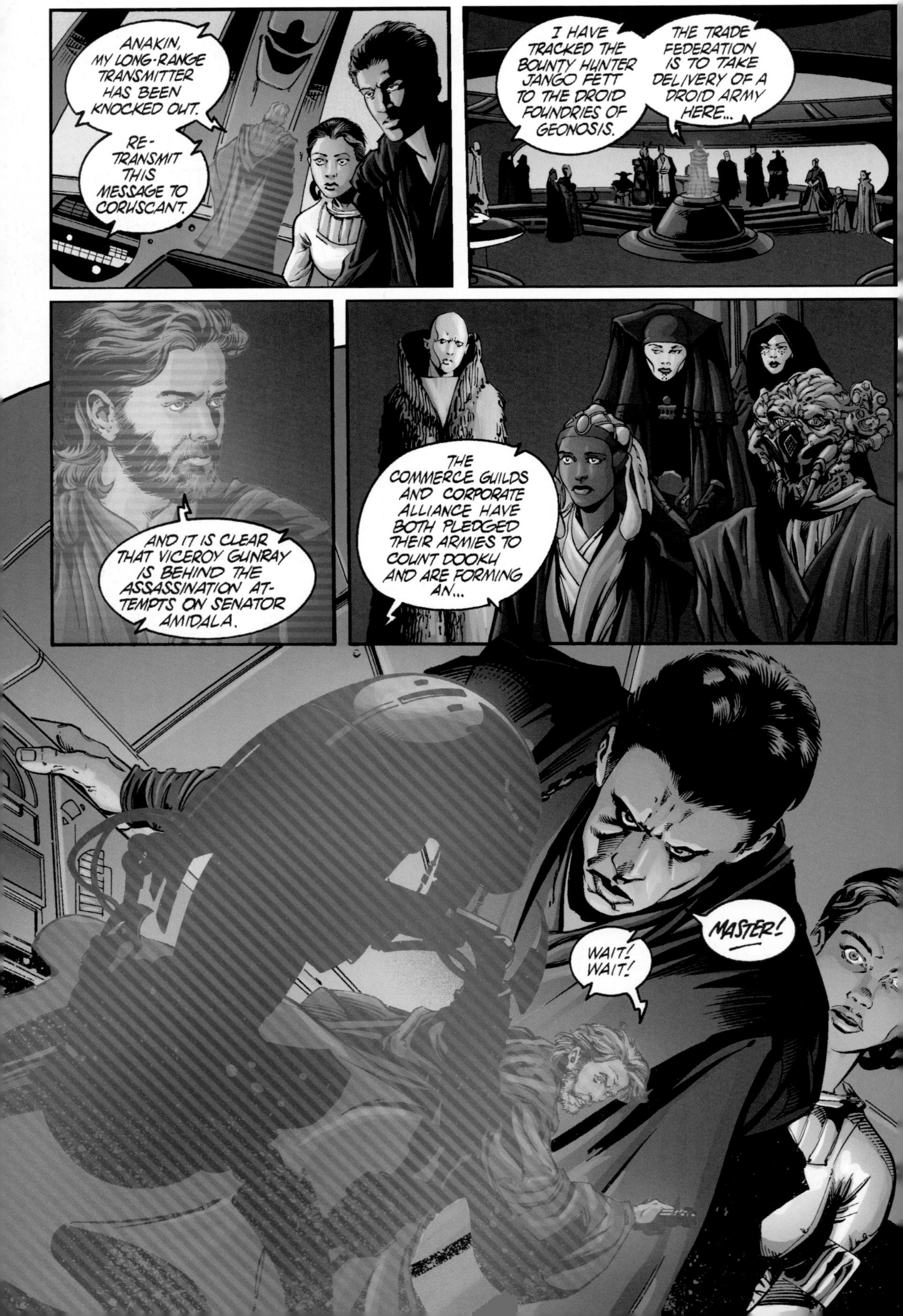
ANAKIN, MY LONG-RANGE TRANSMITTER HAS BEEN KNOCKED OUT.
RE-TRANSMIT THIS MESSAGE TO CORUSCANT.
I HAVE TRACKED THE BOUNTY HUNTER JANGO FETT TO THE DROID FOUNDRIES OF GEONOSIS.
THE TRADE FEDERATION IS TO TAKE DELIVERY OF A DROID ARMY HERE...
AND IT IS CLEAR THAT VICEROY GUNRAY IS BEHIND THE ASSASSINATION AT-TEMPTS ON SENATOR AMIDALA.
THE COMMERCE GUILDS AND CORPORATE ALLIANCE HAVE BOTH PLEDGED THEIR ARMIES TO COUNT DOOKU AND ARE FORMING AN...
MASTER!
WAIT! WAIT!

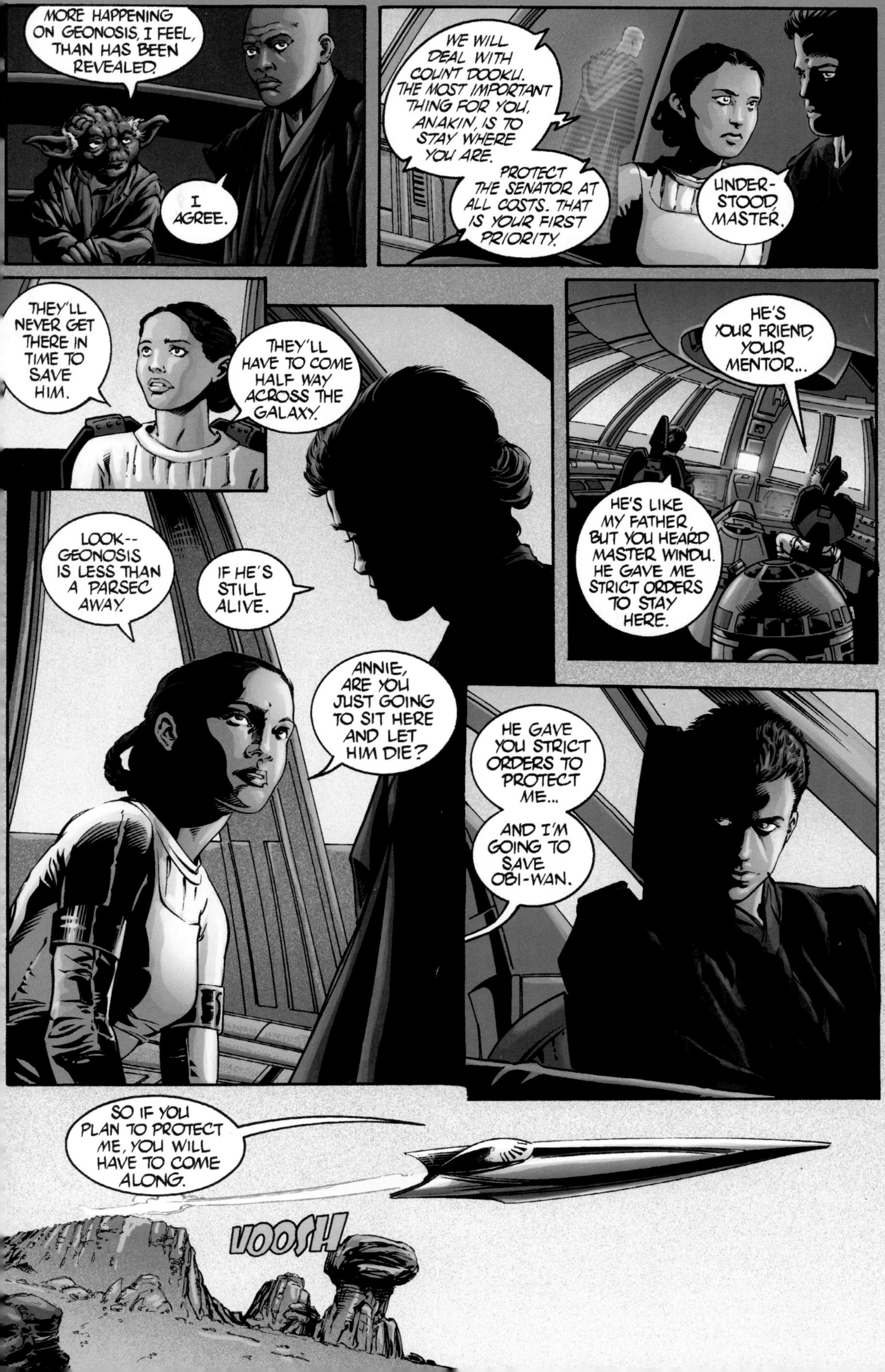
MORE HAPPENING ON GEONOSIS, I FEEL, THAN HAS BEEN REVEALED.
I AGREE.
WE WILL DEAL WITH COUNT DOOKU. THE MOST IMPORTANT THING FOR YOU, ANAKIN, IS TO STAY WHERE YOU ARE.
PROTECT THE SENATOR AT ALL COSTS. THAT IS YOUR FIRST PRIORITY.
UNDER-STOOD, MASTER.
THEY'LL NEVER GET THERE IN TIME TO SAVE HIM.
THEY'LL HAVE TO COME HALF WAY ACROSS THE GALAXY.
HE'S YOUR FRIEND, YOUR MENTOR...
HE'S LIKE MY FATHER, BUT YOU HEARD MASTER WINDU. HE GAVE ME STRICT ORDERS TO STAY HERE.
LOOK-- GEONOSIS IS LESS THAN A PARSEC AWAY.
IF HE'S STILL ALIVE.
ANNIE, ARE YOU JUST GOING TO SIT HERE AND LET HIM DIE?
HE GAVE YOU STRICT ORDERS TO PROTECT ME...
AND I'M GOING TO SAVE OBI-WAN.
SO IF YOU PLAN TO PROTECT ME, YOU WILL HAVE TO COME ALONG.
VOOSH

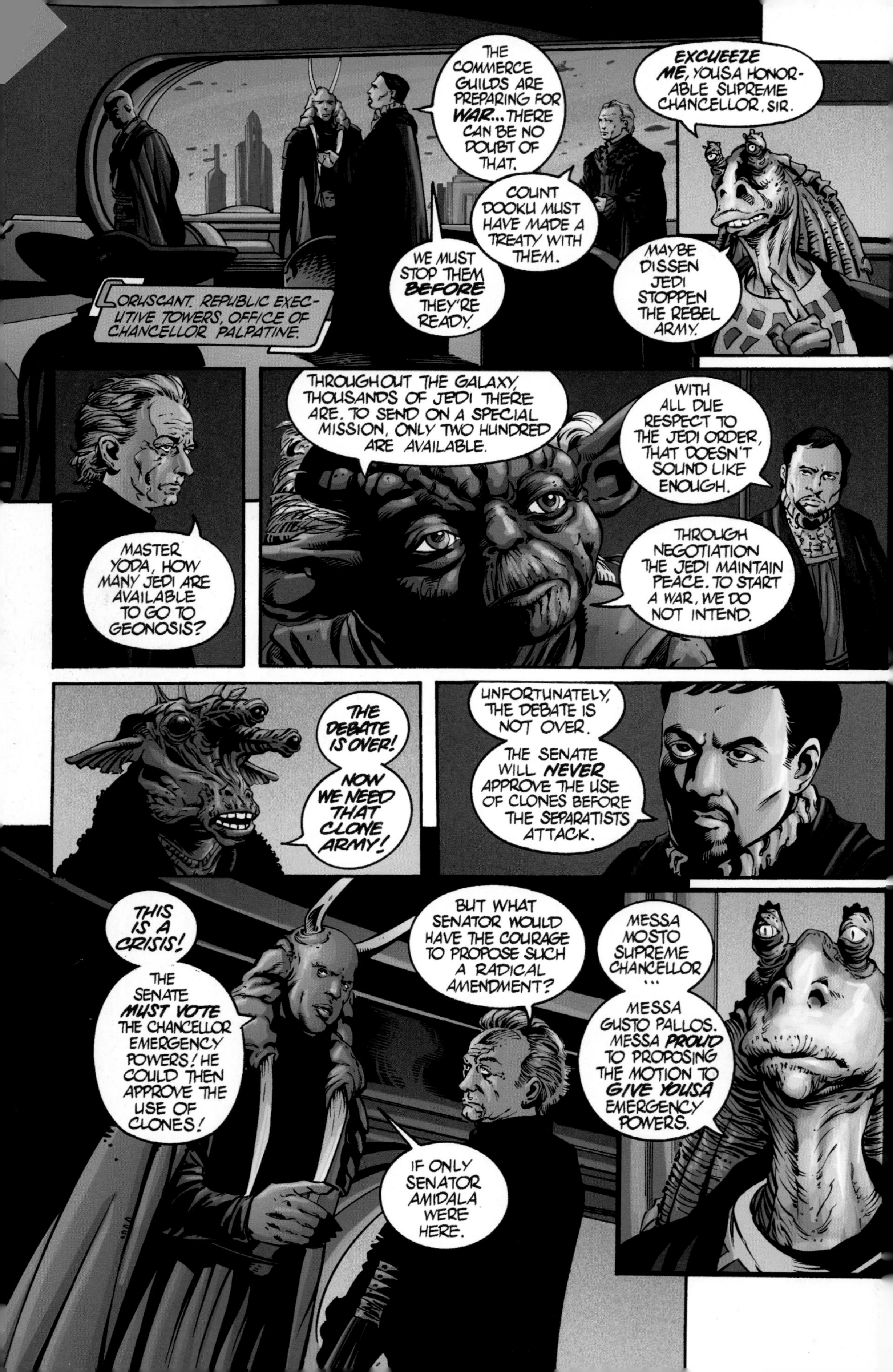
CORUSCANT. REPUBLIC EXECUTIVE TOWERS, OFFICE OF CHANCELLOR PALPATINE.
THE COMMERCE GUILDS ARE PREPARING FOR WAR... THERE CAN BE NO DOUBT OF THAT.
COUNT DOOKU MUST HAVE MADE A TREATY WITH THEM.
WE MUST STOP THEM BEFORE THEY'RE READY.
EXCUEEZE ME, YOUSA HONORABLE SUPREME CHANCELLOR, SIR.
MAYBE DISSEN JEDI STOPPEN THE REBEL ARMY.
MASTER YODA, HOW MANY JEDI ARE AVAILABLE TO GO TO GEONOSIS?
THROUGHOUT THE GALAXY, THOUSANDS OF JEDI THERE ARE. TO SEND ON A SPECIAL MISSION, ONLY TWO HUNDRED ARE AVAILABLE.
WITH ALL DUE RESPECT TO THE JEDI ORDER, THAT DOESN'T SOUND LIKE ENOUGH.
THROUGH NEGOTIATION THE JEDI MAINTAIN PEACE. TO START A WAR, WE DO NOT INTEND.
THE DEBATE IS OVER!
NOW WE NEED THAT CLONE ARMY!
UNFORTUNATELY, THE DEBATE IS NOT OVER.
THE SENATE WILL NEVER APPROVE THE USE OF CLONES BEFORE THE SEPARATISTS ATTACK.
THIS IS A CRISIS!
THE SENATE MUST VOTE THE CHANCELLOR EMERGENCY POWERS! HE COULD THEN APPROVE THE USE OF CLONES!
BUT WHAT SENATOR WOULD HAVE THE COURAGE TO PROPOSE SUCH A RADICAL AMENDMENT?
IF ONLY SENATOR AMIDALA WERE HERE.
MESSA MOSTO SUPREME CHANCELLOR...
MESSA GUSTO PALLOS. MESSA PROUD TO PROPOSING THE MOTION TO GIVE YOUSA EMERGENCY POWERS.

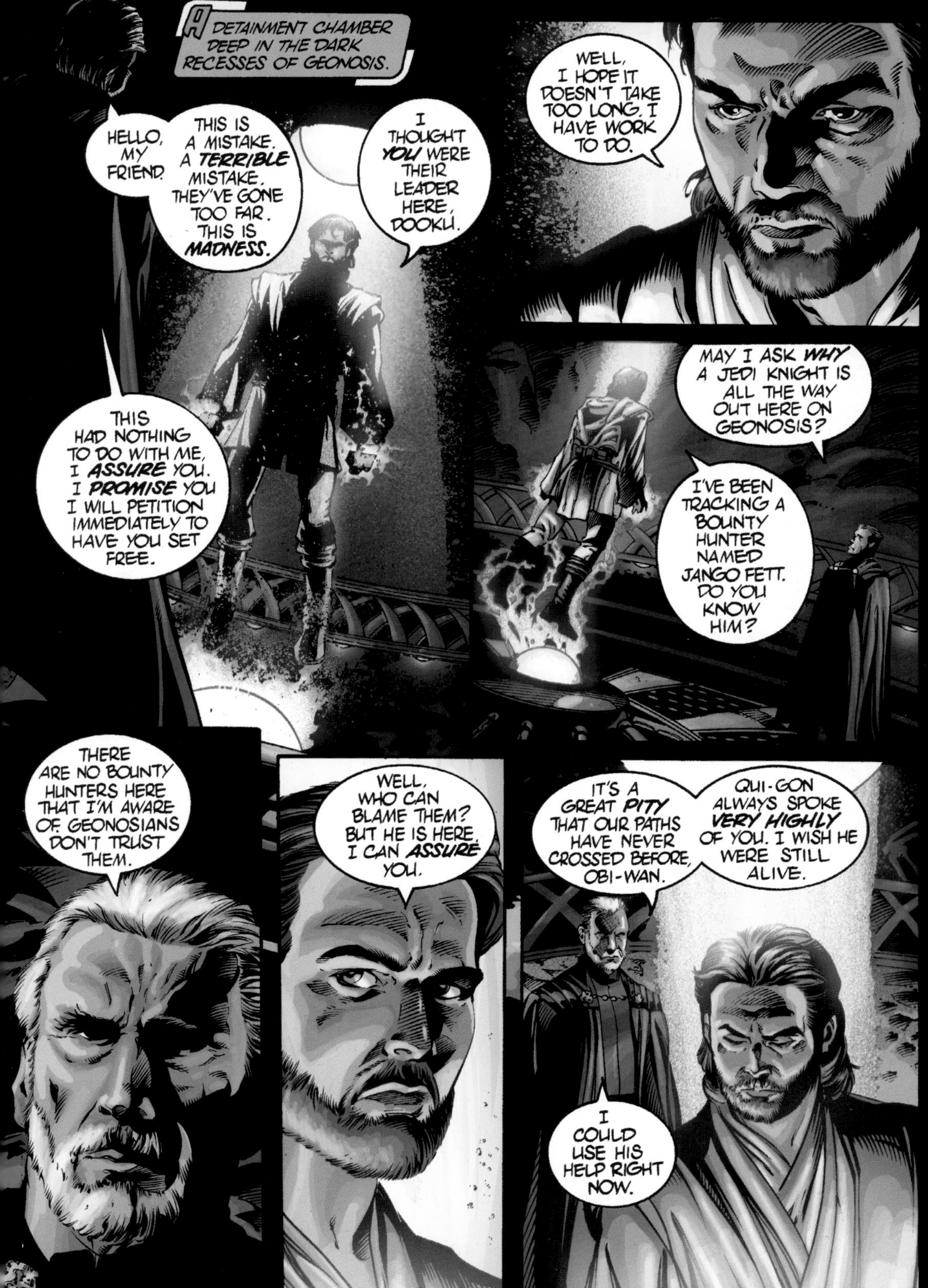
A DETAINMENT CHAMBER DEEP IN THE DARK RECESSES OF GEONOSIS.
HELLO, MY FRIEND.
THIS IS A MISTAKE. A TERRIBLE MISTAKE. THEY'VE GONE TOO FAR. THIS IS MADNESS.
I THOUGHT YOU WERE THEIR LEADER HERE, DOOKU.
THIS HAD NOTHING TO DO WITH ME, I ASSURE YOU. I PROMISE YOU I WILL PETITION IMMEDIATELY TO HAVE YOU SET FREE.
WELL, I HOPE IT DOESN'T TAKE TOO LONG. I HAVE WORK TO DO.
MAY I ASK WHY A JEDI KNIGHT IS ALL THE WAY OUT HERE ON GEONOSIS?
I'VE BEEN TRACKING A BOUNTY HUNTER NAMED JANGO FETT. DO YOU KNOW HIM?
THERE ARE NO BOUNTY HUNTERS HERE THAT I'M AWARE OF. GEONOSIANS DON'T TRUST THEM.
WELL, WHO CAN BLAME THEM? BUT HE IS HERE, I CAN ASSURE YOU.
IT'S A GREAT PITY THAT OUR PATHS HAVE NEVER CROSSED BEFORE, OBI-WAN.
QUI-GON ALWAYS SPOKE VERY HIGHLY OF YOU. I WISH HE WERE STILL ALIVE.
I COULD USE HIS HELP RIGHT NOW.

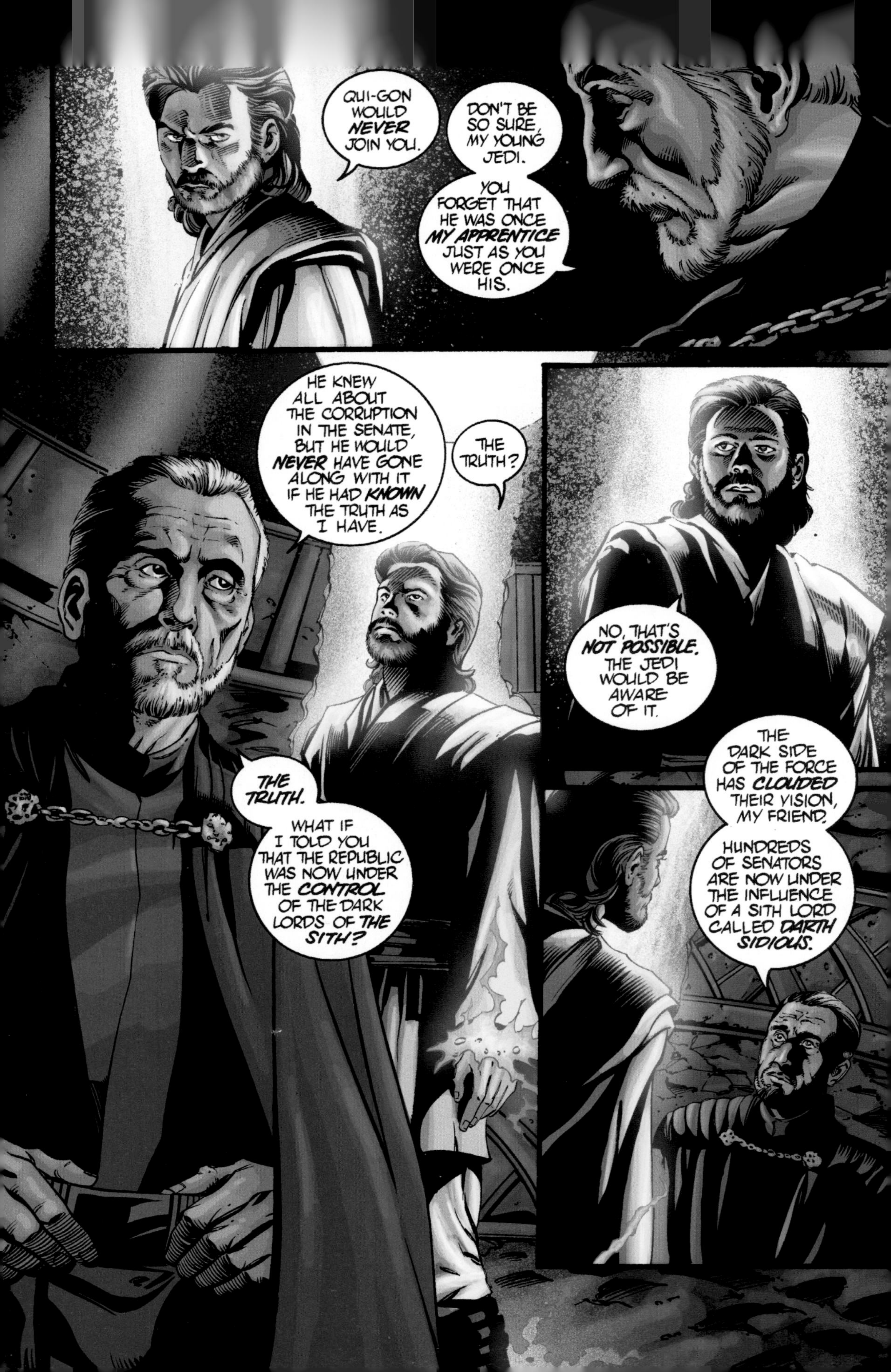
QUI-GON WOULD NEVER JOIN YOU.
DON'T BE SO SURE, MY YOUNG JEDI.
YOU FORGET THAT HE WAS ONCE MY APPRENTICE JUST AS YOU WERE ONCE HIS.
HE KNEW ALL ABOUT THE CORRUPTION IN THE SENATE, BUT HE WOULD NEVER HAVE GONE ALONG WITH IT IF HE HAD KNOWN THE TRUTH AS I HAVE.
THE TRUTH?
THE TRUTH.
WHAT IF I TOLD YOU THAT THE REPUBLIC WAS NOW UNDER THE CONTROL OF THE DARK LORDS OF THE SITH?
NO, THAT'S NOT POSSIBLE. THE JEDI WOULD BE AWARE OF IT.
THE DARK SIDE OF THE FORCE HAS CLOUDED THEIR VISION, MY FRIEND.
HUNDREDS OF SENATORS ARE NOW UNDER THE INFLUENCE OF A SITH LORD CALLED DARTH SIDIOUS.

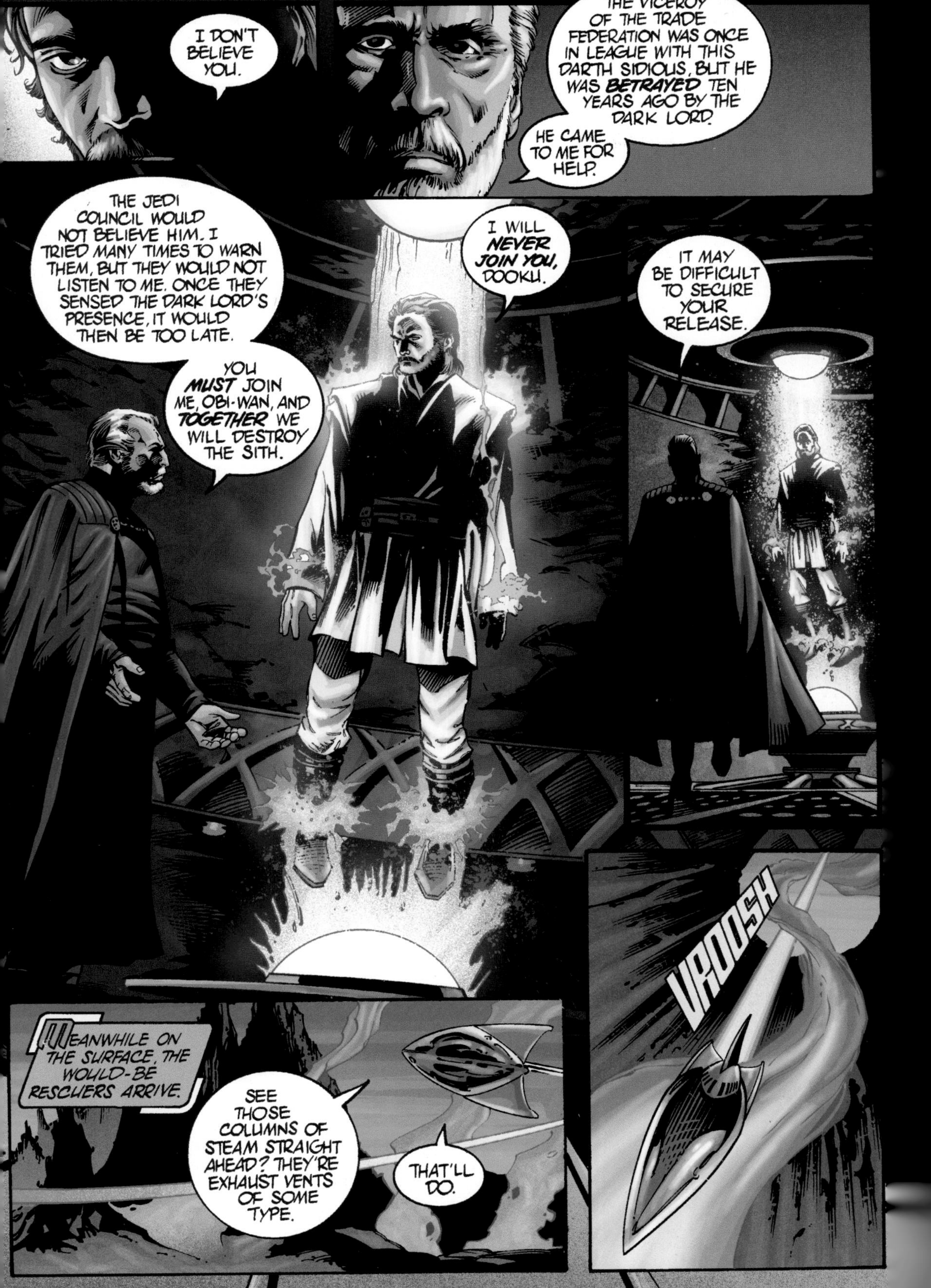
I DON'T BELIEVE YOU.
THE VICEROY OF THE TRADE FEDERATION WAS ONCE IN LEAGUE WITH THIS DARTH SIDIOUS, BUT HE WAS BETRAYED TEN YEARS AGO BY THE DARK LORD.
HE CAME TO ME FOR HELP.
THE JEDI COUNCIL WOULD NOT BELIEVE HIM. I TRIED MANY TIMES TO WARN THEM, BUT THEY WOULD NOT LISTEN TO ME. ONCE THEY SENSED THE DARK LORD'S PRESENCE, IT WOULD THEN BE TOO LATE.
YOU MUST JOIN ME, OBI-WAN, AND TOGETHER WE WILL DESTROY THE SITH.
I WILL NEVER JOIN YOU, DOOKU.
IT MAY BE DIFFICULT TO SECURE YOUR RELEASE.
MEANWHILE ON THE SURFACE, THE WOULD-BE RESCUERS ARRIVE.
SEE THOSE COLUMNS OF STEAM STRAIGHT AHEAD? THEY'RE EXHAUST VENTS OF SOME TYPE.
THAT'LL DO.
VROOSH

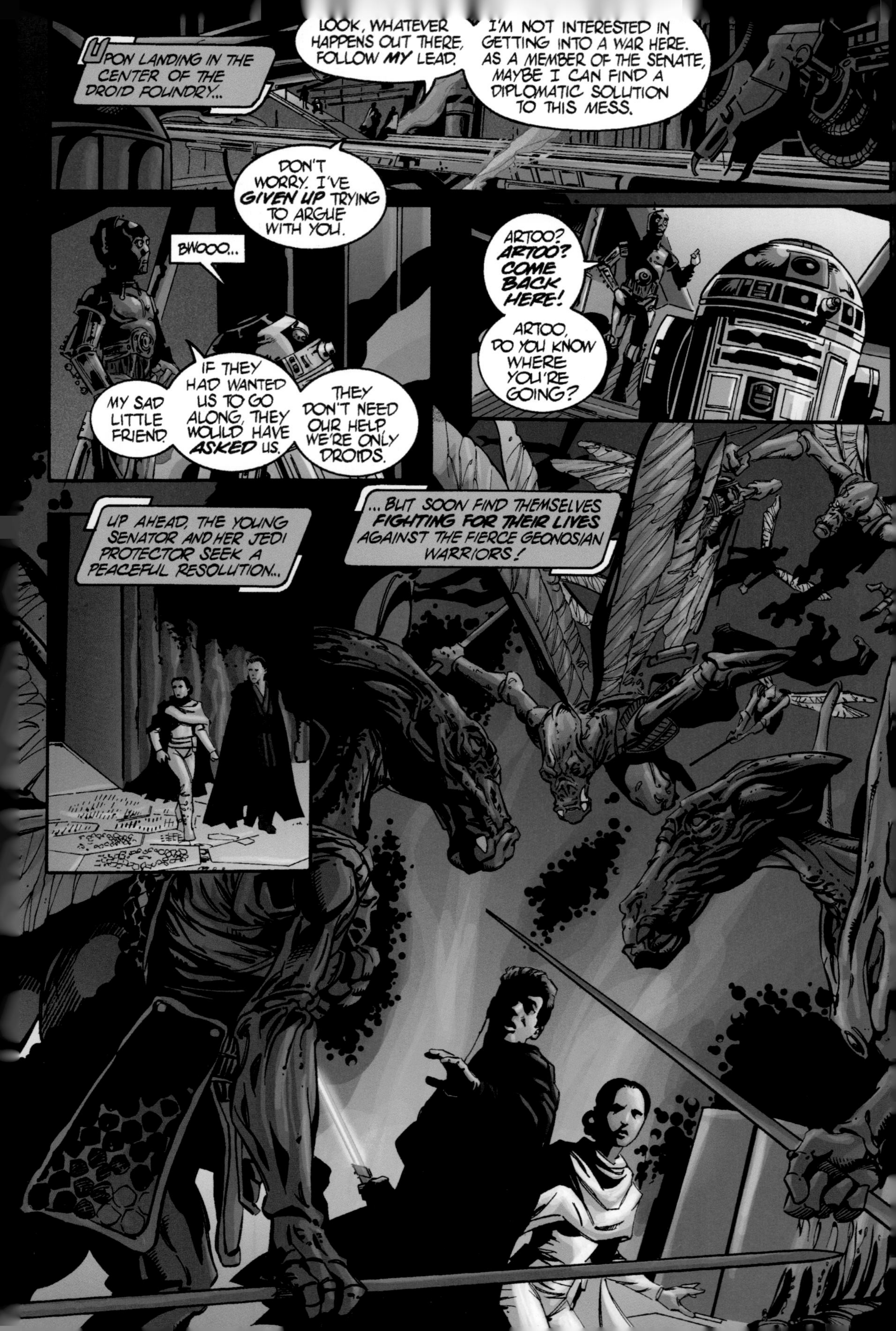
UPON LANDING IN THE CENTER OF THE DROID FOUNDRY...
LOOK, WHATEVER HAPPENS OUT THERE, FOLLOW MY LEAD.
I'M NOT INTERESTED IN GETTING INTO A WAR HERE. AS A MEMBER OF THE SENATE, MAYBE I CAN FIND A DIPLOMATIC SOLUTION TO THIS MESS.
DON'T WORRY. I'VE GIVEN UP TRYING TO ARGUE WITH YOU.
BWOOO...
MY SAD LITTLE FRIEND.
IF THEY HAD WANTED US TO GO ALONG, THEY WOULD HAVE ASKED US.
THEY DON'T NEED OUR HELP. WE'RE ONLY DROIDS.
ARTOO? ARTOO? COME BACK HERE!
ARTOO, DO YOU KNOW WHERE YOU'RE GOING?
UP AHEAD, THE YOUNG SENATOR AND HER JEDI PROTECTOR SEEK A PEACEFUL RESOLUTION...
...BUT SOON FIND THEMSELVES FIGHTING FOR THEIR LIVES AGAINST THE FIERCE GEONOSIAN WARRIORS!

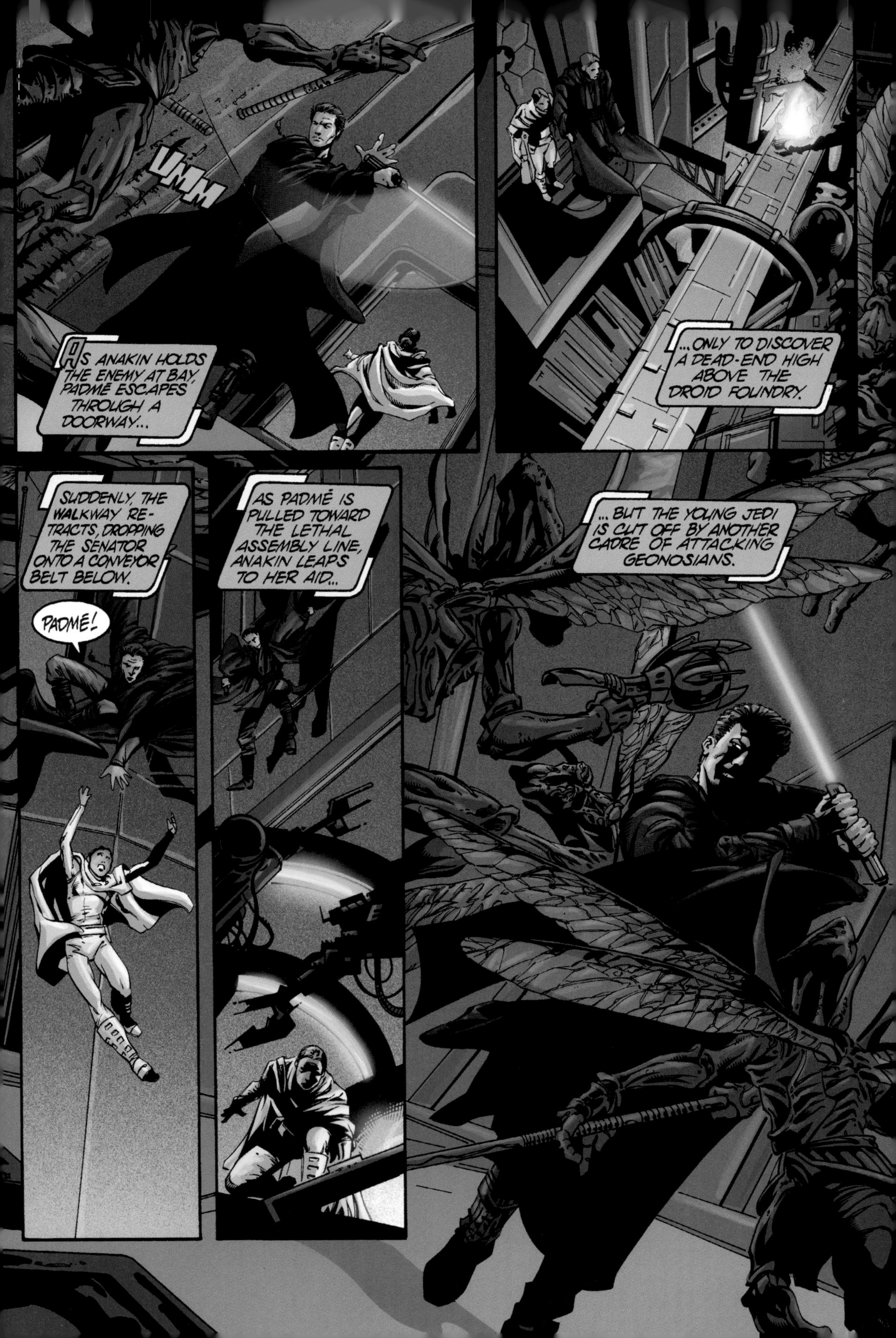
UMM
AS ANAKIN HOLDS THE ENEMY AT BAY, PADMÉ ESCAPES THROUGH A DOORWAY...
...ONLY TO DISCOVER A DEAD-END HIGH ABOVE THE DROID FOUNDRY.
SUDDENLY, THE WALKWAY RETRACTS, DROPPING THE SENATOR ONTO A CONVEYOR BELT BELOW.
PADMÉ!
AS PADMÉ IS PULLED TOWARD THE LETHAL ASSEMBLY LINE, ANAKIN LEAPS TO HER AID...
...BUT THE YOUNG JEDI IS CUT OFF BY ANOTHER CADRE OF ATTACKING GEONOSIANS.

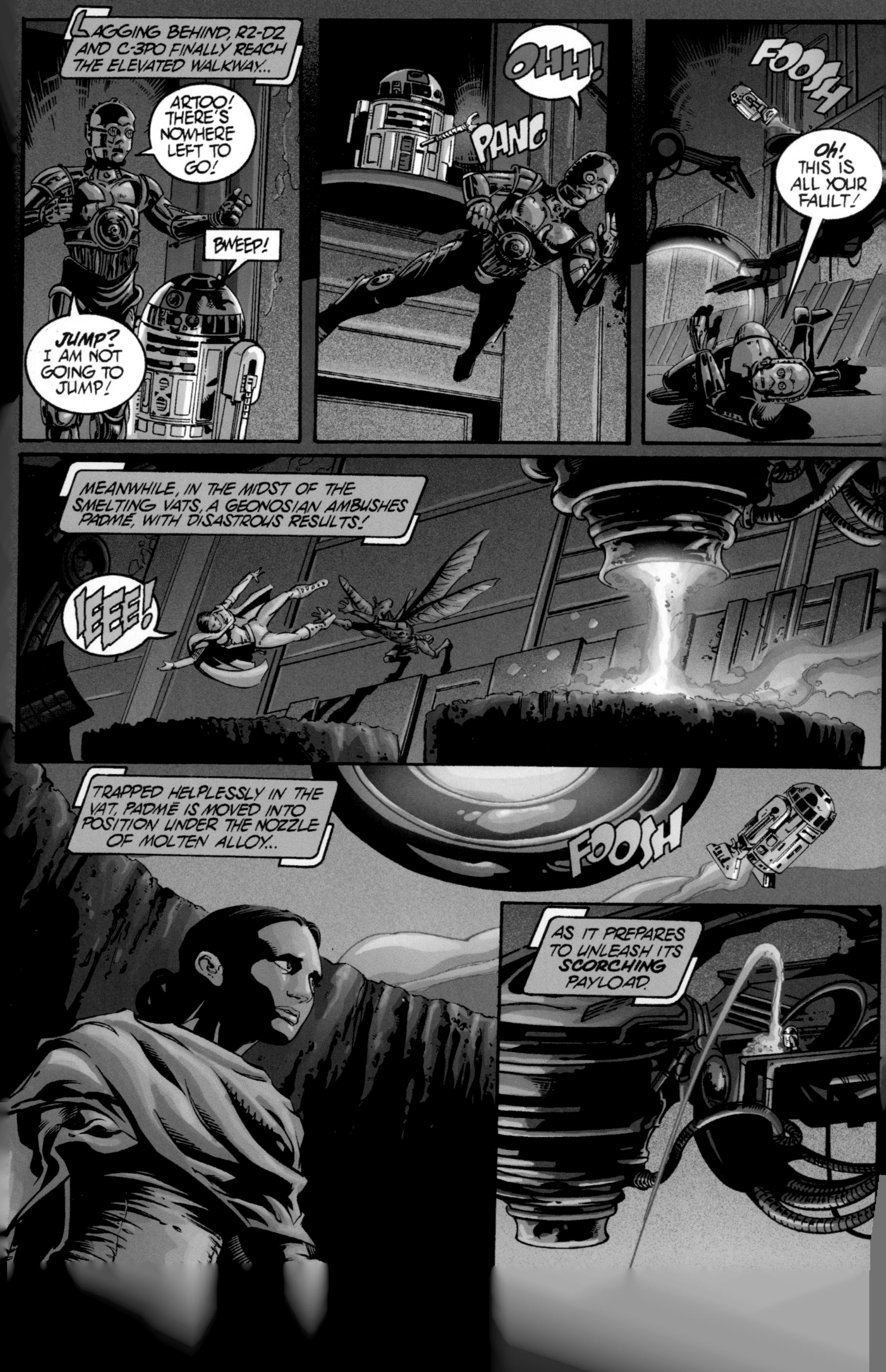
LAGGING BEHIND, R2-D2 AND C-3PO FINALLY REACH THE ELEVATED WALKWAY...
ARTOO! THERE'S NOWHERE LEFT TO GO!
BWEEP!
JUMP? I AM NOT GOING TO JUMP!
OHH!
PANG
FOOSH
Oh! THIS IS ALL YOUR FAULT!
MEANWHILE, IN THE MIDST OF THE SMELTING VATS, A GEONOSIAN AMBUSHES PADMÉ, WITH DISASTROUS RESULTS!
IEEE!
TRAPPED HELPLESSLY IN THE VAT, PADMÉ IS MOVED INTO POSITION UNDER THE NOZZLE OF MOLTEN ALLOY...
FOOSH
AS IT PREPARES TO UNLEASH ITS SCORCHING PAYLOAD.

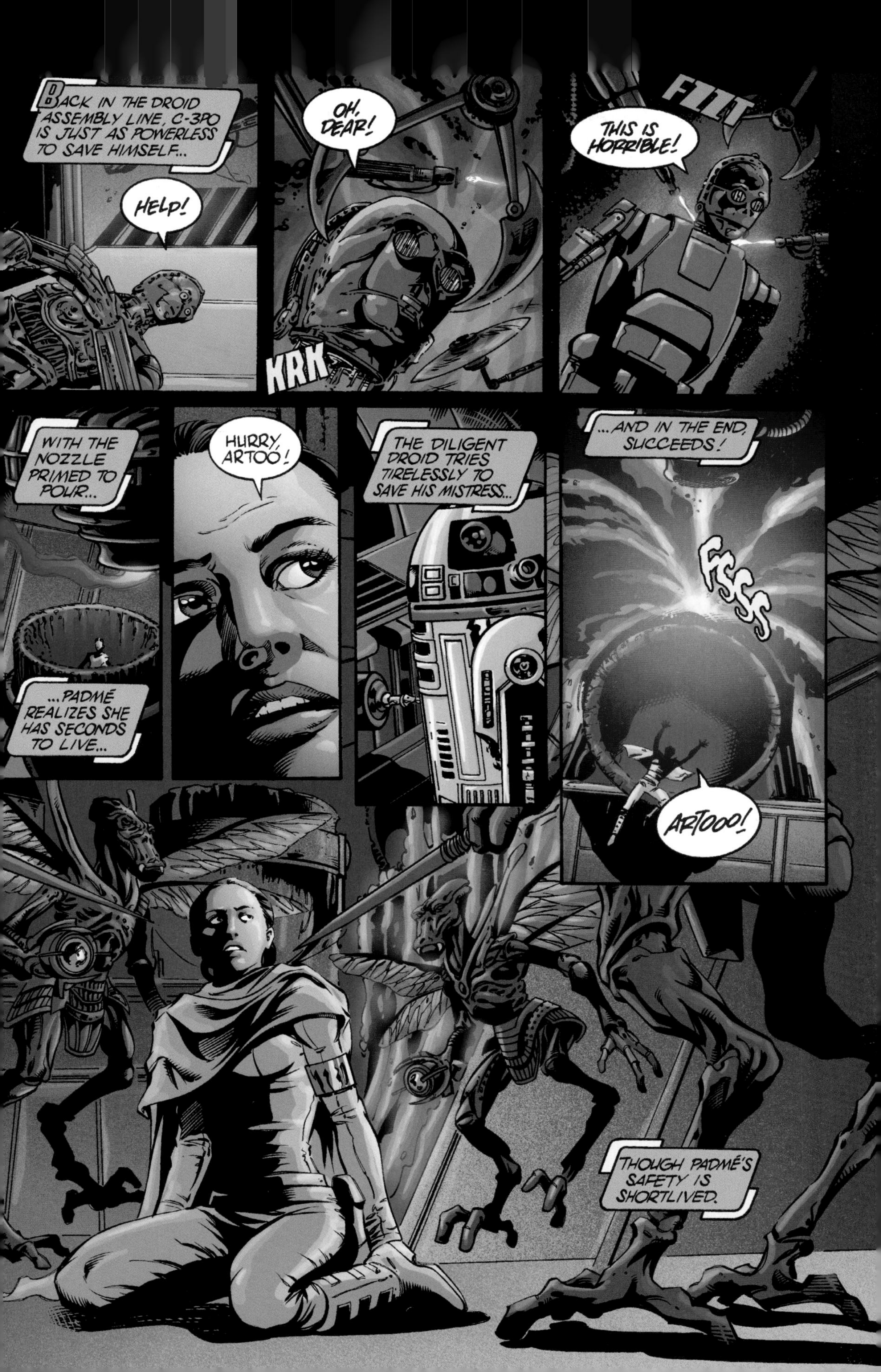
BACK IN THE DROID ASSEMBLY LINE, C-3PO IS JUST AS POWERLESS TO SAVE HIMSELF...
HELP!
OH, DEAR!
KRK
FZZT
THIS IS HORRIBLE!
WITH THE NOZZLE PRIMED TO POUR...
...PADMÉ REALIZES SHE HAS SECONDS TO LIVE...
HURRY, ARTOO!
THE DILIGENT DROID TRIES TIRELESSLY TO SAVE HIS MISTRESS...
...AND IN THE END, SUCCEEDS!
FSSS
ARTOOO!
THOUGH PADMÉ'S SAFETY IS SHORTLIVED.

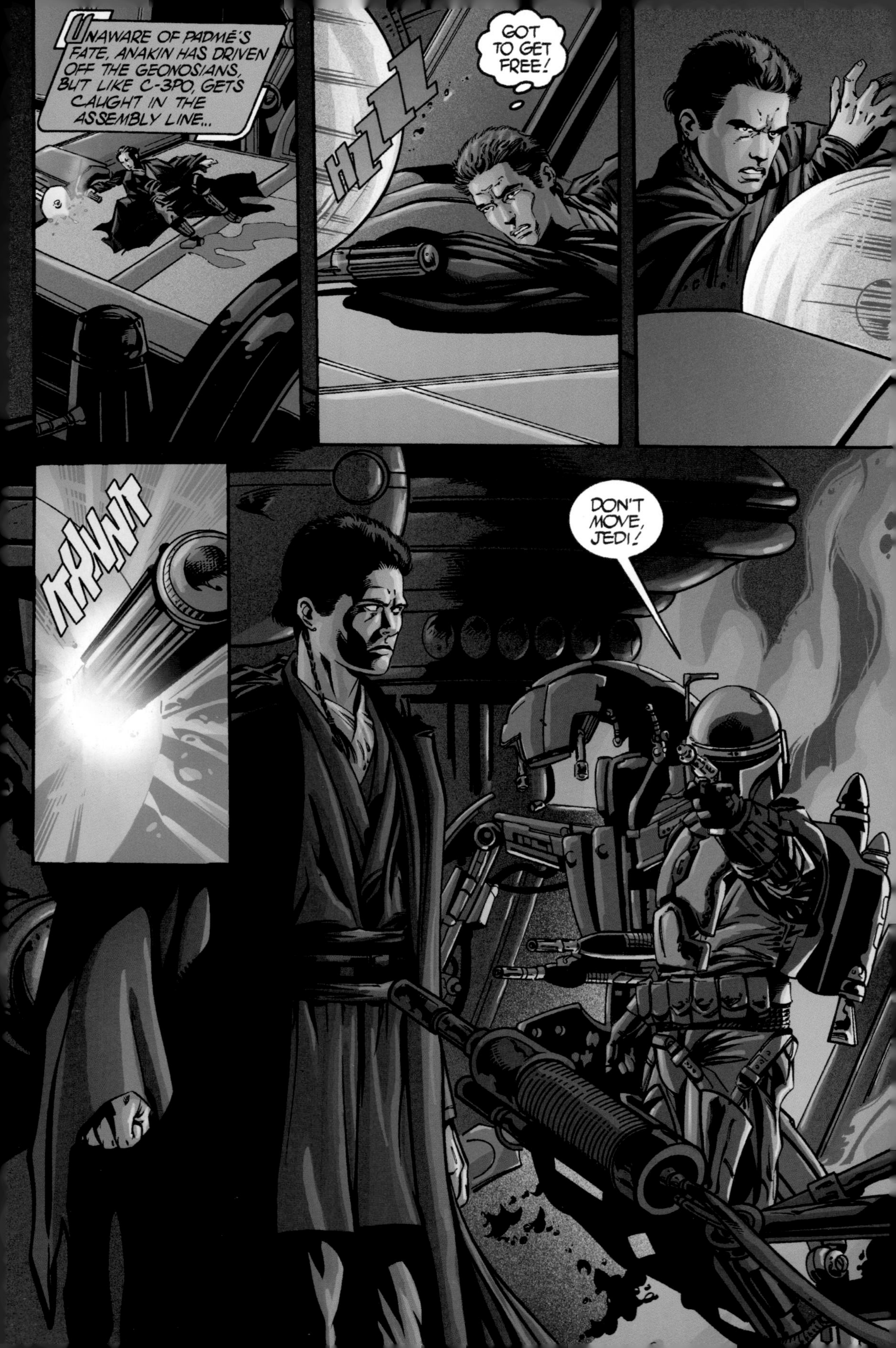

UNAWARE OF PADMÉ'S FATE, ANAKIN HAS DRIVEN OFF THE GEONOSIANS, BUT LIKE C-3PO, GETS CAUGHT IN THE ASSEMBLY LINE...
HZZZZ
GOT TO GET FREE!
KRUNT
DON'T MOVE, JEDI!

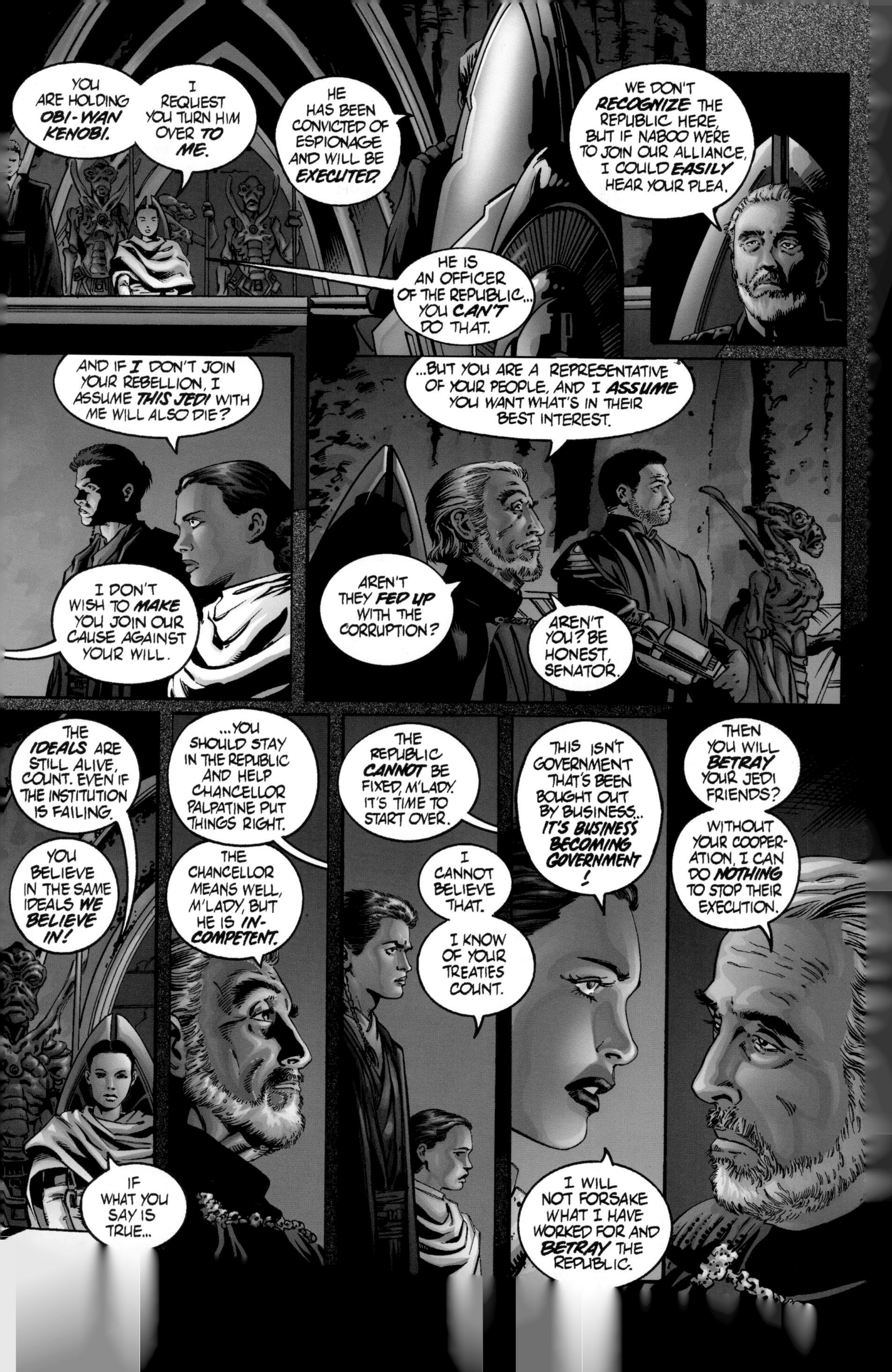
YOU ARE HOLDING OBI-WAN KENOBI.
I REQUEST YOU TURN HIM OVER TO ME.
HE HAS BEEN CONVICTED OF ESPIONAGE AND WILL BE EXECUTED.
HE IS AN OFFICER OF THE REPUBLIC... YOU CAN'T DO THAT.
WE DON'T RECOGNIZE THE REPUBLIC HERE, BUT IF NABOO WERE TO JOIN OUR ALLIANCE, I COULD EASILY HEAR YOUR PLEA.
AND IF I DON'T JOIN YOUR REBELLION, I ASSUME THIS JEDI WITH ME WILL ALSO DIE?
I DON'T WISH TO MAKE YOU JOIN OUR CAUSE AGAINST YOUR WILL.
...BUT YOU ARE A REPRESENTATIVE OF YOUR PEOPLE, AND I ASSUME YOU WANT WHAT'S IN THEIR BEST INTEREST.
AREN'T THEY FED UP WITH THE CORRUPTION?
AREN'T YOU? BE HONEST, SENATOR.
THE IDEALS ARE STILL ALIVE, COUNT. EVEN IF THE INSTITUTION IS FAILING.
YOU BELIEVE IN THE SAME IDEALS WE BELIEVE IN!
IF WHAT YOU SAY IS TRUE...
...YOU SHOULD STAY IN THE REPUBLIC AND HELP CHANCELLOR PALPATINE PUT THINGS RIGHT.
THE CHANCELLOR MEANS WELL, M'LADY, BUT HE IS IN-COMPETENT.
THE REPUBLIC CANNOT BE FIXED, M'LADY. IT'S TIME TO START OVER.
I CANNOT BELIEVE THAT.
I KNOW OF YOUR TREATIES COUNT.
THIS ISN'T GOVERNMENT THAT'S BEEN BOUGHT OUT BY BUSINESS... IT'S BUSINESS BECOMING GOVERNMENT!
I WILL NOT FORSAKE WHAT I HAVE WORKED FOR AND BETRAY THE REPUBLIC.
THEN YOU WILL BETRAY YOUR JEDI FRIENDS?
WITHOUT YOUR COOPER-ATION, I CAN DO NOTHING TO STOP THEIR EXECUTION.

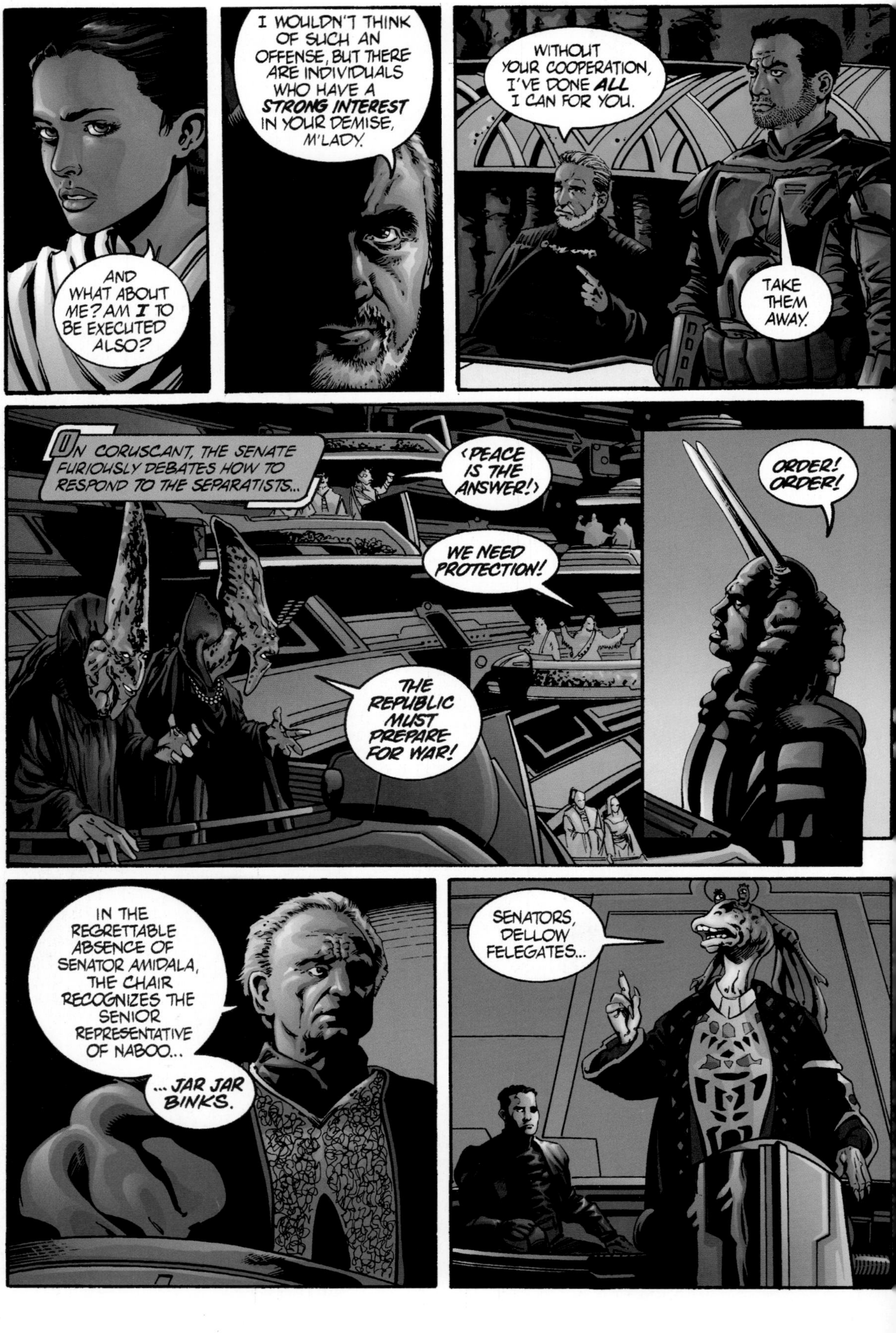
I WOULDN'T THINK OF SUCH AN OFFENSE, BUT THERE ARE INDIVIDUALS WHO HAVE A STRONG INTEREST IN YOUR DEMISE, M'LADY.
AND WHAT ABOUT ME? AM I TO BE EXECUTED ALSO?
WITHOUT YOUR COOPERATION, I'VE DONE ALL I CAN FOR YOU.
TAKE THEM AWAY.
ON CORUSCANT, THE SENATE FURIOUSLY DEBATES HOW TO RESPOND TO THE SEPARATISTS...
‹PEACE IS THE ANSWER!›
WE NEED PROTECTION!
THE REPUBLIC MUST PREPARE FOR WAR!
ORDER! ORDER!
IN THE REGRETTABLE ABSENCE OF SENATOR AMIDALA, THE CHAIR RECOGNIZES THE SENIOR REPRESENTATIVE OF NABOO...
...JAR JAR BINKS.
SENATORS, DELLOW FELEGATES...

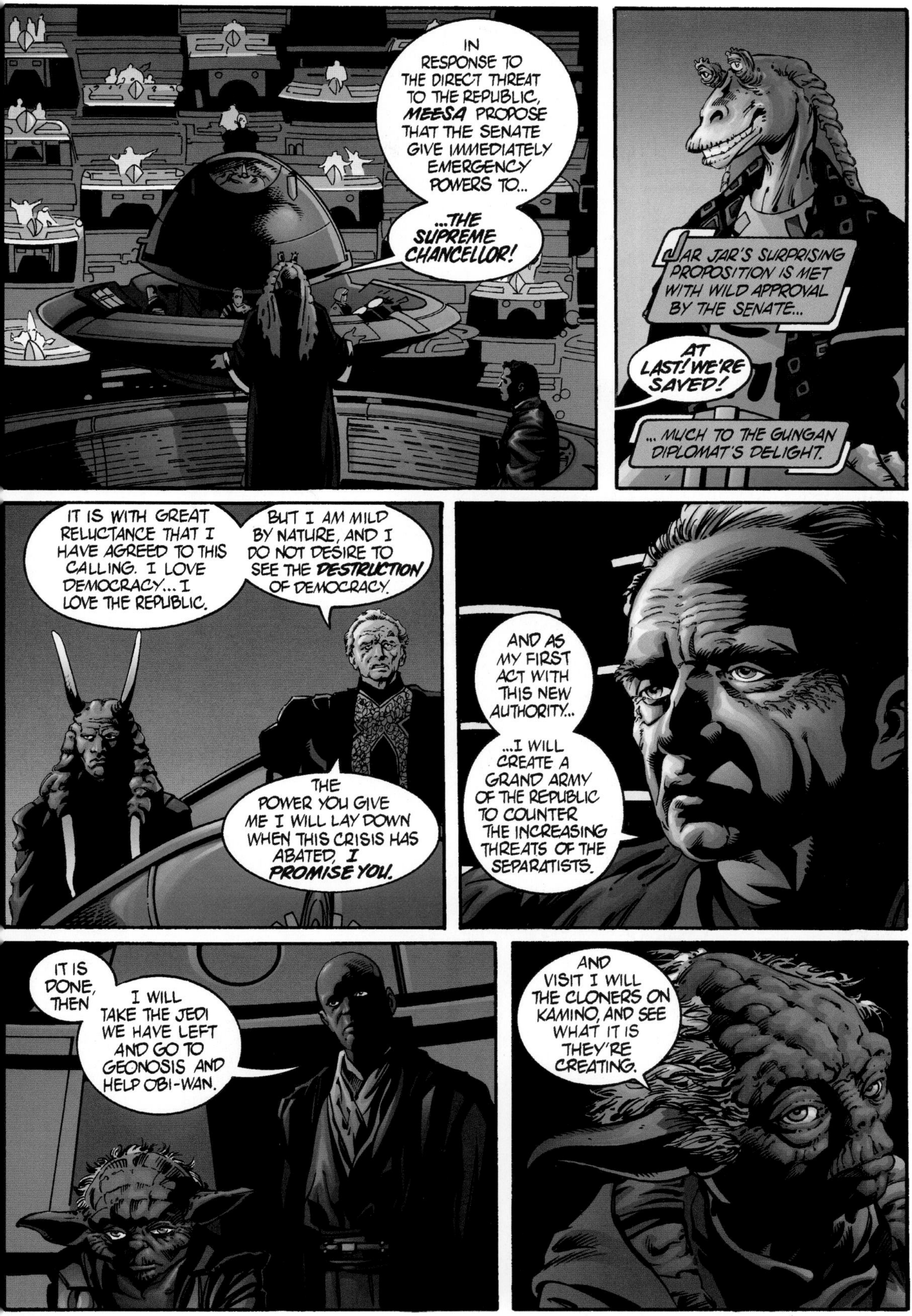
IN RESPONSE TO THE DIRECT THREAT TO THE REPUBLIC, MEESA PROPOSE THAT THE SENATE GIVE IMMEDIATELY EMERGENCY POWERS TO...
...THE SÜPREME CHANCELLOR!
JAR JAR'S SURPRISING PROPOSITION IS MET WITH WILD APPROVAL BY THE SENATE...
AT LAST! WE'RE SAVED!
... MUCH TO THE GUNGAN DIPLOMAT'S DELIGHT.
IT IS WITH GREAT RELUCTANCE THAT I HAVE AGREED TO THIS CALLING. I LOVE DEMOCRACY... I LOVE THE REPUBLIC.
BUT I AM MILD BY NATURE, AND I DO NOT DESIRE TO SEE THE DESTRUCTION OF DEMOCRACY.
THE POWER YOU GIVE ME I WILL LAY DOWN WHEN THIS CRISIS HAS ABATED, I PROMISE YOU.
AND AS MY FIRST ACT WITH THIS NEW AUTHORITY...
...I WILL CREATE A GRAND ARMY OF THE REPUBLIC TO COUNTER THE INCREASING THREATS OF THE SEPARATISTS.
IT IS DONE, THEN
I WILL TAKE THE JEDI WE HAVE LEFT AND GO TO GEONOSIS AND HELP OBI-WAN.
AND VISIT I WILL THE CLONERS ON KAMINO, AND SEE WHAT IT IS THEY'RE CREATING.

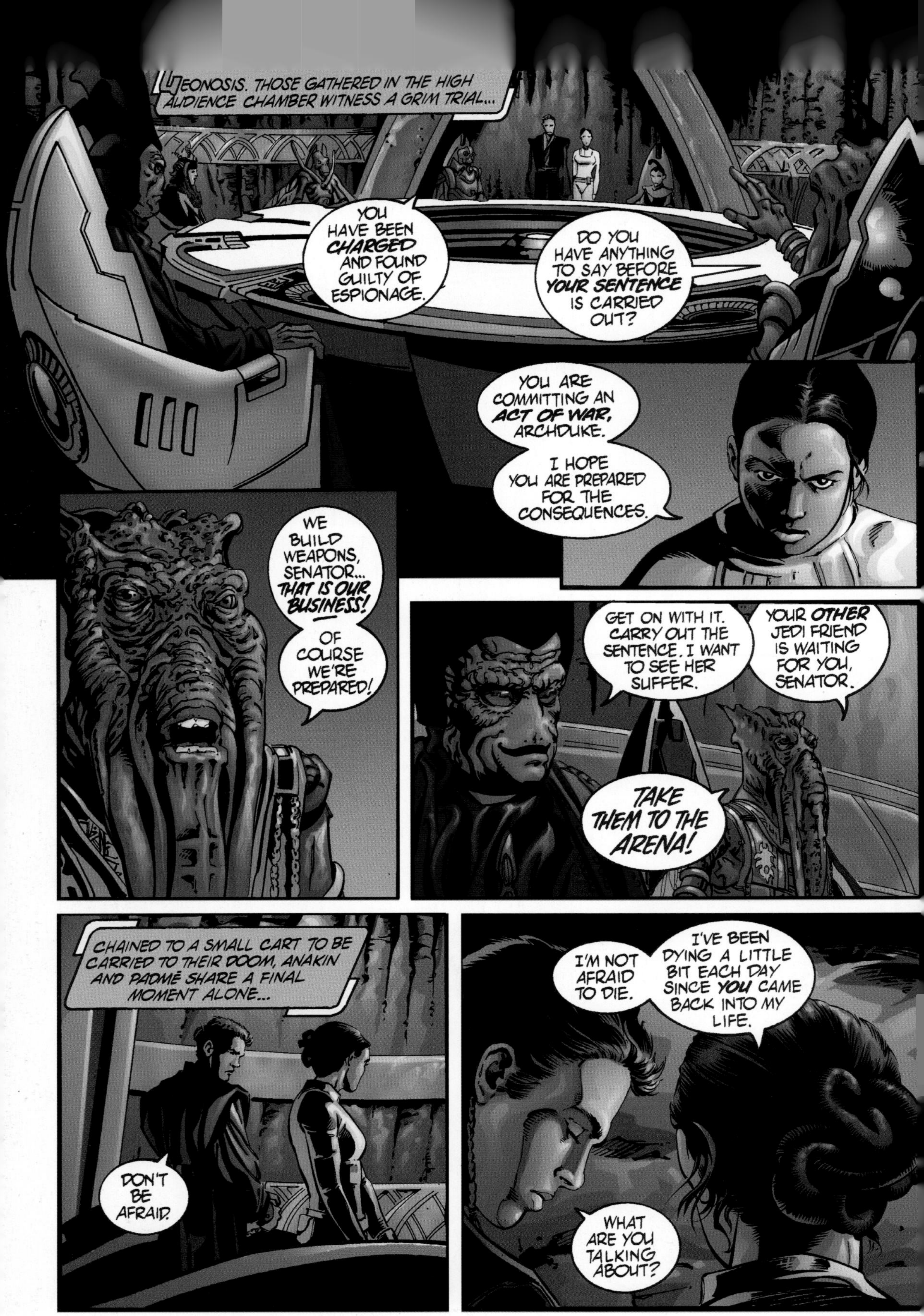
GEONOSIS. THOSE GATHERED IN THE HIGH AUDIENCE CHAMBER WITNESS A GRIM TRIAL...
YOU HAVE BEEN CHARGED AND FOUND GUILTY OF ESPIONAGE.
DO YOU HAVE ANYTHING TO SAY BEFORE YOUR SENTENCE IS CARRIED OUT?
YOU ARE COMMITTING AN ACT OF WAR, ARCHDUKE.
I HOPE YOU ARE PREPARED FOR THE CONSEQUENCES.
WE BUILD WEAPONS, SENATOR... THAT IS OUR BUSINESS!
OF COURSE WE'RE PREPARED!
GET ON WITH IT. CARRY OUT THE SENTENCE. I WANT TO SEE HER SUFFER.
YOUR OTHER JEDI FRIEND IS WAITING FOR YOU, SENATOR.
TAKE THEM TO THE ARENA!
CHAINED TO A SMALL CART TO BE CARRIED TO THEIR DOOM, ANAKIN AND PADMÉ SHARE A FINAL MOMENT ALONE...
DON'T BE AFRAID.
I'M NOT AFRAID TO DIE.
I'VE BEEN DYING A LITTLE BIT EACH DAY SINCE YOU CAME BACK INTO MY LIFE.
WHAT ARE YOU TALKING ABOUT?

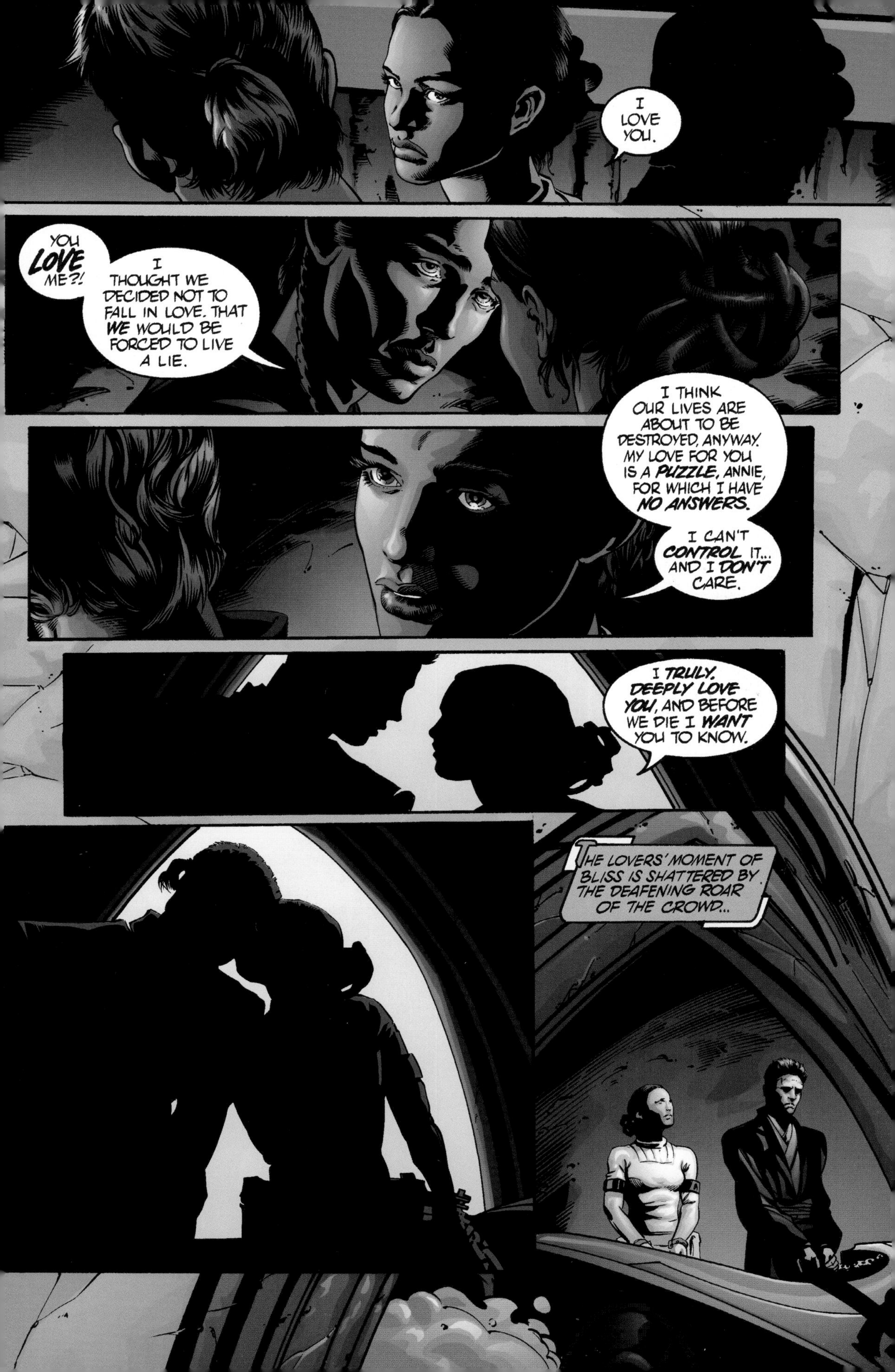
I LOVE YOU.
YOU LOVE ME?!
I THOUGHT WE DECIDED NOT TO FALL IN LOVE. THAT WE WOULD BE FORCED TO LIVE A LIE.
I THINK OUR LIVES ARE ABOUT TO BE DESTROYED, ANYWAY. MY LOVE FOR YOU IS A PUZZLE, ANNIE, FOR WHICH I HAVE NO ANSWERS.
I CAN'T CONTROL IT... AND I DON'T CARE.
I TRULY, DEEPLY LOVE YOU, AND BEFORE WE DIE I WANT YOU TO KNOW.
THE LOVERS' MOMENT OF BLISS IS SHATTERED BY THE DEAFENING ROAR OF THE CROWD...

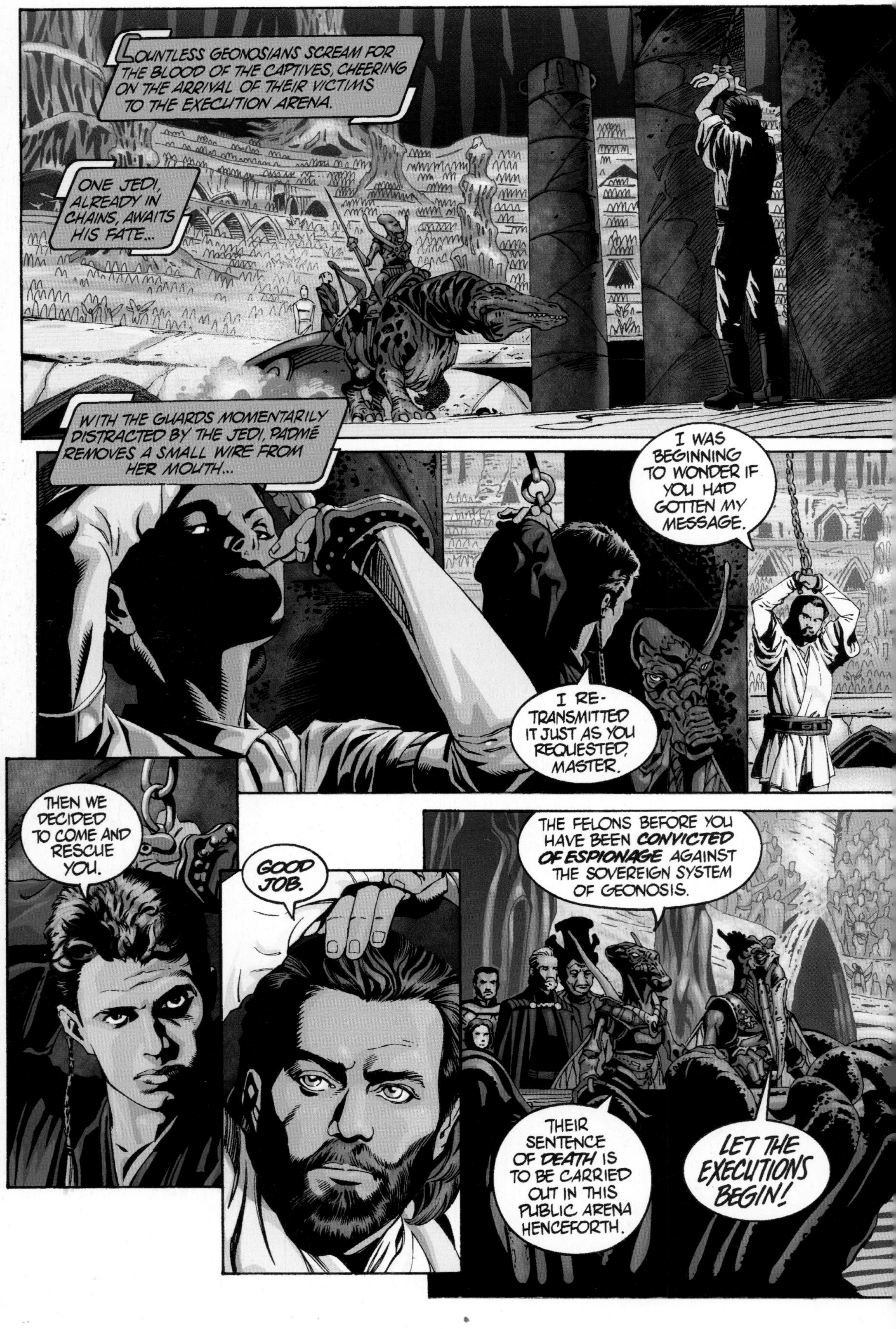
COUNTLESS GEONOSIANS SCREAM FOR THE BLOOD OF THE CAPTIVES, CHEERING ON THE ARRIVAL OF THEIR VICTIMS TO THE EXECUTION ARENA.
ONE JEDI, ALREADY IN CHAINS, AWAITS HIS FATE...
WITH THE GUARDS MOMENTARILY DISTRACTED BY THE JEDI, PADMÉ REMOVES A SMALL WIRE FROM HER MOUTH...
I WAS BEGINNING TO WONDER IF YOU HAD GOTTEN MY MESSAGE.
I RE-TRANSMITTED IT JUST AS YOU REQUESTED, MASTER.
THEN WE DECIDED TO COME AND RESCUE YOU.
GOOD JOB.
THE FELONS BEFORE YOU HAVE BEEN CONVICTED OF ESPIONAGE AGAINST THE SOVEREIGN SYSTEM OF GEONOSIS.
THEIR SENTENCE OF DEATH IS TO BE CARRIED OUT IN THIS PUBLIC ARENA HENCEFORTH.
LET THE EXECUTIONS BEGIN!

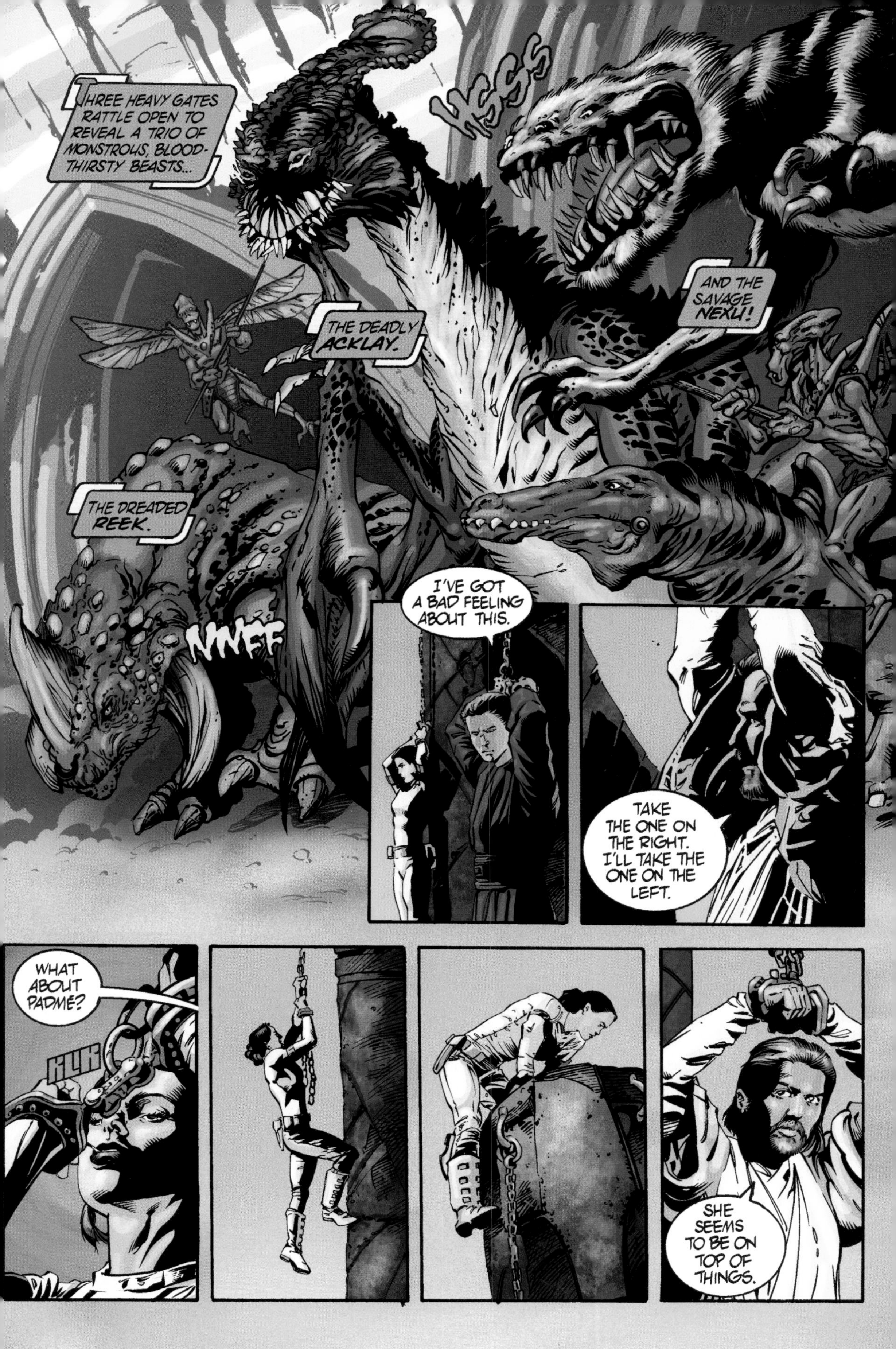
THREE HEAVY GATES RATTLE OPEN TO REVEAL A TRIO OF MONSTROUS, BLOOD-THIRSTY BEASTS...
HSSS
THE DEADLY ACKLAY.
AND THE SAVAGE NEXU!
THE DREADED REEK.
NNFF
I'VE GOT A BAD FEELING ABOUT THIS.
TAKE THE ONE ON THE RIGHT. I'LL TAKE THE ONE ON THE LEFT.
WHAT ABOUT PADME?
KLIK
SHE SEEMS TO BE ON TOP OF THINGS.

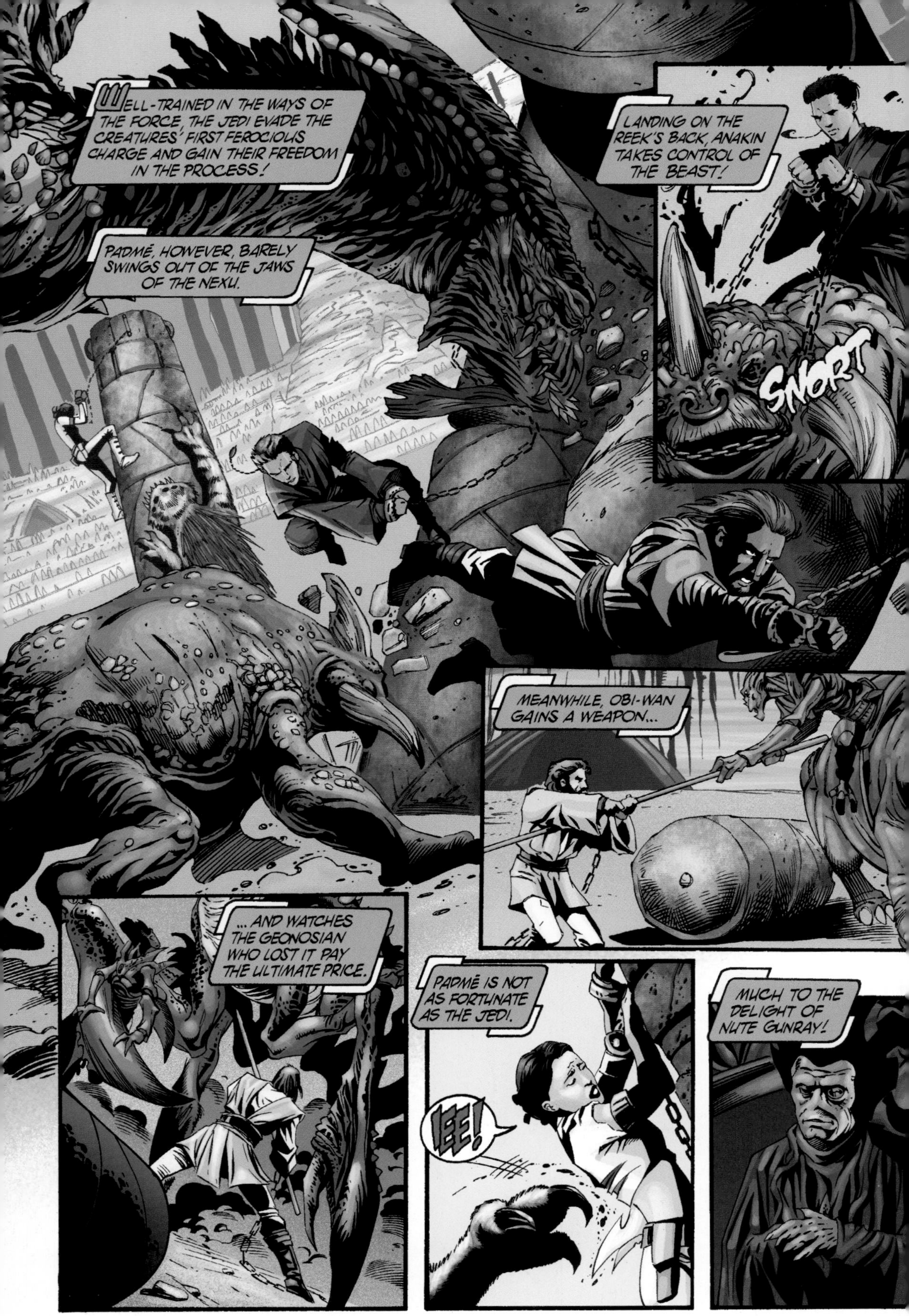
WELL-TRAINED IN THE WAYS OF THE FORCE, THE JEDI EVADE THE CREATURES' FIRST FEROCIOUS CHARGE AND GAIN THEIR FREEDOM IN THE PROCESS!
PADMÉ, HOWEVER, BARELY SWINGS OUT OF THE JAWS OF THE NEXU.
LANDING ON THE REEK'S BACK, ANAKIN TAKES CONTROL OF THE BEAST!
SNORT
MEANWHILE, OBI-WAN GAINS A WEAPON...
...AND WATCHES THE GEONOSIAN WHO LOST IT PAY THE ULTIMATE PRICE.
PADMÉ IS NOT AS FORTUNATE AS THE JEDI.
IEE!
MUCH TO THE DELIGHT OF NUTE GUNRAY!

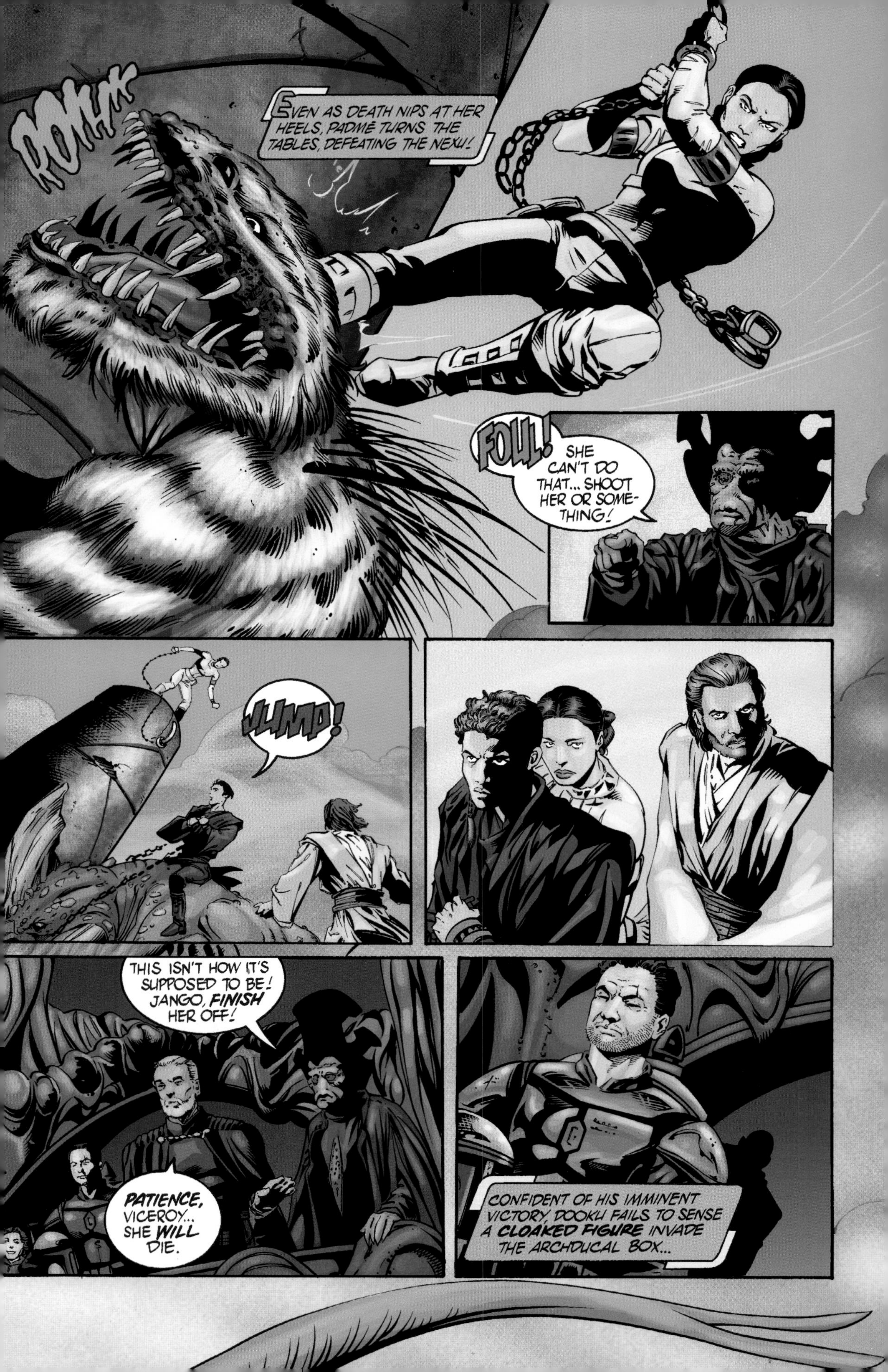
ROWR
EVEN AS DEATH NIPS AT HER HEELS, PADMÉ TURNS THE TABLES, DEFEATING THE NEXU!
FOUL! SHE CAN'T DO THAT... SHOOT HER OR SOME-THING!
JUMP!
THIS ISN'T HOW IT'S SUPPOSED TO BE! JANGO, FINISH HER OFF!
PATIENCE, VICEROY... SHE WILL DIE.
CONFIDENT OF HIS IMMINENT VICTORY, DOOKU FAILS TO SENSE A CLOAKED FIGURE INVADE THE ARCHDUCAL BOX...

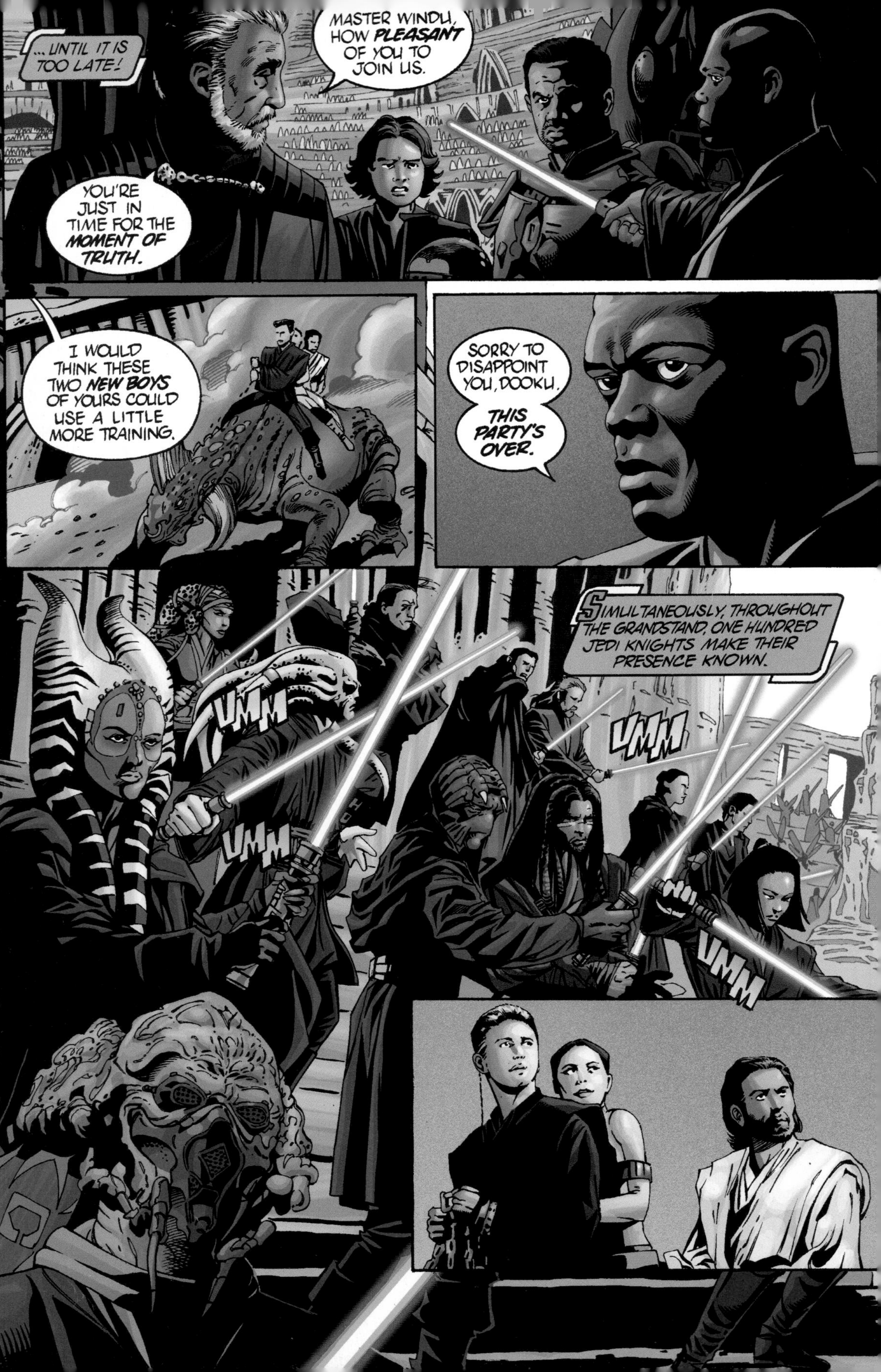
...UNTIL IT IS TOO LATE!
MASTER WINDU, HOW PLEASANT OF YOU TO JOIN US.
YOU'RE JUST IN TIME FOR THE MOMENT OF TRUTH.
I WOULD THINK THESE TWO NEW BOYS OF YOURS COULD USE A LITTLE MORE TRAINING.
SORRY TO DISAPPOINT YOU, DOOKU.
THIS PARTY'S OVER.
SIMULTANEOUSLY, THROUGHOUT THE GRANDSTAND, ONE HUNDRED JEDI KNIGHTS MAKE THEIR PRESENCE KNOWN.
UMM
UMM
UMM
UMM

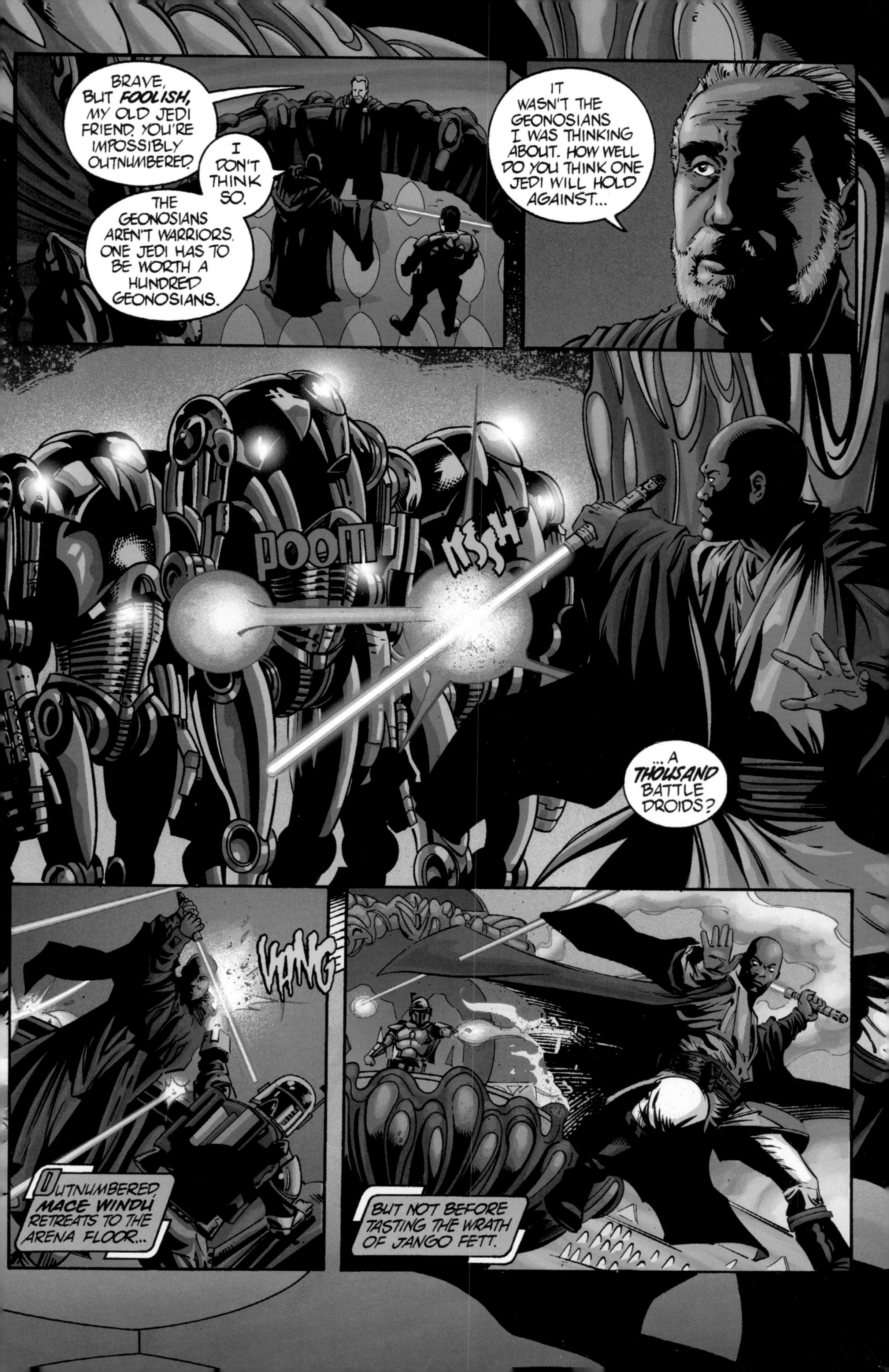

BRAVE, BUT FOOLISH, MY OLD JEDI FRIEND. YOU'RE IMPOSSIBLY OUTNUMBERED.
I DON'T THINK SO.
THE GEONOSIANS AREN'T WARRIORS. ONE JEDI HAS TO BE WORTH A HUNDRED GEONOSIANS.
IT WASN'T THE GEONOSIANS I WAS THINKING ABOUT. HOW WELL DO YOU THINK ONE JEDI WILL HOLD AGAINST...
POOM
KSSH
...A THOUSAND BATTLE DROIDS?
VANG
OUTNUMBERED, MACE WINDU RETREATS TO THE ARENA FLOOR...
BUT NOT BEFORE TASTING THE WRATH OF JANGO FETT.

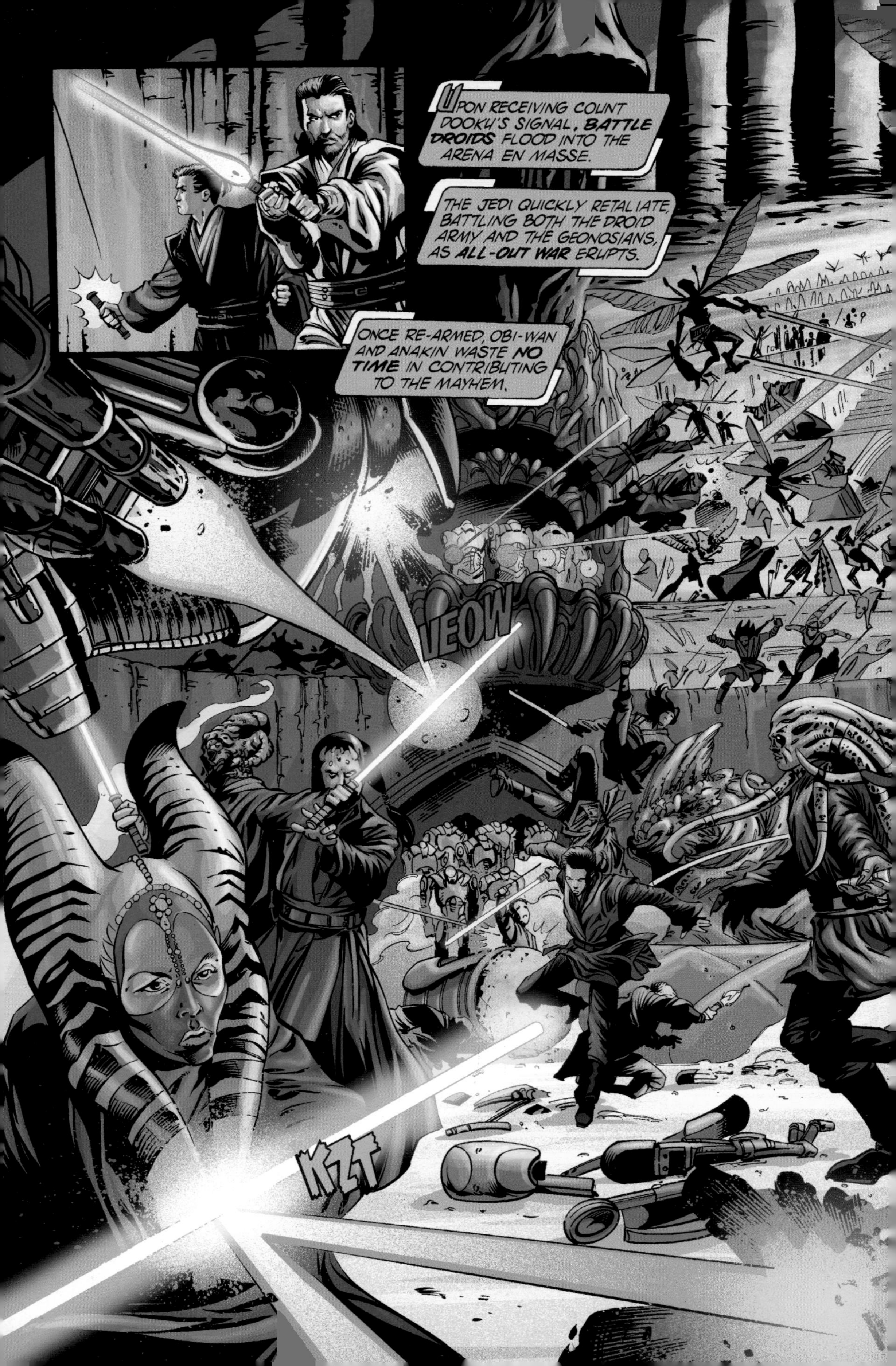
UPON RECEIVING COUNT DOOKU'S SIGNAL, BATTLE DROIDS FLOOD INTO THE ARENA EN MASSE.
THE JEDI QUICKLY RETALIATE, BATTLING BOTH THE DROID ARMY AND THE GEONOSIANS, AS ALL-OUT WAR ERUPTS.
ONCE RE-ARMED, OBI-WAN AND ANAKIN WASTE NO TIME IN CONTRIBUTING TO THE MAYHEM.
VEOW
KZT

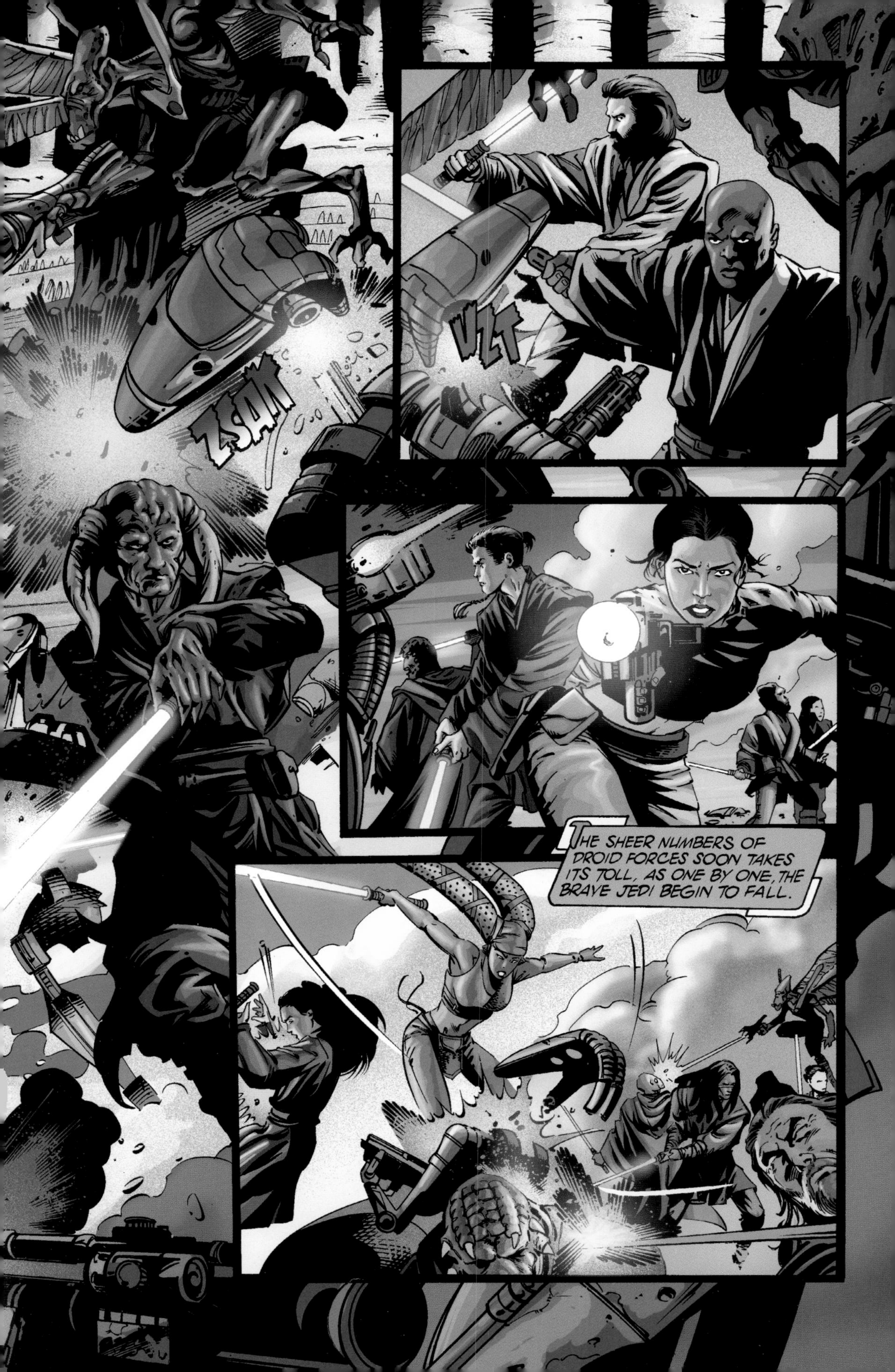
ZSAK
VZT
THE SHEER NUMBERS OF DROID FORCES SOON TAKES ITS TOLL, AS ONE BY ONE, THE BRAVE JEDI BEGIN TO FALL.

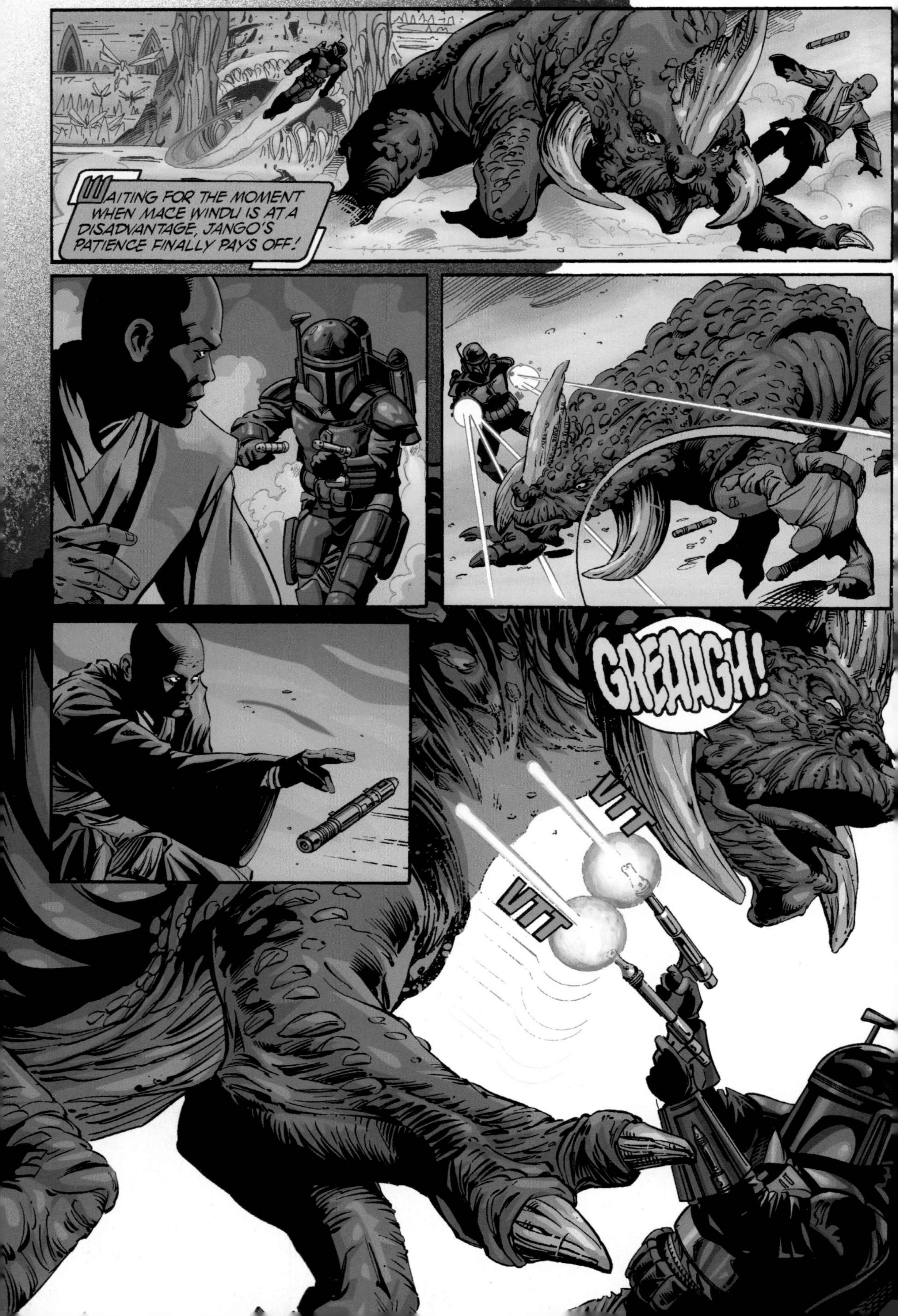
WAITING FOR THE MOMENT WHEN MACE WINDU IS AT A DISADVANTAGE, JANGO'S PATIENCE FINALLY PAYS OFF!
GREAAGH!
VTT
VTT

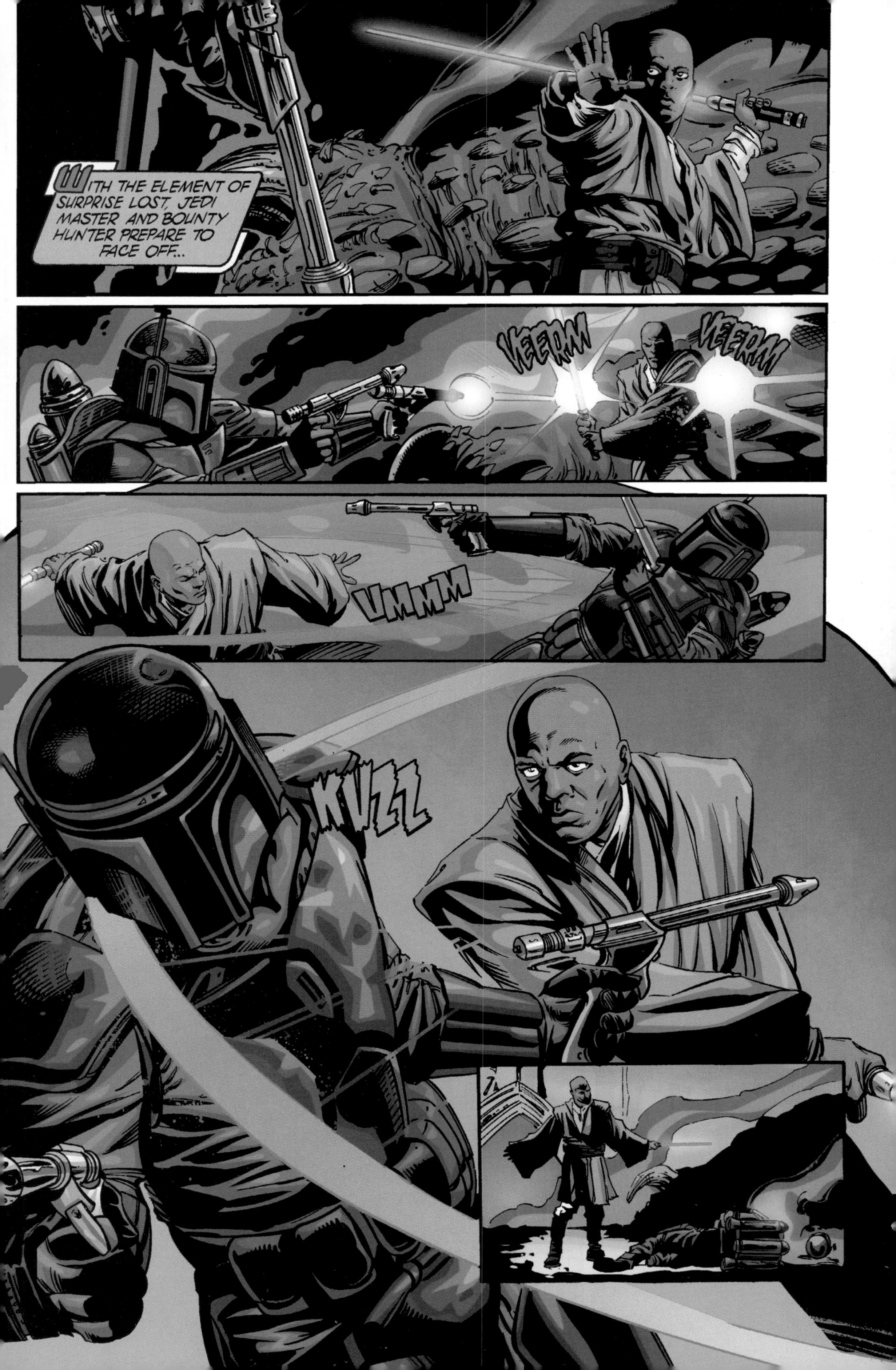
WITH THE ELEMENT OF SURPRISE LOST, JEDI MASTER AND BOUNTY HUNTER PREPARE TO FACE OFF...
VEERM
VEERM
UMMMM
KVZZ

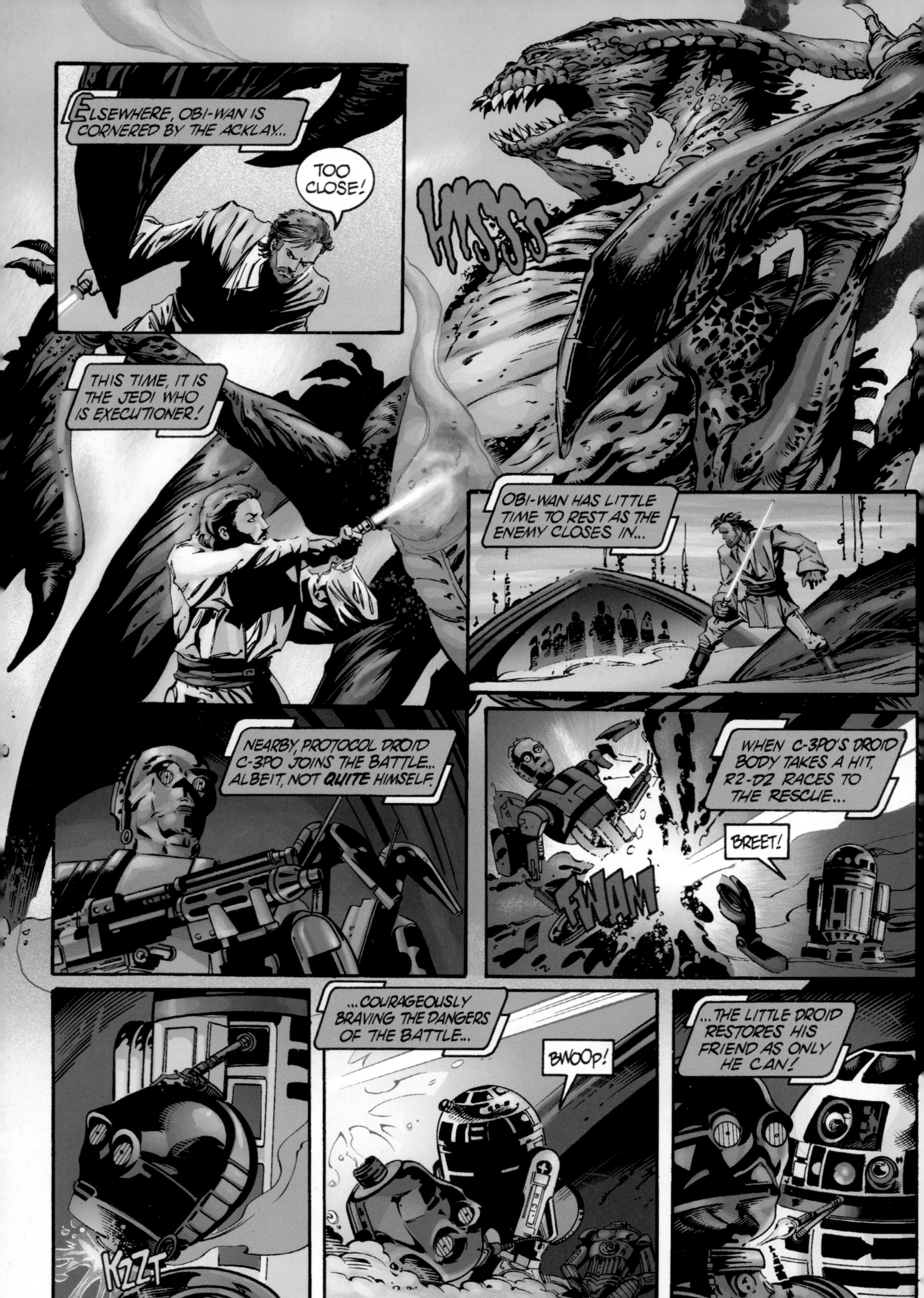
ELSEWHERE, OBI-WAN IS CORNERED BY THE ACKLAY...
TOO CLOSE!
HISSS
THIS TIME, IT IS THE JEDI WHO IS EXECUTIONER!
OBI-WAN HAS LITTLE TIME TO REST AS THE ENEMY CLOSES IN...
NEARBY, PROTOCOL DROID C-3PO JOINS THE BATTLE... ALBEIT, NOT QUITE HIMSELF.
WHEN C-3PO'S DROID BODY TAKES A HIT, R2-D2 RACES TO THE RESCUE...
BREET!
FWAM
KZZT
...COURAGEOUSLY BRAVING THE DANGERS OF THE BATTLE...
BWOOP!
...THE LITTLE DROID RESTORES HIS FRIEND AS ONLY HE CAN!

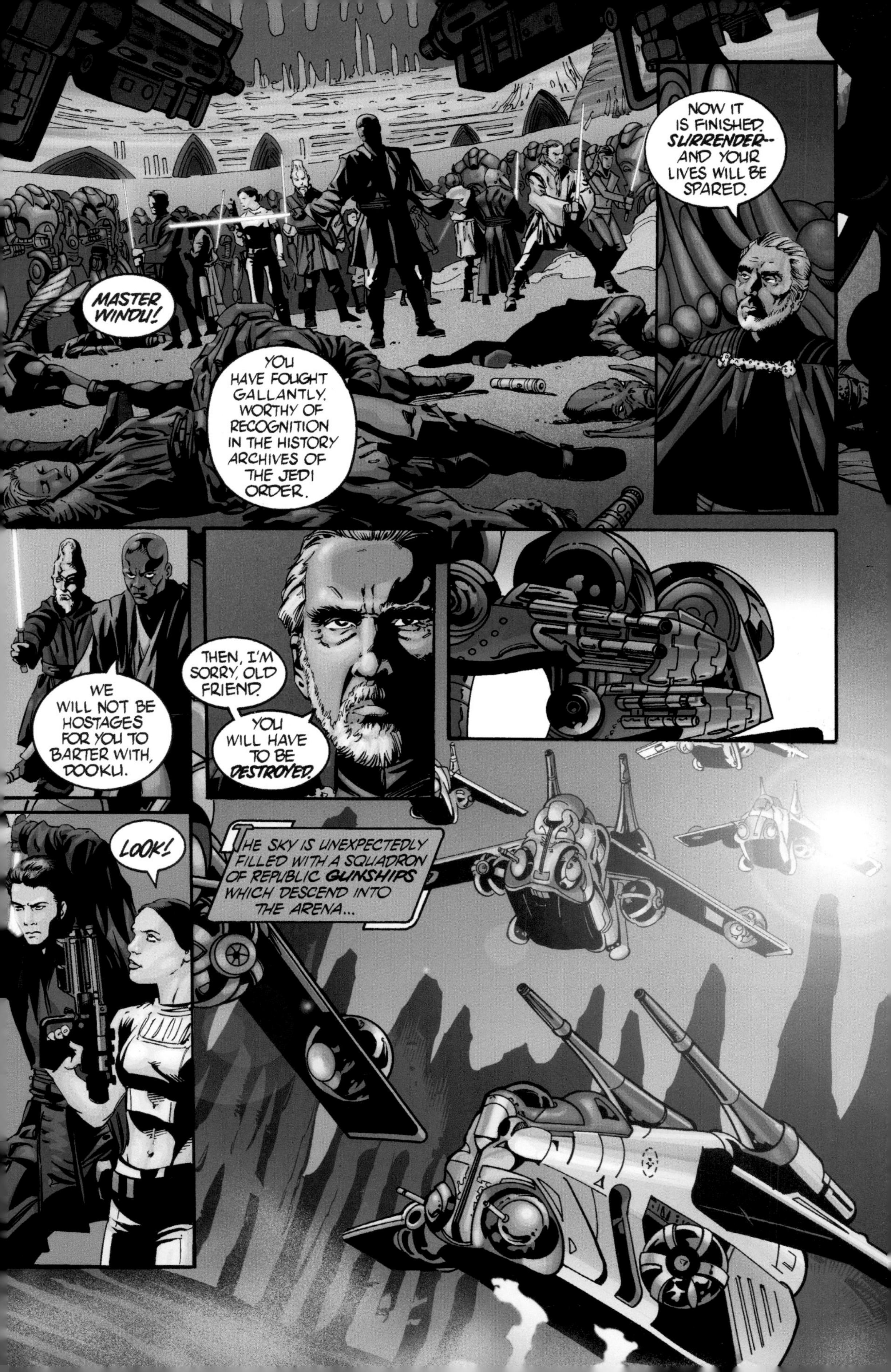
NOW IT IS FINISHED. SURRENDER-- AND YOUR LIVES WILL BE SPARED.
MASTER WINDU!
YOU HAVE FOUGHT GALLANTLY. WORTHY OF RECOGNITION IN THE HISTORY ARCHIVES OF THE JEDI ORDER.
WE WILL NOT BE HOSTAGES FOR YOU TO BARTER WITH, DOOKU.
THEN, I'M SORRY, OLD FRIEND.
YOU WILL HAVE TO BE DESTROYED.
LOOK!
THE SKY IS UNEXPECTEDLY FILLED WITH A SQUADRON OF REPUBLIC GUNSHIPS WHICH DESCEND INTO THE ARENA...

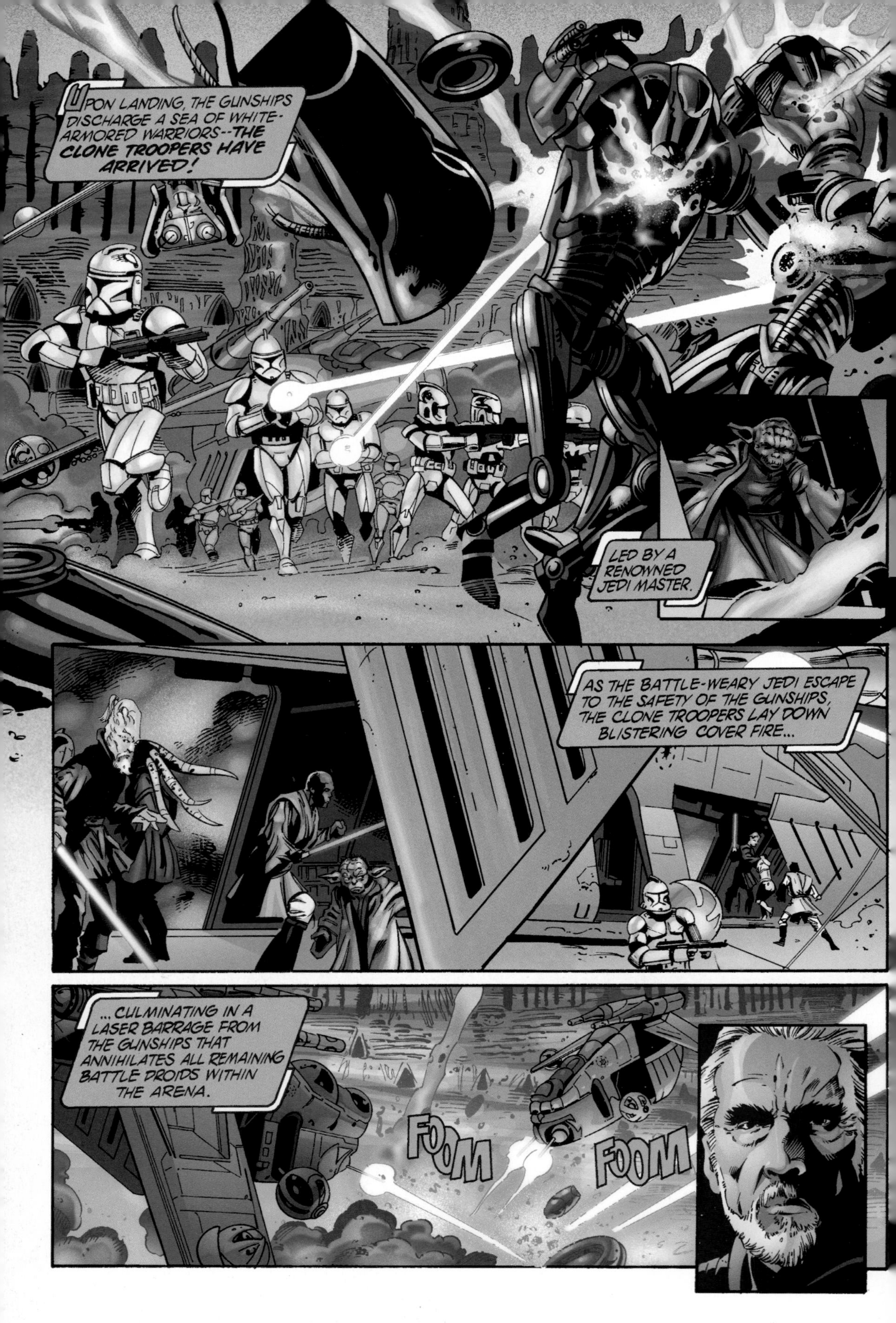
UPON LANDING, THE GUNSHIPS DISCHARGE A SEA OF WHITE-ARMORED WARRIORS--THE CLONE TROOPERS HAVE ARRIVED!
LED BY A RENOWNED JEDI MASTER.
AS THE BATTLE-WEARY JEDI ESCAPE TO THE SAFETY OF THE GUNSHIPS, THE CLONE TROOPERS LAY DOWN BLISTERING COVER FIRE...
...CULMINATING IN A LASER BARRAGE FROM THE GUNSHIPS THAT ANNIHILATES ALL REMAINING BATTLE DROIDS WITHIN THE ARENA.
FOOM
FOOM

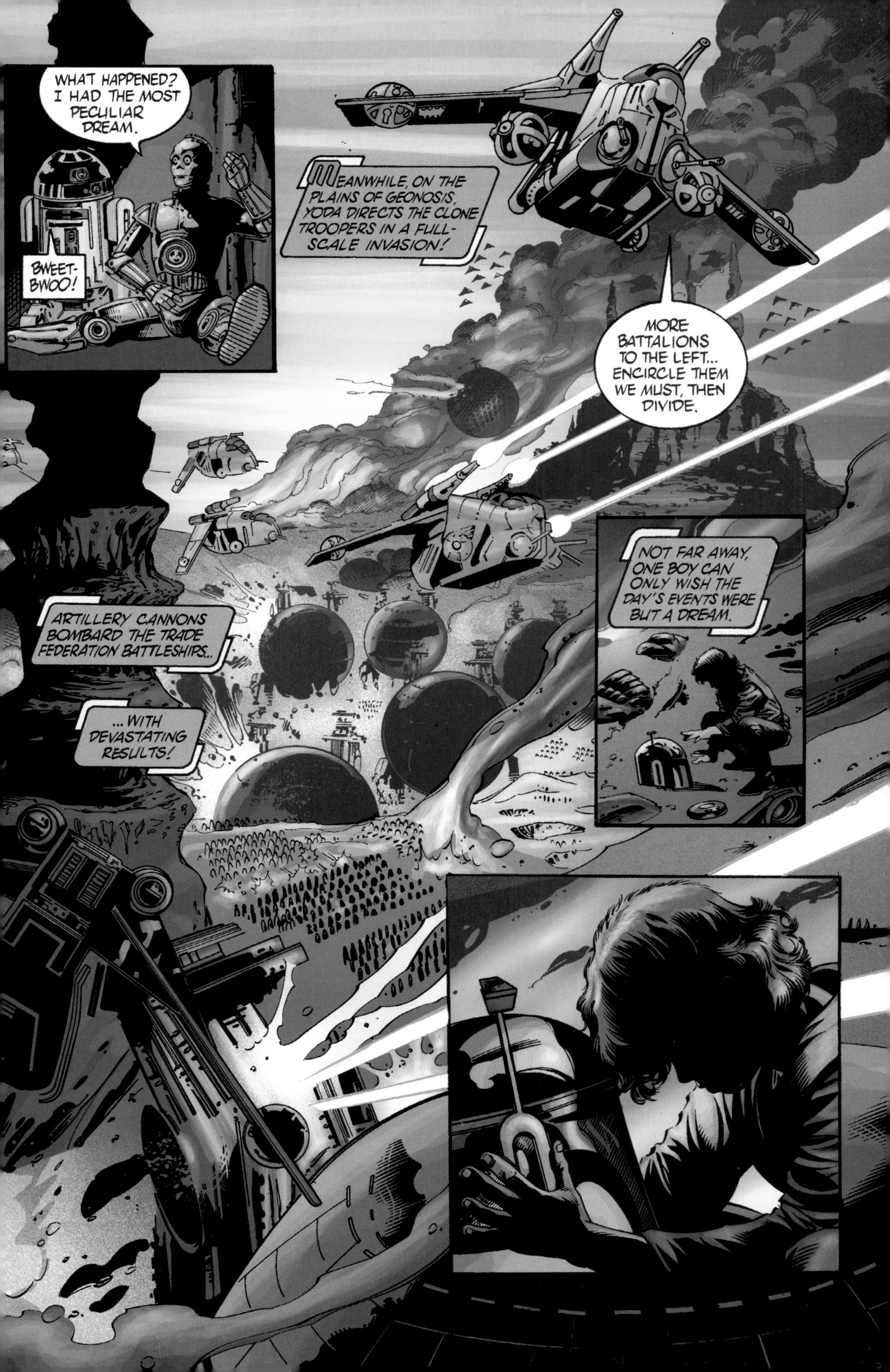
WHAT HAPPENED? I HAD THE MOST PECULIAR DREAM.
BWEET-BWOO!
MEANWHILE, ON THE PLAINS OF GEONOSIS, YODA DIRECTS THE CLONE TROOPERS IN A FULL-SCALE INVASION!
MORE BATTALIONS TO THE LEFT... ENCIRCLE THEM WE MUST, THEN DIVIDE.
ARTILLERY CANNONS BOMBARD THE TRADE FEDERATION BATTLESHIPS...
...WITH DEVASTATING RESULTS!
NOT FAR AWAY, ONE BOY CAN ONLY WISH THE DAY'S EVENTS WERE BUT A DREAM.

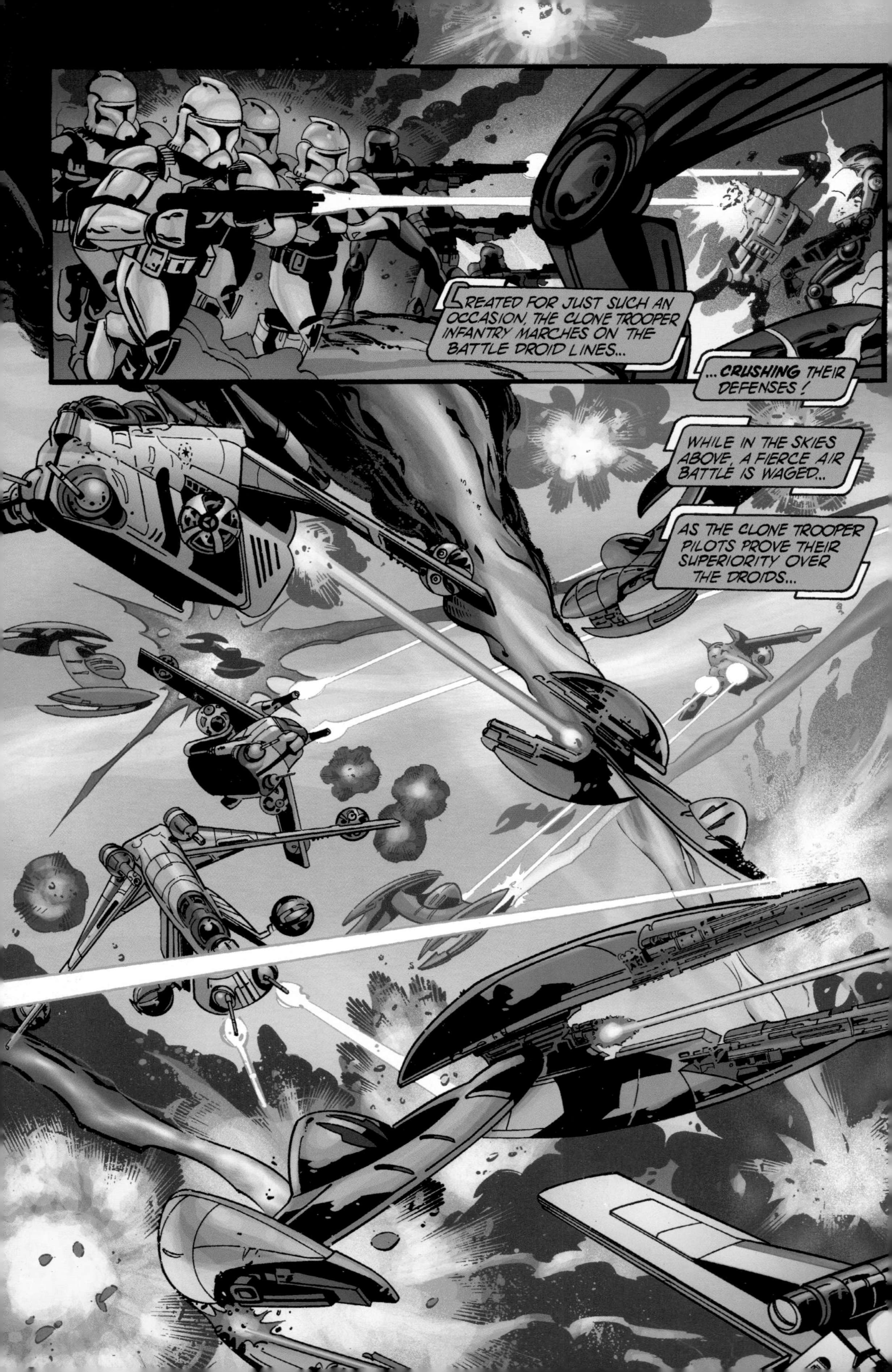
CREATED FOR JUST SUCH AN OCCASION, THE CLONE TROOPER INFANTRY MARCHES ON THE BATTLE DROID LINES...
...CRUSHING THEIR DEFENSES!
WHILE IN THE SKIES ABOVE, A FIERCE AIR BATTLE IS WAGED...
AS THE CLONE TROOPER PILOTS PROVE THEIR SUPERIORITY OVER THE DROIDS...

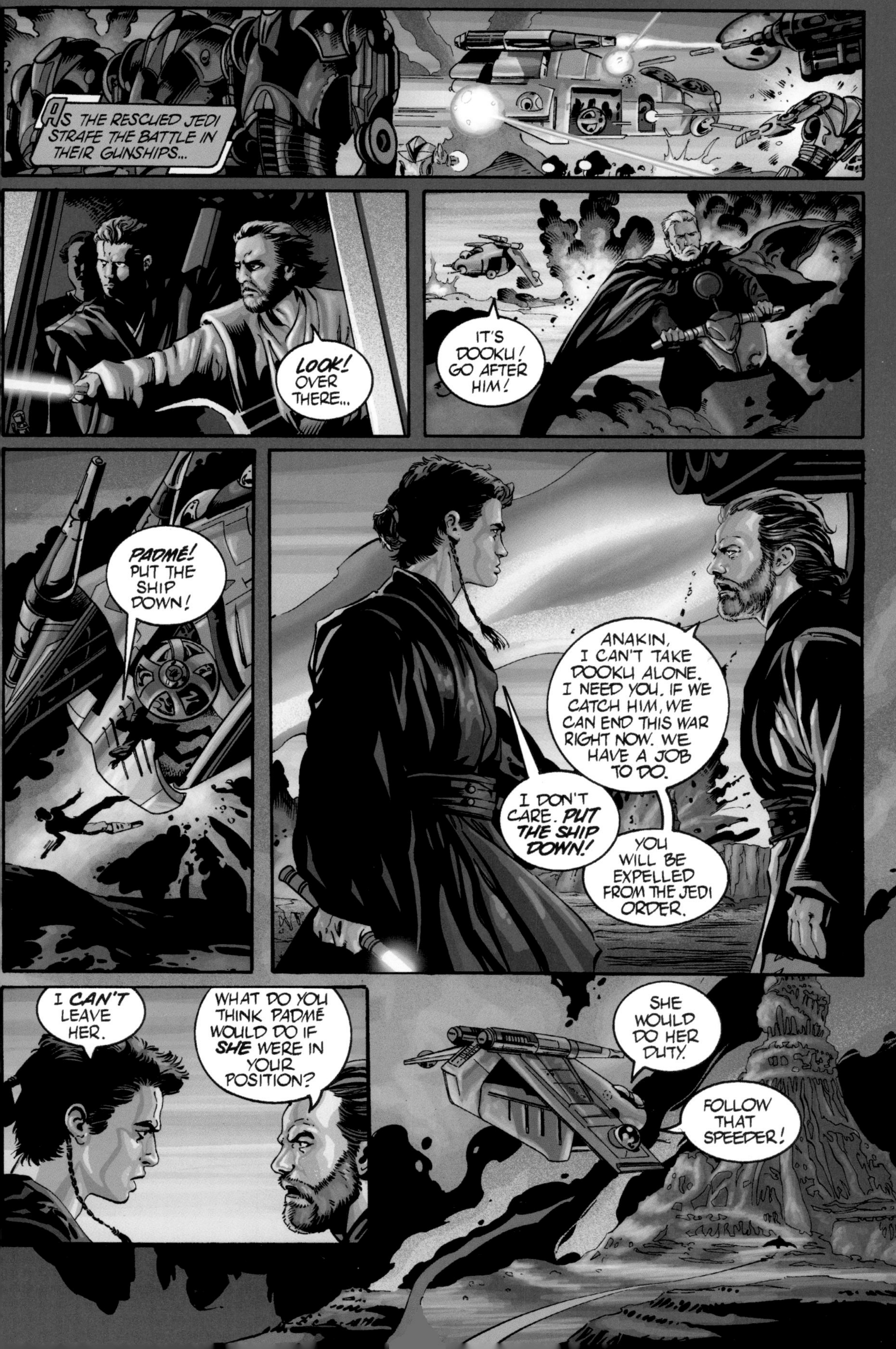
AS THE RESCUED JEDI STRAFE THE BATTLE IN THEIR GUNSHIPS...
LOOK! OVER THERE...
IT'S DOOKU! GO AFTER HIM!
PADMÉ! PUT THE SHIP DOWN!
ANAKIN, I CAN'T TAKE DOOKU ALONE. I NEED YOU. IF WE CATCH HIM, WE CAN END THIS WAR RIGHT NOW. WE HAVE A JOB TO DO.
I DON'T CARE. PUT THE SHIP DOWN!
YOU WILL BE EXPELLED FROM THE JEDI ORDER.
I CAN'T LEAVE HER.
WHAT DO YOU THINK PADMÉ WOULD DO IF SHE WERE IN YOUR POSITION?
SHE WOULD DO HER DUTY.
FOLLOW THAT SPEEDER!

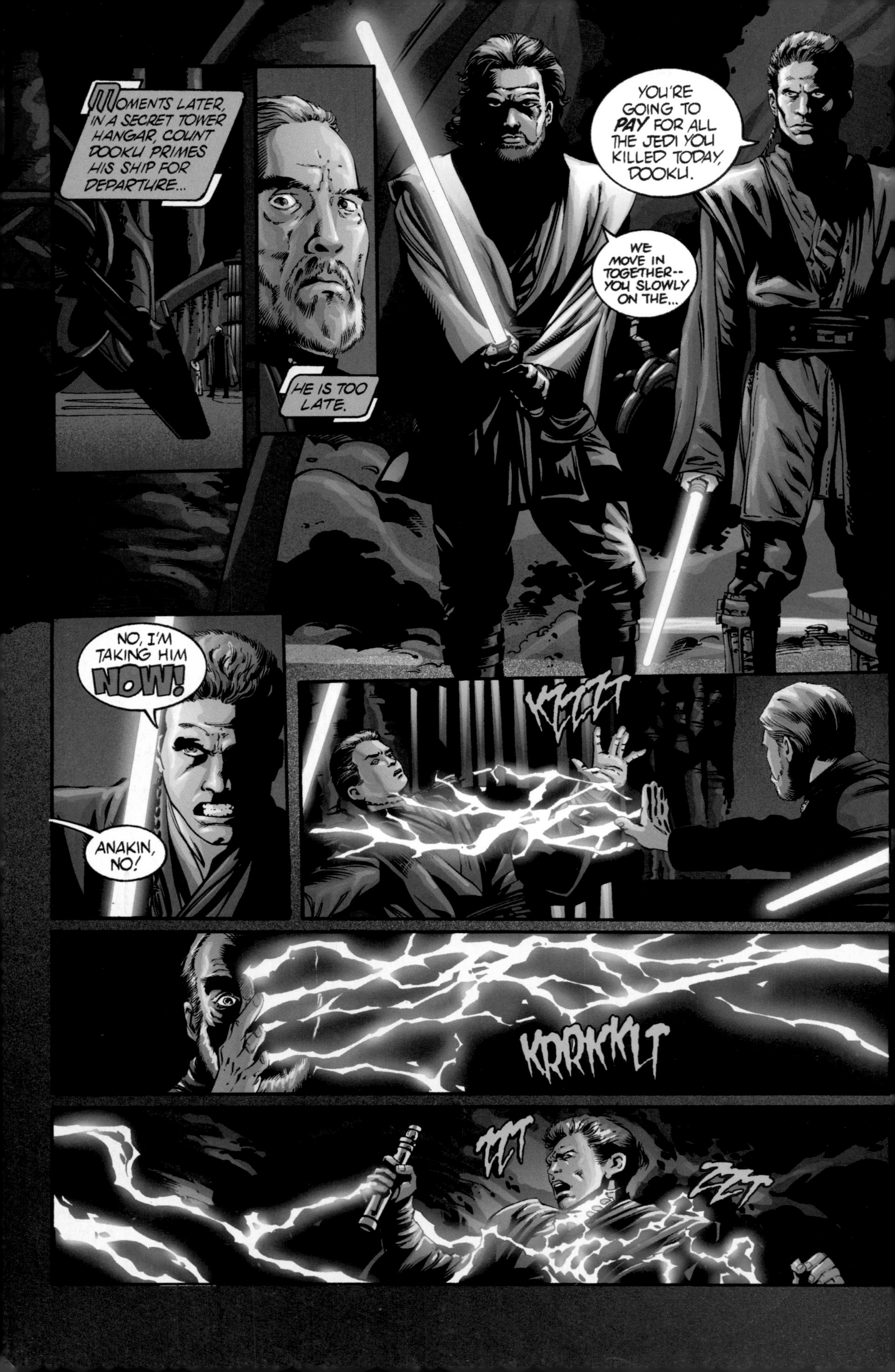
MOMENTS LATER, IN A SECRET TOWER HANGAR, COUNT DOOKU PRIMES HIS SHIP FOR DEPARTURE...
HE IS TOO LATE.
YOU'RE GOING TO PAY FOR ALL THE JEDI YOU KILLED TODAY, DOOKU.
WE MOVE IN TOGETHER-- YOU SLOWLY ON THE...
NO, I'M TAKING HIM NOW!
ANAKIN, NO!
KZZZT
KRRKKLT
ZZT
ZZZT

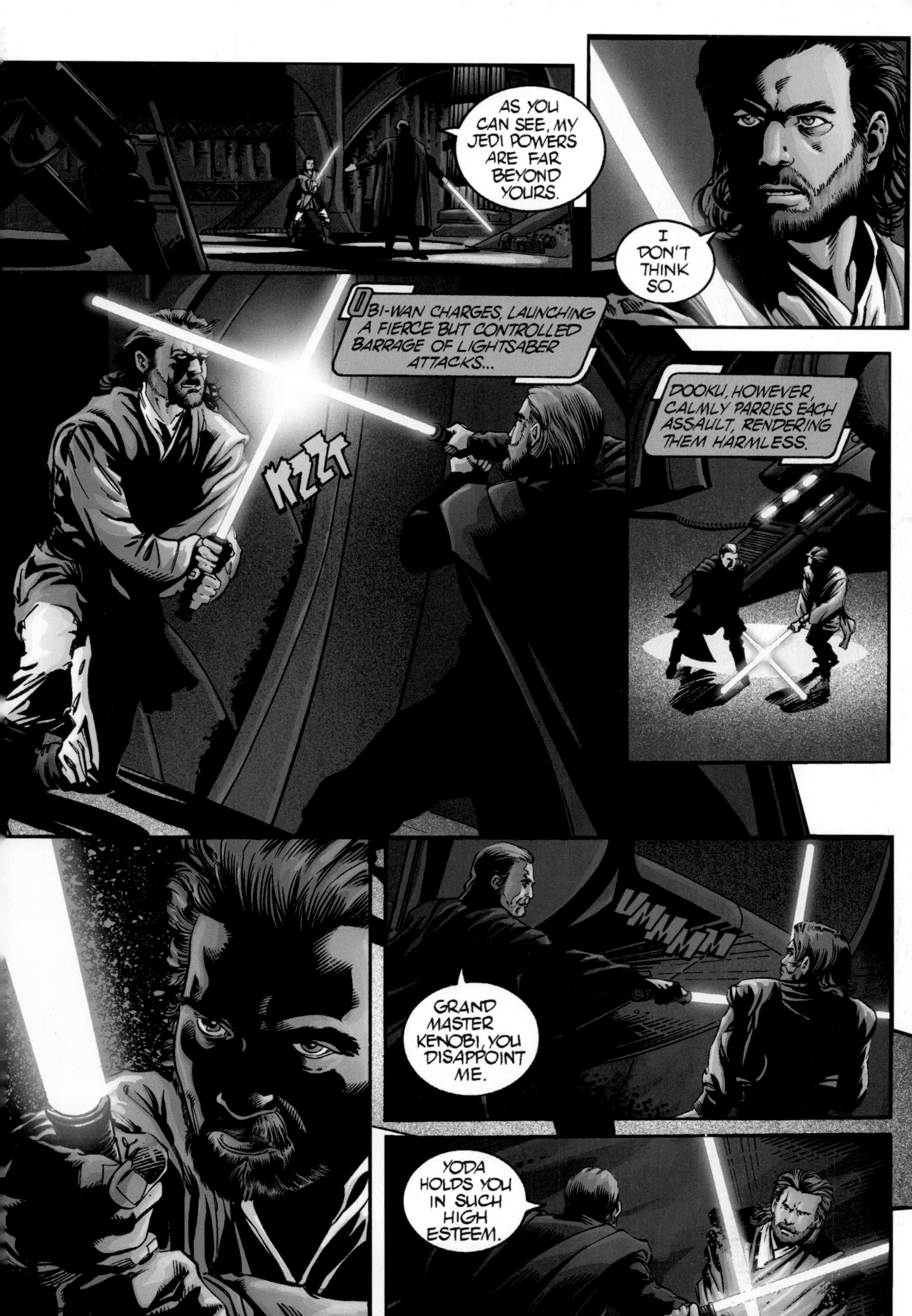

AS YOU CAN SEE, MY JEDI POWERS ARE FAR BEYOND YOURS.
I DON'T THINK SO.
OBI-WAN CHARGES, LAUNCHING A FIERCE BUT CONTROLLED BARRAGE OF LIGHTSABER ATTACKS...
KZZT
DOOKU, HOWEVER, CALMLY PARRIES EACH ASSAULT, RENDERING THEM HARMLESS.
UMMMM
GRAND MASTER KENOBI, YOU DISAPPOINT ME.
YODA HOLDS YOU IN SUCH HIGH ESTEEM.

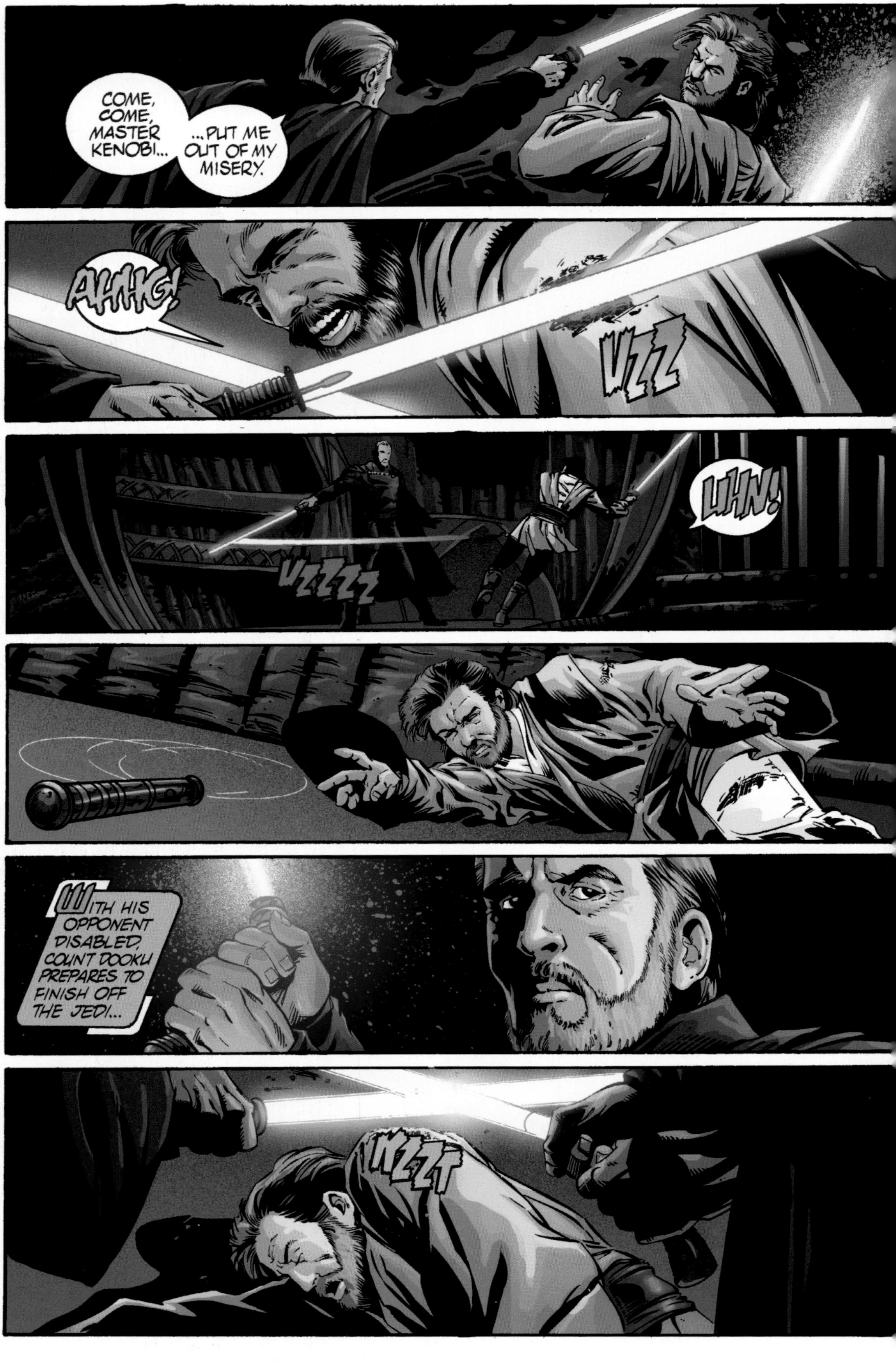
COME, COME, MASTER KENOBI...
...PUT ME OUT OF MY MISERY.
AHHG!
VZZ
UHN!
VZZZZZ
WITH HIS OPPONENT DISABLED, COUNT DOOKU PREPARES TO FINISH OFF THE JEDI...
NZZT

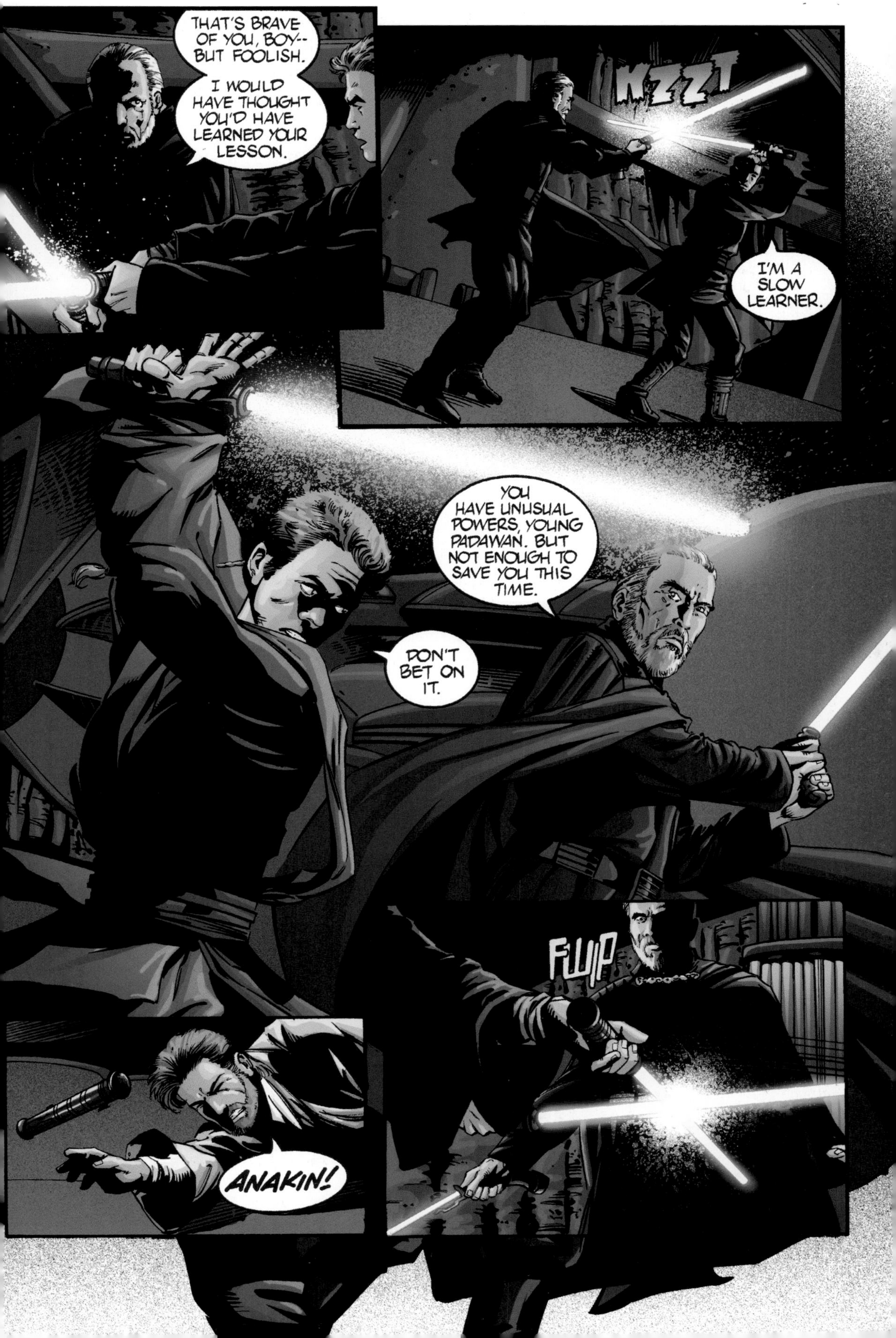
THAT'S BRAVE OF YOU, BOY-- BUT FOOLISH.
I WOULD HAVE THOUGHT YOU'D HAVE LEARNED YOUR LESSON.
NZZT
I'M A SLOW LEARNER.
YOU HAVE UNUSUAL POWERS, YOUNG PADAWAN. BUT NOT ENOUGH TO SAVE YOU THIS TIME.
DON'T BET ON IT.
FWIP
ANAKIN!

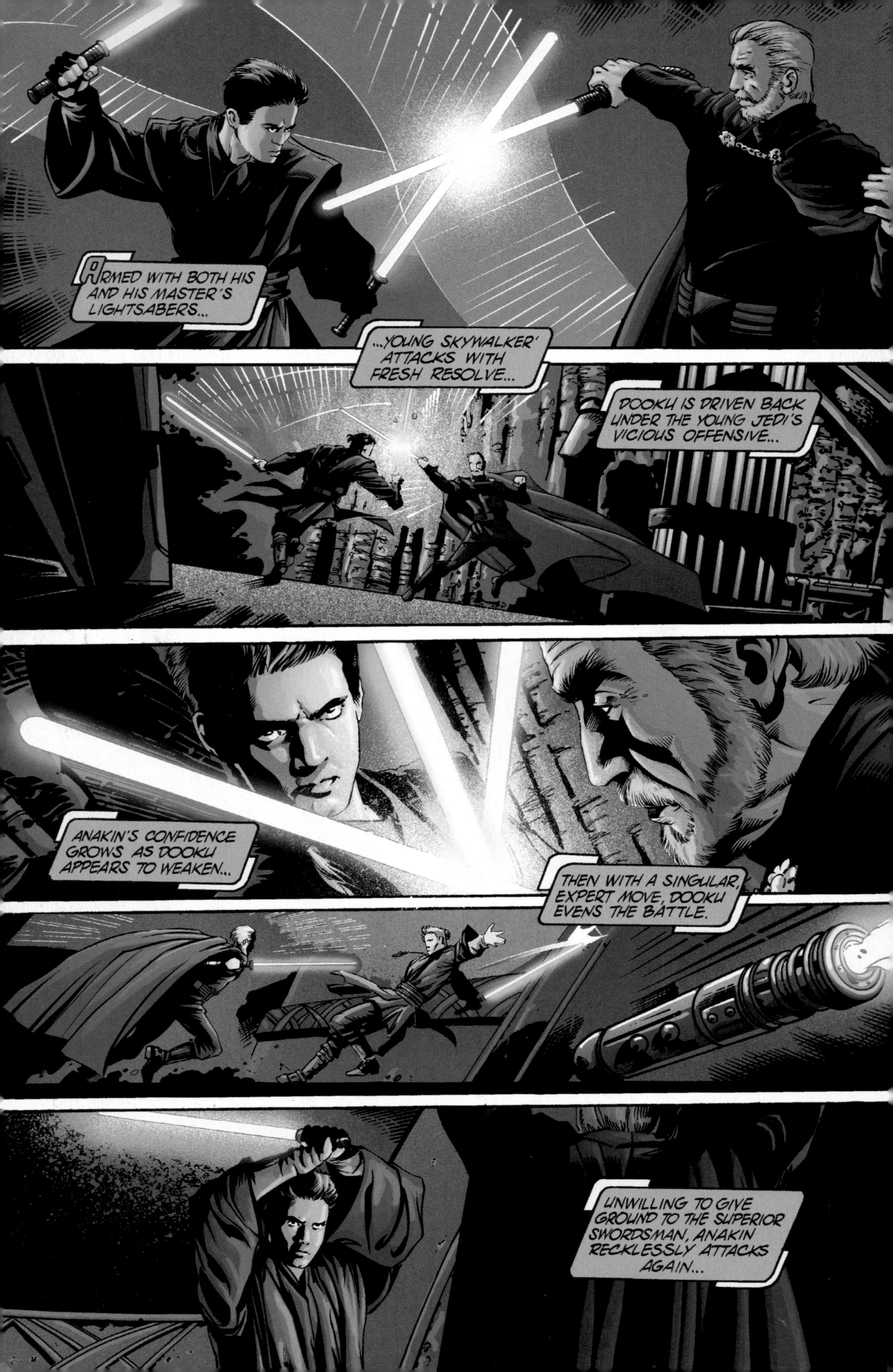
ARMED WITH BOTH HIS AND HIS MASTER'S LIGHTSABERS...
...YOUNG SKYWALKER' ATTACKS WITH FRESH RESOLVE...
DOOKU IS DRIVEN BACK UNDER THE YOUNG JEDI'S VICIOUS OFFENSIVE...
ANAKIN'S CONFIDENCE GROWS AS DOOKU APPEARS TO WEAKEN...
THEN WITH A SINGULAR, EXPERT MOVE, DOOKU EVENS THE BATTLE.
UNWILLING TO GIVE GROUND TO THE SUPERIOR SWORDSMAN, ANAKIN RECKLESSLY ATTACKS AGAIN...

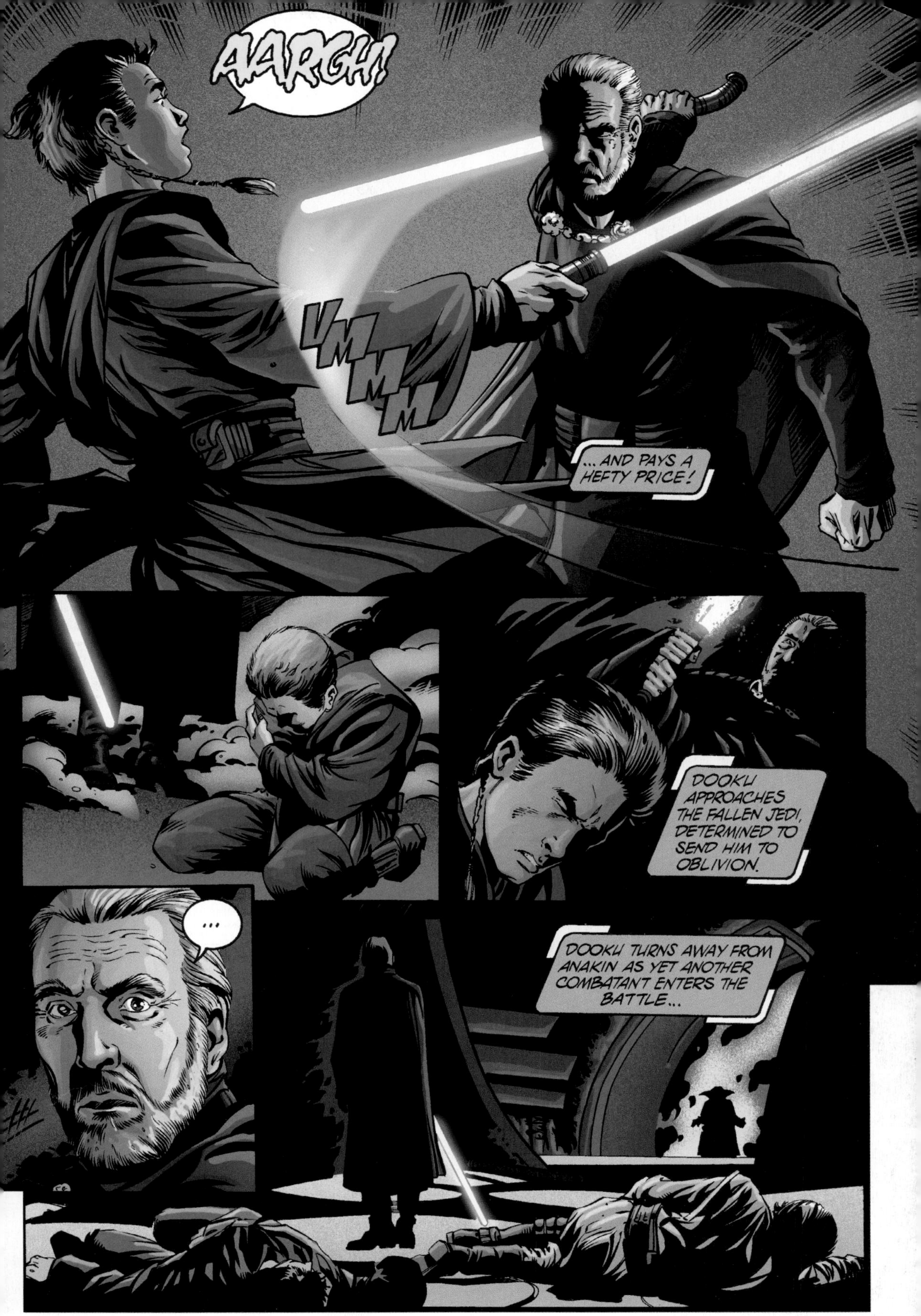
AARGH!
VMMMM
...AND PAYS A HEFTY PRICE!
DOOKU APPROACHES THE FALLEN JEDI, DETERMINED TO SEND HIM TO OBLIVION.
...
DOOKU TURNS AWAY FROM ANAKIN AS YET ANOTHER COMBATANT ENTERS THE BATTLE...

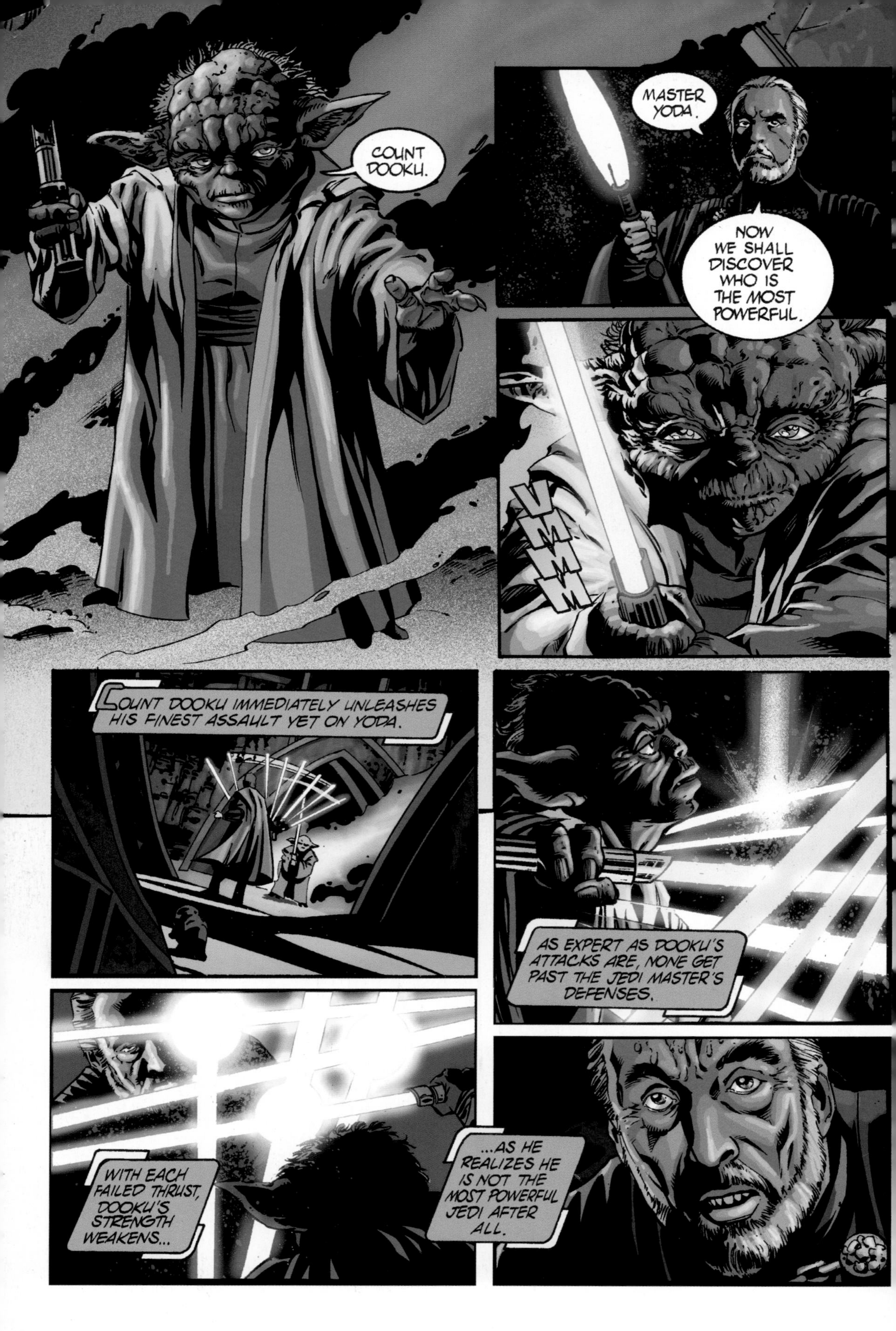
COUNT DOOKU.
MASTER YODA.
NOW WE SHALL DISCOVER WHO IS THE MOST POWERFUL.
VMMM
COUNT DOOKU IMMEDIATELY UNLEASHES HIS FINEST ASSAULT YET ON YODA.
AS EXPERT AS DOOKU'S ATTACKS ARE, NONE GET PAST THE JEDI MASTER'S DEFENSES.
WITH EACH FAILED THRUST, DOOKU'S STRENGTH WEAKENS...
...AS HE REALIZES HE IS NOT THE MOST POWERFUL JEDI AFTER ALL.

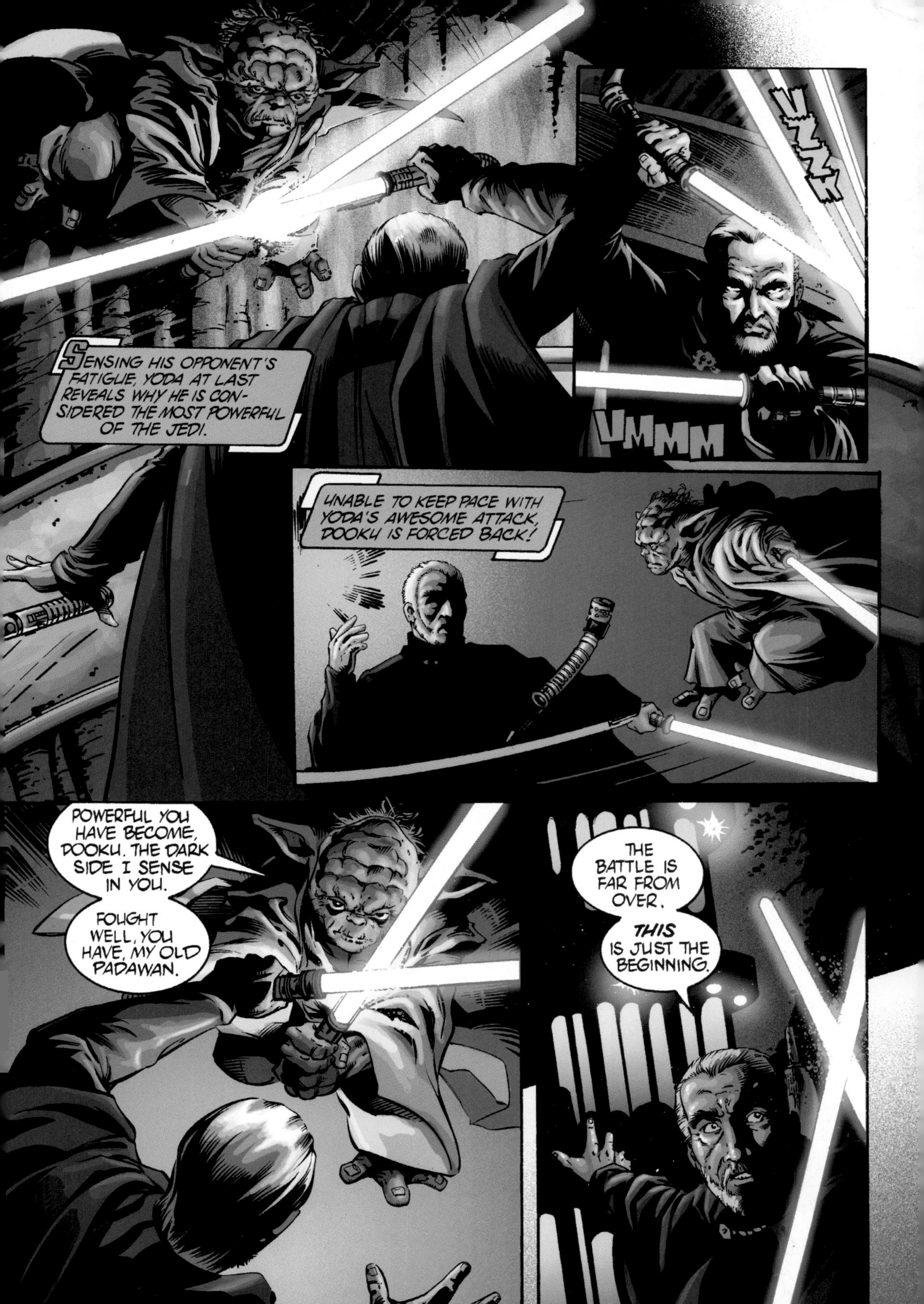

SENSING HIS OPPONENT'S FATIGUE, YODA AT LAST REVEALS WHY HE IS CONSIDERED THE MOST POWERFUL OF THE JEDI.
VVZZZ
UMMMM
UNABLE TO KEEP PACE WITH YODA'S AWESOME ATTACK, DOOKU IS FORCED BACK!
POWERFUL YOU HAVE BECOME, DOOKU. THE DARK SIDE I SENSE IN YOU.
FOUGHT WELL, YOU HAVE, MY OLD PADAWAN.
THE BATTLE IS FAR FROM OVER.
THIS IS JUST THE BEGINNING.

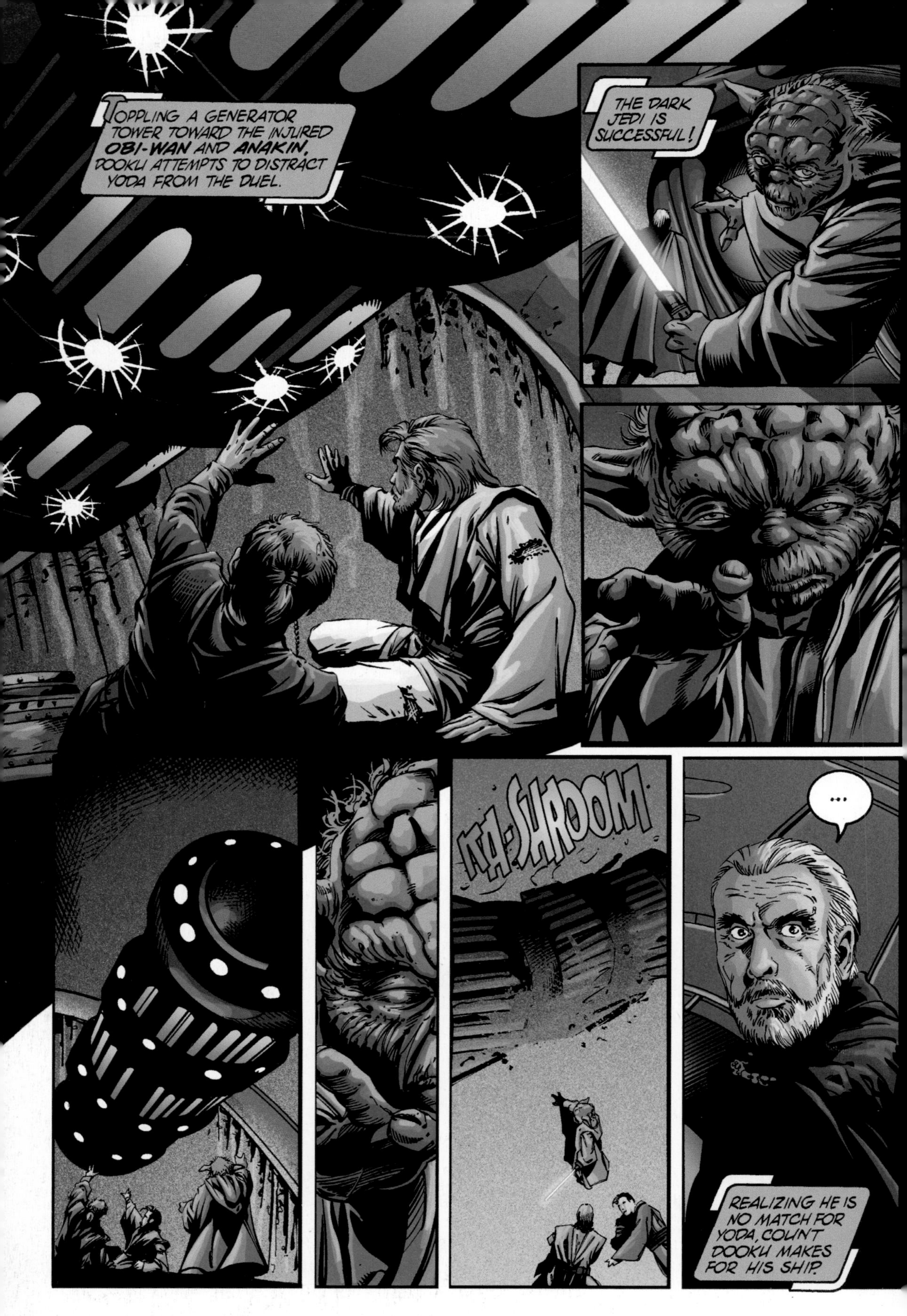
TOPPLING A GENERATOR TOWER TOWARD THE INJURED OBI-WAN AND ANAKIN, DOOKU ATTEMPTS TO DISTRACT YODA FROM THE DUEL.
THE DARK JEDI IS SUCCESSFUL!
KA-SHROOM
...
REALIZING HE IS NO MATCH FOR YODA, COUNT DOOKU MAKES FOR HIS SHIP.

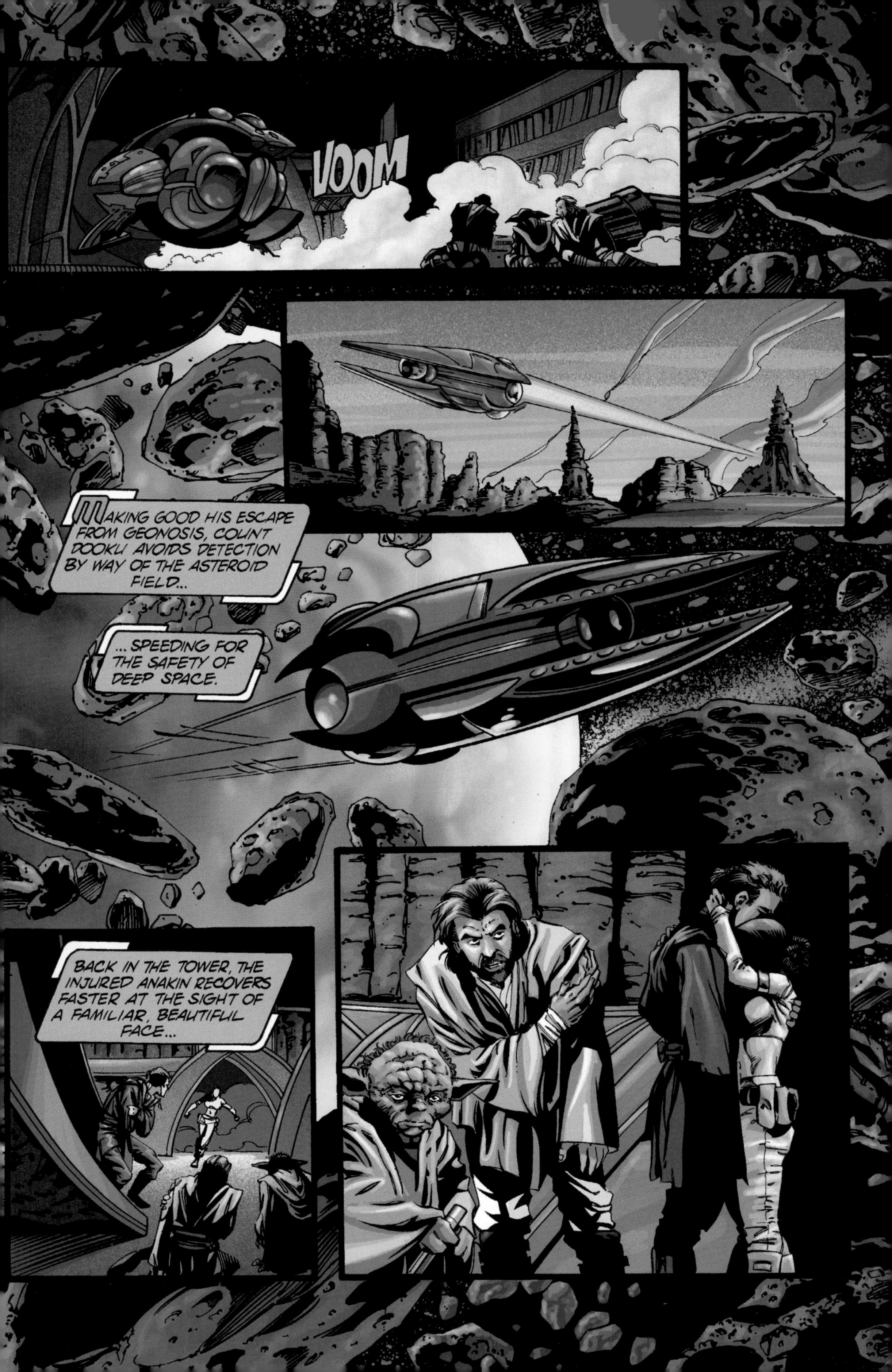
VOOM
MAKING GOOD HIS ESCAPE FROM GEONOSIS, COUNT DOOKU AVOIDS DETECTION BY WAY OF THE ASTEROID FIELD...
...SPEEDING FOR THE SAFETY OF DEEP SPACE.
BACK IN THE TOWER, THE INJURED ANAKIN RECOVERS FASTER AT THE SIGHT OF A FAMILIAR, BEAUTIFUL FACE...

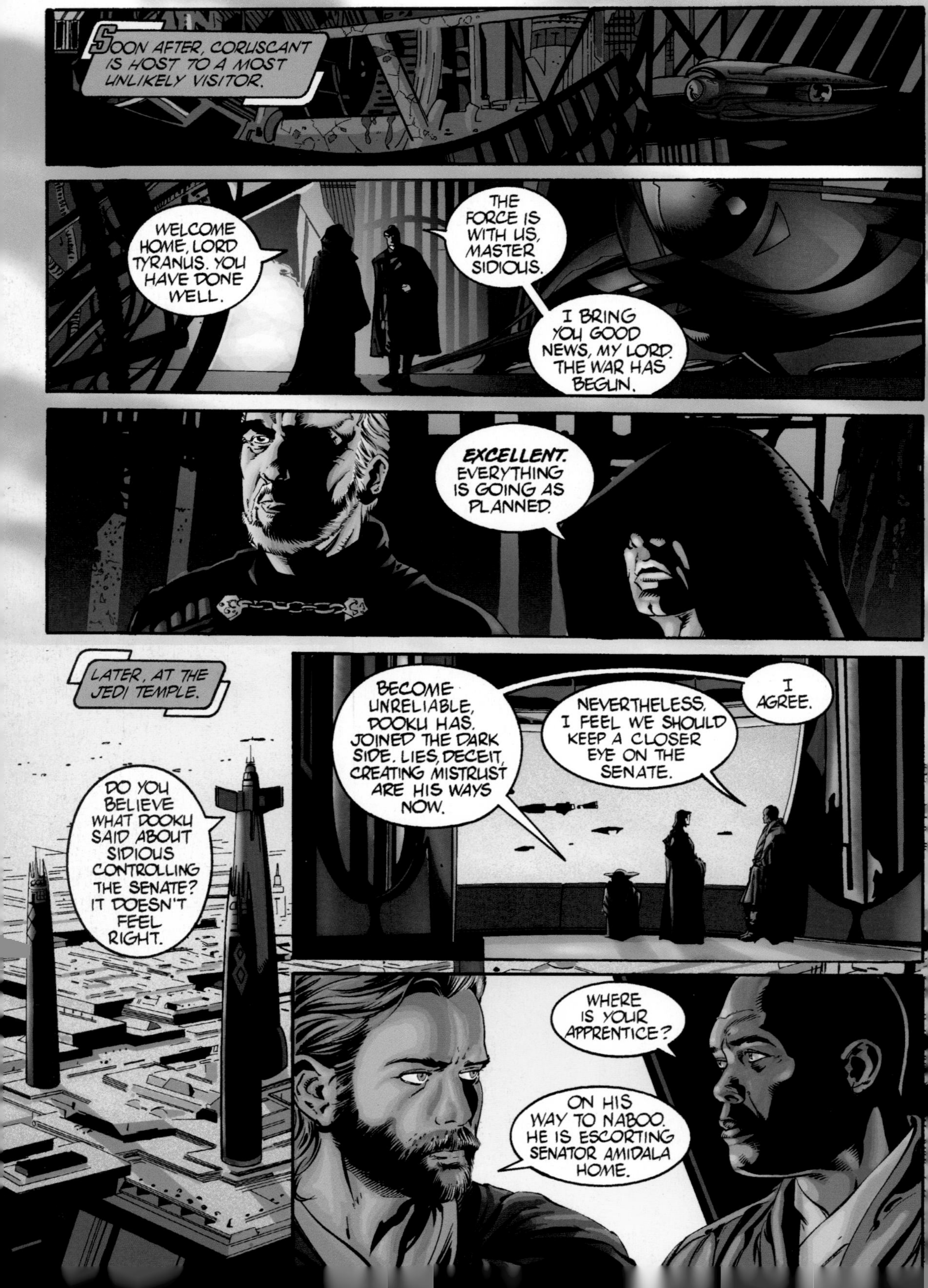
SOON AFTER, CORUSCANT IS HOST TO A MOST UNLIKELY VISITOR.
WELCOME HOME, LORD TYRANUS. YOU HAVE DONE WELL.
THE FORCE IS WITH US, MASTER SIDIOUS.
I BRING YOU GOOD NEWS, MY LORD. THE WAR HAS BEGUN.
EXCELLENT. EVERYTHING IS GOING AS PLANNED.
LATER, AT THE JEDI TEMPLE.
DO YOU BELIEVE WHAT DOOKU SAID ABOUT SIDIOUS CONTROLLING THE SENATE? IT DOESN'T FEEL RIGHT.
BECOME UNRELIABLE, DOOKU HAS. JOINED THE DARK SIDE. LIES, DECEIT, CREATING MISTRUST ARE HIS WAYS NOW.
NEVERTHELESS, I FEEL WE SHOULD KEEP A CLOSER EYE ON THE SENATE.
I AGREE.
WHERE IS YOUR APPRENTICE?
ON HIS WAY TO NABOO. HE IS ESCORTING SENATOR AMIDALA HOME.

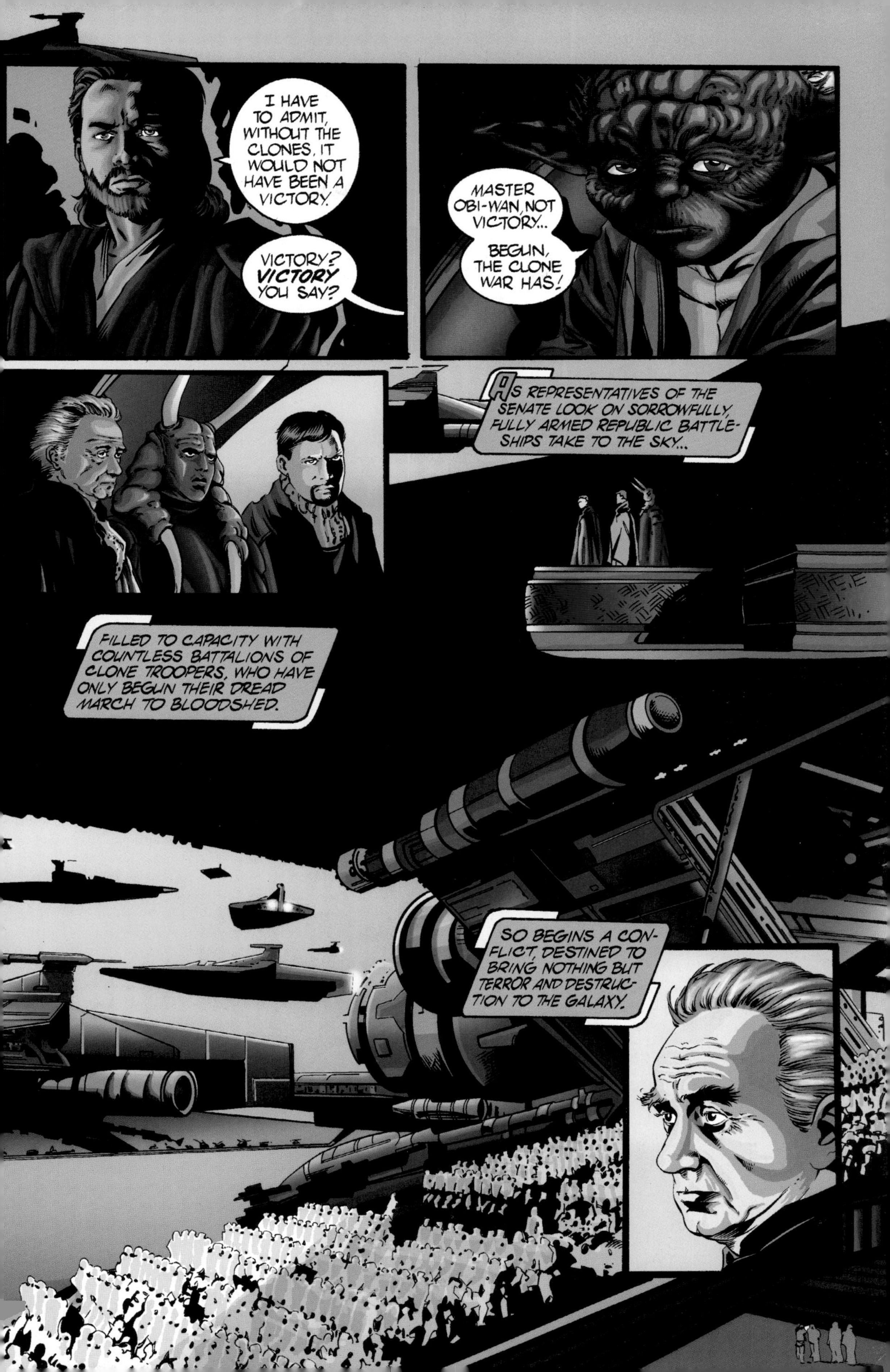
I HAVE TO ADMIT, WITHOUT THE CLONES, IT WOULD NOT HAVE BEEN A VICTORY.
VICTORY? **VICTORY** YOU SAY?
MASTER OBI-WAN, NOT VICTORY...
BEGUN, THE CLONE WAR HAS!
AS REPRESENTATIVES OF THE SENATE LOOK ON SORROWFULLY, FULLY ARMED REPUBLIC BATTLE-SHIPS TAKE TO THE SKY...
FILLED TO CAPACITY WITH COUNTLESS BATTALIONS OF CLONE TROOPERS, WHO HAVE ONLY BEGUN THEIR DREAD MARCH TO BLOODSHED.
SO BEGINS A CONFLICT, DESTINED TO BRING NOTHING BUT TERROR AND DESTRUCTION TO THE GALAXY.

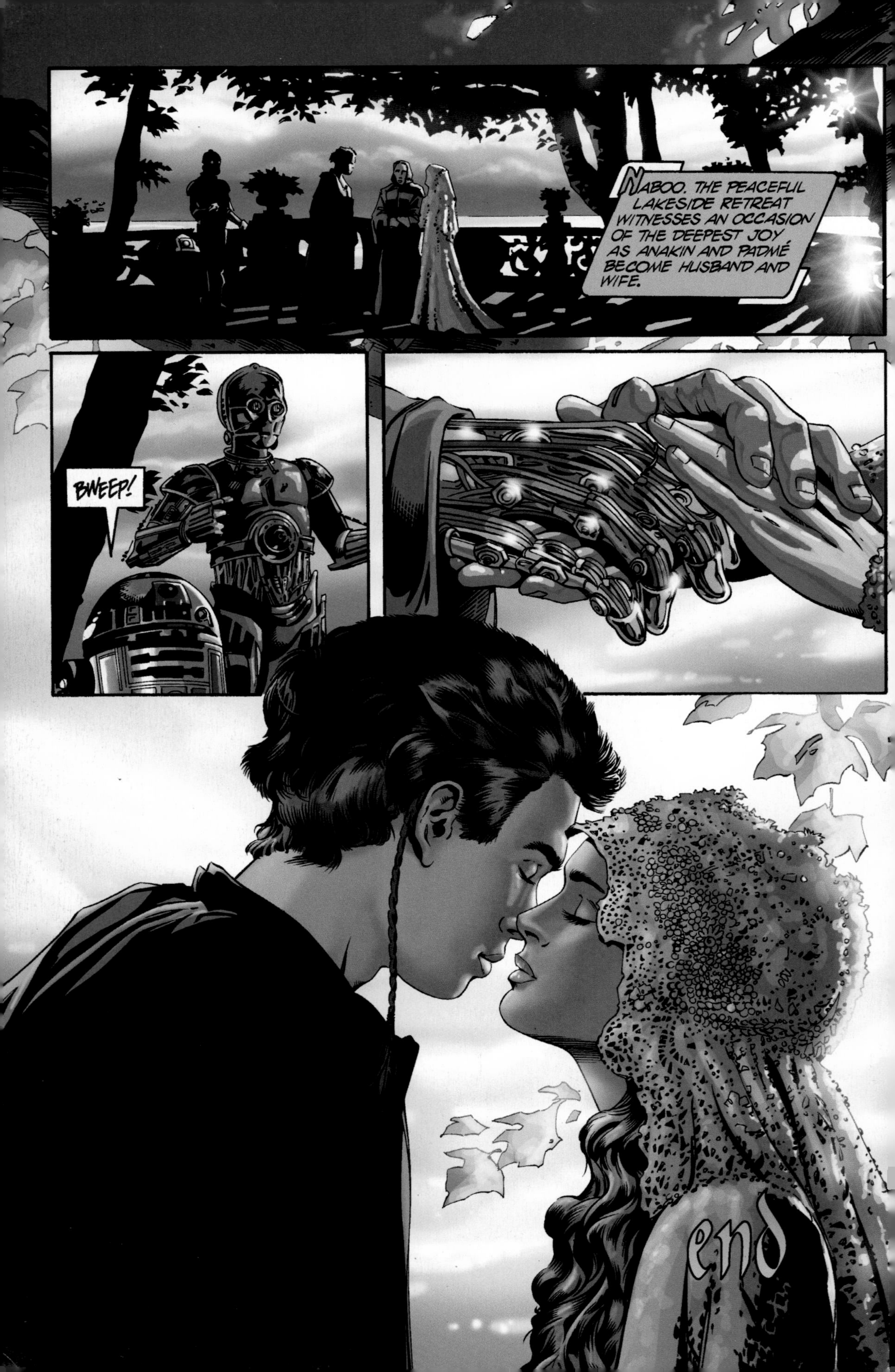
NABOO. THE PEACEFUL LAKESIDE RETREAT WITNESSES AN OCCASION OF THE DEEPEST JOY AS ANAKIN AND PADMÉ BECOME HUSBAND AND WIFE.
BWEEP!
end

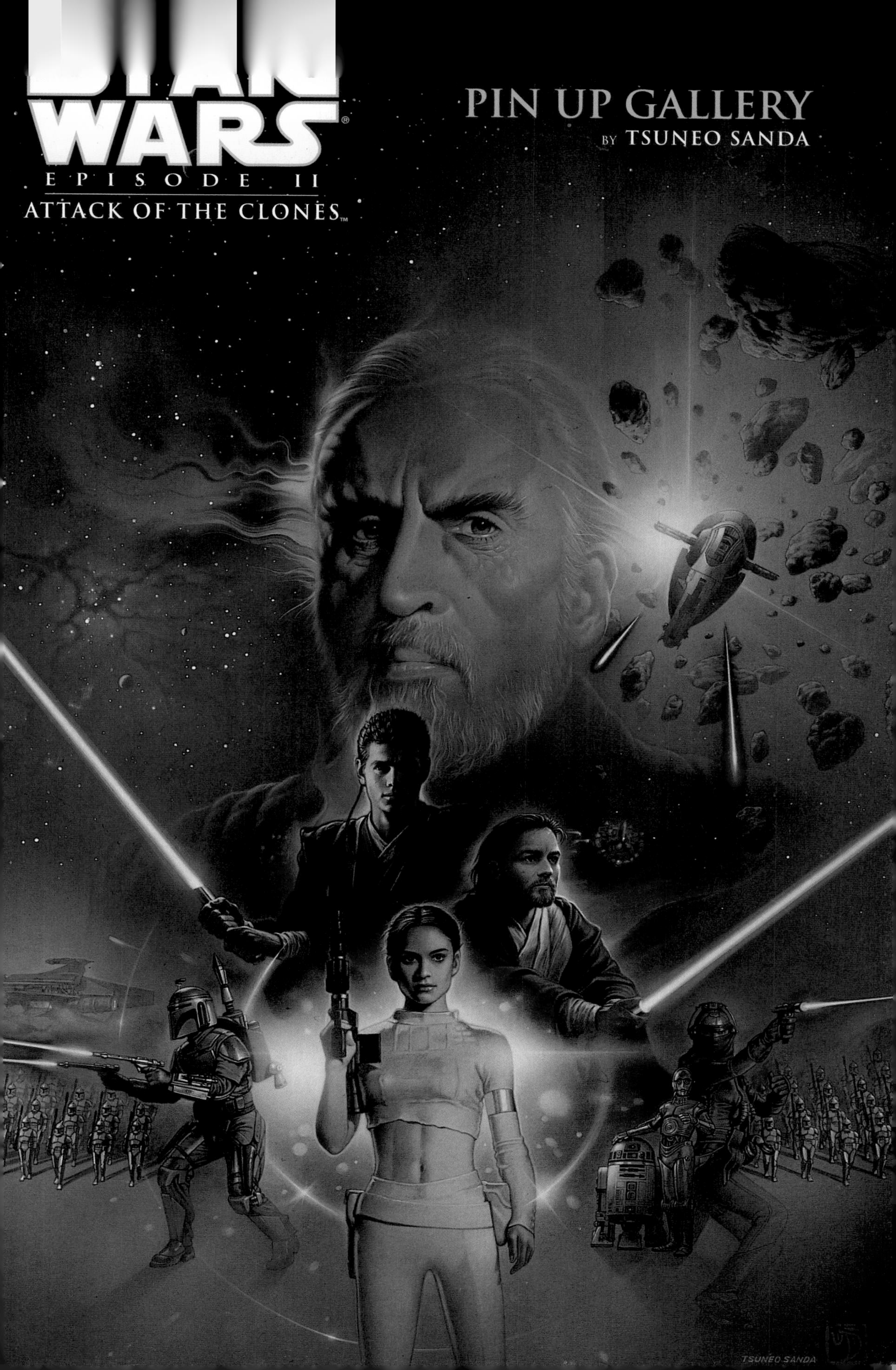
WARS
EPISODE II
ATTACK OF THE CLONES
PIN UP GALLERY
BY TSUNEO SANDA
TSUNEO SANDA

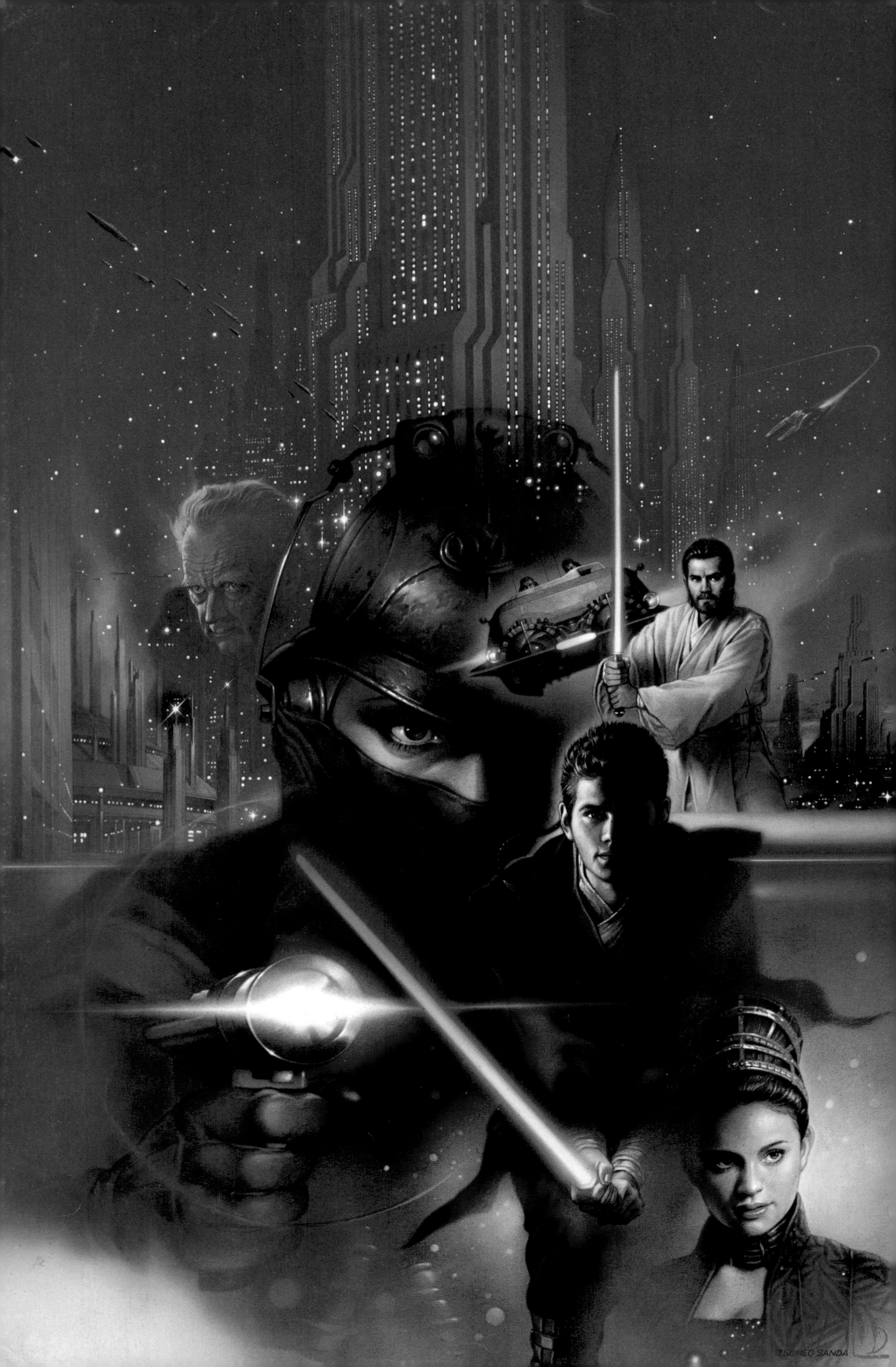
TSUNEO SANDA